HITLER'S
CHILDREN

HITLER'S CHILDREN

The Story of the
Baader-Meinhof Terrorist Gang

JILLIAN BECKER

J. B. LIPPINCOTT COMPANY
Philadelphia and New York

The following sources are acknowledged with thanks:

Translated and reprinted by permission of the heirs to the estate of Ulrike Meinhof: quotations on pages 34, 36, 136, 139, 141–42, 143–44, 147, 151, 157, 161, 162, and 165, from Ulrike Meinhof's columns in *Konkret*.

Translated and reprinted by permission of Kiepenheuer & Witsch GmbH & Co. KG: quotations on pages 129, 131–32, 137, 138, 150–51, 153, 162, 164–65, 166–67, and 167–68, from *Fünf Finger sind keine Faust* by Klaus Rainer Röhl (Cologne: Verlag Kiepenheuer & Witsch, 1974), pages 130, 131, 151, 156, 285–86, 289, 331, 347, and 373.

Reprinted by permission of Holt, Rinehart and Winston, Publishers: quotations on page 120, from *Steppenwolf* by Hermann Hesse, translated by Basil Creighton. Copyright 1929, © 1957 by Holt, Rinehart and Winston.

Translated and reprinted by permission of Rowohlt Taschenbuch Verlag GmbH: quotations on pages 140, 144, 152–53, 159–60, and 164, from *Die Jahre die Ihr kennt* by Peter Rühmkorf, pages 133, 171, 224, 225–26, and 227, from the series "das neue buch" © Rowohlt Taschenbuch Verlag GmbH, Reinbeck bei Hamburg, 1972.

Translated and reprinted by permission of the Spiegel-Verlag Rudolf Augstein GmbH & Co. KG: quotations on pages 85, 89, 94, 96, 97, 170, 180, 183–84, 186, 193–94, 196, 199, 201, 203, and 265 from various issues of *Der Spiegel*.

Translated and reprinted by permission of *Die Welt*: quotations on pages 181–85, 186–88, 190, and 192–99, from "Karl-Heinz Ruhland: Baader-Meinhof und ich," in issues of *Die Welt*, May 20 to June 7, 1975.

U.S. LIBRARY OF CONGRESS CATALOGING IN PUBLICATION DATA

Becker, Jillian, birth date
    Hitler's children: the story of the baader-meinhof terrorist gang.

    Bibliography: p.
    Includes index.
    1. Terrorism—Germany, West. 2. Anarchism and anarchists—Germany, West—Biography. 3. Baader, Andreas, 1943–   4. Meinhof, Ulrike Marie.
5. Rote Armee Fraktion. I. Title.
HV6433.G3B43   3641'06   76-55730
ISBN-0-397-01153-9

52/31

Contents

PART FIVE: THE DEVIL TO PAY

A section of photographs follows page 204

Acknowledgments

The author wishes to acknowledge with thanks the help of Professor Ossip Flechtheim of the Free University, Berlin; Bernd C. Hesslein of North German Radio and Television; Herbert Kadel of the University Library of Marburg and Mrs. Kadel; Professor Harold Hurwitz, Tilman Fichter, and Siegward Lönnendonker of the Central Institute for Social Science Research, Berlin; Peg Cameron; Rex Gribble and Warren H. Jones of the Public Affairs Division of USAEUR, Heidelberg; Professor Helmut Krauch of the University of Kassel; Heinrich and Hertha Götz; Thierry Dudreuilh and Christophe Olivier; Klaus and Anne Koch; Erich Fried; Friedrich Glöckner, Hermann Kunz, and Dr. Heinrich Schwing, formerly of the Gymnasium Philippinum, Weilburg; David Mutch of the *Christian Science Monitor*, Bonn; Sabine Reichel.

The author especially thanks the numerous persons who gave her information and whose names appear in the pages of this book, above all Professor Renate Riemeck, Klaus Rainer Röhl, Stefan Aust; and also Peter and Eva Rühmkorf; Monika Seifert; Professor Werner Link; Gertrud Lorenz of the German Institute for Social Questions, Dahlem, Berlin; Erich Kuby; Marlene Vesper; Professor Jürgen Habermas of the Max Planck Institute, Starnberg; Herbert Faller of the Frankfurt Youth Office; Professor Reinhard Redhardt; Dr. Lothar Wallek; and those who were helpful and generous with information but asked that they should not be named as helpers.

Lastly but most importantly, the author acknowledges with deep gratitude the indispensable, tireless, and superbly efficient aid and support of her translator-and-research-assistant extraordinary, Bernhard Adamczewski.

Abbreviations used in this book refer to the following organizations:

APO   Ausser-Parliamentarische Opposition (Extraparliamentary Opposition)

AStA   Allgemeiner Studenten Ausschuss (General Students Council)

CDU   Christlich-Demokratische Union (Christian Democratic Union, the conservative party of West Germany)

CSU   Christlich-Sozialistische Union (Christian Socialist Union, the CDU's Bavarian partner)

DDR   Deutsche Demokratische Republik (German Democratic Republic—i.e., East Germany)

DFU   Deutsche Friedens Union (German Peace Union)

DKP   Deutsche Kommunistische Partei (German Communist Party, formed as legal party 1968)

FDP   Freie Demokratische Partei (Free Democratic Party, the Liberal Party of West Germany)

IZRU   Information Zentrum Rote [Volks-] Universität (Information Center Red [People's] University, name given as of July 1971 to the SPK of Heidelberg)

KPD   Kommunistische Partei Deutschlands (Communist Party of Germany, banned 1956)

LSD   Liberaler Studentenbund Deutschlands (the Student Liberal Party of Germany)

NPD   Nationaldemokratische Partei Deutschlands (National Democratic Party of Germany, the successor to Hitler's NSDAP)

NSDAP   Nationalsozialistische Deutsche Arbeiterpartei (National Socialist German Workers' Party, the defunct Nazi Party)

RAF   Rote Armee Fraktion (Red Army Faction, the Baader-Meinhof terrorist gang)

SDS   Sozialistischer Deutscher Studentenbund (Socialist German Students Union)

SPD   Sozialdemokratische Partei Deutschlands (Social Democratic Party of Germany, the West German socialist party)

SPK   Sozialistisches Patienten Kollektiv (Socialist Patients' Collective)

VDS   Verband Deutscher Studentenschaften (Union of German Student Associations)

Prologue

In March 1973 the Saudi Arabian ambassador at Khartoum was giving a farewell party for a United States diplomat, George Curtis Moore. Some Arab gunmen of Black September, the military arm of Yasser Arafat's Palestine Liberation Organization (PLO), burst in with Kalashnikov machine guns. They held five men as hostages: the Saudi ambassador, American ambassador Cleo Noel, George Curtis Moore, and a Jordanian and a Belgian diplomat. Their demands were: the release of one of their men from prison in Jordan, believed to have been an organizer of the massacre of Israeli athletes at the 1972 Olympic Games in Munich, and the release by the United States government of Sirhan Sirhan, the assassin of Robert Kennedy, by Israel of certain imprisoned women terrorists, and by West Germany of the imprisoned members of a terrorist group known as the Baader-Meinhof gang. None of their demands were acceded to. The terrorists cold-bloodedly killed the Belgian and the two Americans, who faced their murderers with calm courage.

Why the gunmen should want the release of their fellow Arabs is not mysterious, but how the lives of two Americans and a Belgian should have been made in this bizarre plot to depend, in part, on the freeing of some imprisoned gangsters in West Germany needs an explanation, and is part of a story which has frightening implications for the Western world.

The Baader-Meinhof gang was the first group in West Germany to organize itself into an underground urban guerrilla movement. Soon after its inception in 1970, it made world headlines with bank raids and street gun battles, and later with bombings and widespread hell-raising in West Germany and even beyond its borders. Many members of the gang were captured by the police, some within the first few months of its existence. At their trials they were all accused of common crimes—murder, bank robbery, shooting, bombing, kidnapping, criminal conspiracy—and none were charged with political offenses; but they called themselves "political prisoners" because they claimed exclusively political motivation. They said they were fighting fascism, imperialism, and capitalist exploitation—and this claim secured for them a fairly sympathetic treatment by the liberal and leftist press outside of West Germany. Some foreign newspapers took the view that their aims—though never specified, and at best hinted at in references to the group's being "against an imperfect society"—were not unrespectable, and that only their methods were wrong. And then, after the arrest of the gang leaders, disturbing tales of their maltreatment in prison spread abroad through the press and television and helped to preserve or increase the sympathy.

The three leaders of the gang were all caught and imprisoned in June 1972. Andreas Baader, with his fellow gangsters Holger Meins and Jan-Carl Raspe, was arrested in Frankfurt on June 1. Less than a week later, on June 7, Baader's lover, Gudrun Ensslin, was arrested in Hamburg, and a week after that, on June 15, Ulrike Meinhof, the woman whose name was joined with Baader's to make the popular designation of the group, was found by police in Hanover. Of these five, four were brought to trial three years later in Stuttgart, the capital of Baden-Württemberg, because that was the state in which the most serious crimes they were charged with had been committed: the murder by means of time bombs of four United States servicemen. The fifth prisoner was to have stood trial with them, but he—Holger Meins—had died as a result of a hunger strike six months before the trial began.

The other main charges against the four were the murder of a policeman, the attempted murder of fifty-four persons, robbery, and the forming of a criminal association. The trial was predicted to last months, if not years.

One of the reasons for the long delay in bringing them to trial was that an exceptionally secure courthouse was considered necessary to try such dangerous people. There was none secure enough, so they built one. It was erected in a field adjacent to a prison in the Stammheim district of Stuttgart, at a cost of some 12 million Deutschmarks (about $4 million), two thirds of which was spent on the building and the rest on its special equipment for this one particular trial, after which it would be converted for some use by the prison.

The single-story building was surrounded by high steel fences and floodlit at night, and armed policemen patrolled it with guard dogs. On the roof was spread a steel-reinforced plastic net as a defense against bombs. Newspaper reports of an underground passage through which the prisoners would pass from the prison to their courthouse a few hundred yards away turned out to be untrue—an ordinary police van was used to get them there and back—but so dangerous was their terrorist gang believed to be by the public that perhaps no security arrangements, however extreme, would have been considered too exaggerated or too expensive.

"The most important trial in the history of the Federal Republic of West Germany" was what some foreign newspapers called it; "the trial of West German democracy . . . of West German justice."

Certain lawyers briefed for the defense were excluded shortly before the trial, accused of complicity with their clients. Their names, which belong in the story, are Klaus Croissant, Kurt Groenewold, and Hans Christian Ströbele. Their complaints against their exclusion carried as far as England, where lawyers handed in written protests on their behalf at the German embassy.

The defense team which assembled at the opening of the trial on May 21, 1975, consisted—apart from one well-known liberal, Hans Heinz Heldmann, acting for Andreas Baader—of lawyers whose political views seemed to agree more or less closely with those of the accused. Gudrun Ensslin had two defenders: Otto Schily, who had formed part of the defense at an earlier trial where she had stood accused, and Marieluise Becker, whose lawyer husband, Eberhard, was himself a wanted terrorist. For Ulrike Meinhof there was Helmut Riedel (dismissed and replaced six months later). His partner, Rupert von Plottnitz, was for Jan-Carl Raspe.

Of von Plottnitz a state witness and former member of the gang was to declare, in his testimony before the court in July 1976, that he "kept members in line with leadership policy." This witness was one Gerhard Müller, a young man who had been arrested with Ulrike Meinhof in Hanover. His evidence ravaged the defense. He told exactly who had laid bombs, where, and how. Until then criticism of the trial both in Germany and abroad had been severe, some commentators going so far as to contend that it ought to be abandoned, because it had been prejudged by the press and by leading politicians, who had declared the accused guilty in public speeches; but after Müller's evidence the voices of objection became more subdued. The proceedings were scrupulously conducted. It was clear that there was nothing wrong with West Germany's democratic institutions, and there was no cause to be found, for all the passionate denunciations by the Baader-Meinhof gang of the State's "fascism," for West Germans to have anything less than full confidence in their democracy and their justice.

Inside the windowless, artificially lit, technologically well-equipped,

utilitarian, and atmospherically space-age courtroom, the prisoners sat in
a row, on three days a week at most, dressed in similar blue jeans and
loose black sweaters, thin from their hunger strikes and with prison pallor
on their faces. The skin of swarthy, shadow-jowled, yet boyish-faced
Baader had turned a citrus yellow. Gudrun Ensslin, with lank blond
locks, had become quite haggard. She would shriek from time to time at
the five judges (there was no jury), and Baader would yell obscene abuse.
Jan-Carl Raspe wore a droopy moustache and sat quietly, his eyes rolled
up so that the white of his eyeballs showed under the irises; he seemed
withdrawn mentally from his present circumstances. Ulrike Meinhof, her
brown hair hanging in a braid over one shoulder, gazed through austere
round spectacles and complained from time to time that she could not
concentrate on the proceedings for so many hours (up to three) at a sitting. Sometimes the four absented themselves from the court on the
ground that they were too weak to appear. But it was ruled that they
could be tried in absentia if the ill health they blamed had been self-in-
duced, as by hunger strikes.

Outside the court and the prison, the gang continued to command
attention with acts of violence and destruction. It had the romantic, aesthetic, and even erotic fascination for many people which bandit gangs
have always had—especially and predictably, though not exclusively, for
the young.

The gang called itself the Red Army Faction (Rote Armee Fraktion,
or RAF). The name was chosen in imitation of the Japanese "Red Army"
(Rengo Sekigun), a similar organization much admired by one of the
founders of the West German group, a lawyer named Horst Mahler. (It
was the Japanese "Red Army" which mowed down a party of Puerto
Rican pilgrims, among others, with machine guns at Lod airport near Tel
Aviv in May 1972.)

There were other, similar organizations in Italy, the United States,
several South American countries, and England. The first link between
these movements was ideological. They all grew out of the student protest
movements of the late sixties, and they all claimed the same revolutionary aim, the overthrow of capitalism. They equated capitalism with
fascism, imperialism, and exploitation. The chief characteristic of the
student movements and the New Left everywhere was a morally ambitious identification by affluent rebels with the poor, the victimized, and
the socially outcast, and especially with the people of Vietnam, on whose
behalf they protested that the United States was waging aggressive war
against them.

In addition to all this, the West German movement had a special antagonism to what it called "authoritarianism." All authority, without distinction, was considered "fascist" by the German rebels. And fascism in Germany meant Nazism. So in West Germany the movement became essentially a violent backlash against the totalitarian state of the preceding generation. There the students' violence died down when their genuine grievances over unsatisfactory conditions in the universities were removed by the granting of reforms. But it was then that terrorist activities began, at first in the name of Vietnam, but also—and, when the Vietnam War came to an end in 1975, predominantly—in the name of the Palestinians. They were always chiefly directed against the "imperialism" of the United States, the archenemy, and its capitalist empire, and so also against all the governments and the law- and peace-keeping forces of the Western democracies, primarily, of course, those of West Germany itself.

Members of the Baader-Meinhof group began early on to associate with the Palestinians, especially with the People's Front for the Liberation of Palestine (PFLP), which declared itself to be for world Marxist revolution. Some of them went to the Middle East to train with Palestinian guerrillas. And later some who fled from West Germany became prominent and active members of ad hoc guerrilla bands formed under the auspices of, and paid by, Arab politicians, to carry out particular acts of terrorism. Working from the Middle East with members of similar organizations from other parts of the world, the West German revolutionaries helped to promote that international terrorism which has become an increasing menace in many parts of the world, outside of the communist bloc. The Palestinian cause provided Japanese, South Americans, and Germans with a moral excuse to perform acts of extreme violence in a spirit of unshakable self-righteousness. But whether the idealistic moral-political motives claimed by these rebellious children of the free Western democracies, styling themselves an avant-garde of world communist revolution, are plausible, or whether quite different and personal motives were more likely to have impelled the young gangsters to their acts of violence, is one of the questions which a close inquiry into their histories should help to decide.

The international links were sought after and strengthened as a matter of policy by the German groups. In Hamburg, in the summer of 1973, police raided the office of a lawyer and found material which left them in no doubt that it served as an information center through which terrorist organizations abroad kept in touch with the Baader-Meinhof gang. The lawyer, the son of a multimillionaire property owner, was Kurt

Groenewold, one of those excluded from the trial at Stammheim. Through such an "info-center of the RAF prisoners" the international "solidarity" of terrorist groups of the extreme Left could be established and maintained.

It was only a few months before the "info-center" was discovered in Hamburg that the Black September raid on the Saudi Arabian embassy at Khartoum took place and Cleo Noel and George Curtis Moore and their Belgian colleague were killed.

But the discovery of the "info-center" did not noticeably hamper international cooperation in terrorist activities. The direct links were well established.

A traffic in arms between the groups had been carried on across borders for some time. This was made evident after a raid on the French embassy at The Hague in September 1974. The Japanese raiders secured the release of a member of their gang held in France, a large sum of money from the Dutch government, and a free plane ride to Damascus, where not only impunity but a hero's welcome awaited them. They left behind in the embassy some U.S. Army M26 grenades from a 1971 theft in West Germany which had also supplied the Baader-Meinhof gang.

In January 1976 the Vienna office of the Organization of Petroleum Exporting Countries (OPEC) was invaded by five raiders while in session. The leader was Ilich Ramirez Sanchez, the son of a Venezuelan millionaire and anticapitalist capitalist. He used the cover name of "Carlos" and was already wanted in both Britain and France for terrorist activities. He had assisted in the raid on the embassy at The Hague, and it was he who had supplied the Japanese with the American grenades. He was accompanied by four others, one of whom was Gabriele Kröcher-Tiedemann, elegant in gray coat with fur collar and matching gray cap, who had been a member of a weird group called the Socialist Patients' Collective of Heidelberg—an organization which had joined itself to the Baader-Meinhof gang. She had been arrested and imprisoned in Germany, but released in exchange for the kidnapped political leader Peter Lorenz. And another of the raiders was Hans-Joachim Klein, who also had Baader-Meinhof connections (and was the driver of the car which took lawyer Klaus Croissant to meet Jean-Paul Sartre at Stuttgart airport when the great philosopher arrived to visit Baader in prison).

The representatives of the oil-producing countries were held at gunpoint. Although by then total success had been achieved several times against terrorists holding hostages in Holland, Ireland, and England by a "freezing-out" method (surround the place with armed police, send in supplies, and wait), Austrian Chancellor Kreisky gave in within a few hours to the terrorists' demand to be flown with their hostages to a destination of their choice. So the political playboys and smart young Gabriele flew to safety in Algeria. There the hostages were set free, but so were the terrorists, although they had left three people dead in Vienna, two of them, according to surviving eyewitnesses, shot by Gabriele. Klein, however, did not get off unscathed. During the shooting he was severely wounded in the stomach.

The hostages this time had mostly been Arabs, and Sheikh Yamani of Saudi Arabia was among them. He gave it as his opinion that "Carlos" had intended to kill him and an Iranian minister in order to warn their pro-Western states against taking a "soft" line with Israel. He believed they had the Algerian government to thank for their survival. And it was believed generally that the instigator of the raid, the kidnapping, and the probable murder plan, was Colonel Qadhafi, President of Libya, who had earned the title of "the paymaster of terrorism."

"Carlos" had made contact with the Baader-Meinhof gang long before the OPEC raid. In May 1975 he had gone to Frankfurt to see one Wilfried Böse, who worked for a little leftist publishing house called Red Star and lived in the same commune as Hans-Joachim Klein and other urban guerrillas, such as Joannes Weinrich, director of Red Star, who had hired a car used by the attackers of an El-Al plane at Orly airport near Paris in January of that year.

"Carlos" (according to Böse's later "confession" to the French police) wanted him to go to Spain and gather information for the Basque separatist movement. Böse (whose name means "evil") agreed, and in June he went to Paris to get a false passport from "Carlos." But he was arrested by the French police before he set off for Spain, and they handed him over to the West German authorities. The local border-town magistrate knew nothing of him and let him go, back underground.

He surfaced again, briefly and for the last time.

On June 27, 1976, an Air France airbus was hijacked on its way from Tel Aviv to Paris, after a touchdown in Athens, where evil had been awaiting it. One of the hijackers was Wilfried Böse. He and his comrades forced the pilot to fly to the airport of Entebbe, a town in Uganda. It was expected by Uganda's President Idi Amin, an outspoken admirer of Hitler's genocidal massacre of the Jews. After two days the Jews were separated from the rest of the passengers. The others were released, the Jews held as hostages. In return for their lives and freedom, the terrorists demanded the release of forty prisoners held in Israel, five in Kenya, one in France, one in Switzerland (a woman member of an Italian terrorist group closely resembling the Baader-Meinhof gang, who had sold weapons to a Baader-Meinhof member, a lawyer named Siegfried Haag), and six in West Germany—Jan-Carl Raspe, Fritz Teufel (a member of a group affiliated to the Baader-Meinhof, called the Movement Second June), Ralf Reinders and his girl friend Inge Viett (Movement Second June), Ingrid Schubert, and Werner Hoppe (both Baader-Meinhof). The new leadership of the RAF did not, apparently, want Baader or Ensslin out again and back in control. And Ulrike Meinhof, to whom the same reluctance might have been applied, was by that time dead.

Among the hostages at Entebbe there were a few who had been in Hitler's concentration camps. Once again they found themselves being sorted out, Jews from non-Jews, the Jews selected to die. Once again they were ordered about by guards with guns, shouted at to move quickly—"*Schnell!*"—this time by a German woman hijacker, who also felt it was necessary to slap them. One of the captives went up to Böse and showed him a number indelibly branded on his arm. He told him that he had got it in a Nazi concentration camp. He said he had supposed that a new and different generation had grown up in Germany, but with this experience of Böse and his girl comrade, he found it difficult to believe that the Nazi movement had died.

Böse replied that this was something quite different from Nazism: that he was a member of the Baader-Meinhof group, and what they wanted was world Marxist revolution.

To the hostages at Entebbe the difference was hard to see.

The hostages did not die. As all the world knows, armed Israelis descended out of the sky on the day set for the slaughter, gathered them up, and carried them back through the air to safety in Israel. It was Böse and his comrades who were shot dead.

But with their ordeal over, and even with the distance of time and space, the hijack victims might still find it difficult to believe in the distinction which Böse insisted upon.

This book will not make it any easier.

PART ONE
A GAME WITH TERROR

1
Play the Devil

During the 1960s student politics in West Germany moved from pacifism through "passive provocation" to violence. West Berlin was where the most significant events marking this development took place. There, in the middle of the decade, a group of "happenings" satirists formed a commune and launched a campaign of provocative, leftist, but nonviolent anti-Establishment criticism. They won supporters, but enemies too.

They had first gathered together in the southern town of Kochel, on the shores of the lake called the Kochelsee. There nine men and five women, with a couple of small communal children, had met in a country house for a week's discussion of the prospects for a revolutionary movement in western Europe and of the merits of living collectively. They named themselves the "Viva Maria group," after the film by Louis Malle in which Brigitte Bardot and Jeanne Moreau became beautifully involved in a revolution of fun and style in Mexico, with all the rulers rich and cruel and all the rebels poor and lovable.

Among them was one Rudi Dutschke, who had come from West Berlin, where he had taken refuge from the communist East because as an ardent pacifist he had refused to join the National Army of the People for which it was then compulsory to "volunteer." Dutschke was a young man with black straight hair, a gaunt-boned Slavic face, and amber, inflammable eyes.

Another of them was Fritz Teufel (his surname means "devil"). He was twenty-four and said to be shy when he came with the group to live communally in West Berlin, where they tried to put their political and social ideas into practice, sharing all with all.

Rudi Dutschke did not remain long with the group, as he was unwilling to share his girl friend, an American theology student who in time became his wife. But one Rainer Langhans joined them. He had just been released from national service, and he used his new freedom to grow a wide mop of thick curly hair.

The group studied at, or at least became involved in the student affairs of, the Free University. Now they called themselves Kommune I and soon became notorious as a troupe of political jesters, trend setters, student leaders, convention defiers.

It was not long before they had their imitators, though it was more their communal life-style than their methods of political criticism that became fashionable. To make authority look absurd by staging satirical "happenings" required a special talent, but to make a commune, all that was needed was a consenting circle and a large enough apartment. A Kommune II had in fact been started earlier than Kommune I, but was named later. This Kommune II further described itself as a "Psychoanalytic-Amateur-Dramatic Society," which gave fair warning of its deeper earnestness.

But sometimes the satirical methods were imitated too, especially in the service of the cause which was nearest to students all over the country, the cause in which they genuinely believed because it genuinely affected them: university reform.

After the war the universities had been purged of professors tainted with a Nazi past, but many had to be reinstated because of the dearth of teachers and administrators which resulted. Students protested not just because such men were back in power, but against the way they used their power, and many younger teachers, inspired less with reverence than frustration by the all-too-traditional hierarchies of authority, supported the students' quite reasonable demands for reform. The postwar baby boom had grown up to become a student boom in the second half of the sixties, but for all its predictability, no forethought had been given to it. Buildings and facilities were inadequate, courses were antiquated, and academic administration was traditional to the point of petrifaction. The universities had emerged from the war with their pre-Nazi independence strengthened, and the authorities were more concerned with preserving their powers than with making their institutions viable. It was hard enough to get them even to listen to the complaints of students, let alone to allow students to have some say in the making of decisions which vitally affected their careers. Only at the Free University of Berlin, which was built after the war, was there a constitution which allowed two students to sit on the council. It was an inadequate provision. And it was in that anomalous, nervous city that the German student movement became most turbulent.

To the generation born after the war and raised in the reeducation policies of the conquering powers to respect and uphold the values of democracy, including free speech, it was obviously unjust that they were denied simple democratic rights like a say in the making of the rules that governed them, or even freedom to express their ideas on certain important issues. They did have university student councils (Allgemeiner Studenten Ausschuss, AStA), representing all students, and the national Union of Student Associations (Verband Deutscher Studentenschaften, VDS). But though these organizations promoted democracy in a general way after the war, they were not supposed to take sides over distinctly political issues. They did try to prevent the re-formation of the old *Korps*, the dueling fraternities which had been in their time a breeding ground of Prussian militarism, and, though officially forbidden by the power-monopolizing Nazis, of Nazi-type elitist ideals; but they did not succeed, and young men with the duelers' beribboned cap and rapier are still to be seen about the university towns.

There were also the student political parties: most notably, as a force in the student movement, the Socialist Student Union—Sozialistischer Deutscher Studentenbund, or SDS (coincidentally, the same as the initials of the American Students for a Democratic Society but having no connection with it). Certainly the SDS made itself heard, though its membership reached only about twenty-five hundred, and at the Free University where it was strongest it seldom, even with the cooperation of liberal and other left groups, rallied more than about 5 percent of the students to the active support of any cause. It was a most significant force all over the country in the agitation for university reform. But it concerned itself with wider issues, too, and hoped and tried to politicize students generally.

In 1959 an SDS congress had declared itself against the atom bomb, militarism, and the rearmament of Germany. The pacifism of the young delegates at that time was vehement, but not threatening. By holding opinions against violence they may have felt they had achieved pacifism, but of course these pacifists had not yet been subjected to much temptation to be anything else. Such political action as they took was peaceful enough, however loud with challenging conviction. "Protest" was the first key word of the student movement—protest written on placards, demonstrated by crowds marching through city streets, shouted in chorus, and sung.

The year 1961 was a time of crisis in Berlin. It was the year the Berlin Wall was built by the German Democratic Republic, to keep its citizens from voting against communism with their feet. A hundred days after it was erected, about forty thousand protesters, many of them students, marched silently through the streets of West Berlin, in mourning for a student who had leaped from a high window to escape from the East, missed the blanket held for him, and died. Then, after the quiet official march, about a thousand students tried to storm the Wall. "Away with Ulbricht and Mao!" they shouted. And the West Berlin police moved in with tear gas and rubber truncheons to keep them back. To the students this was an outrage.

By way of justification, the Berlin Senate issued a confusing statement approving the demonstrators' motives while reproving their action. While the Senate was able to plead that the demonstrators trying to storm the Wall had been kept back for their own safety, the students nevertheless insisted indignantly that the official reaction was in every respect undemocratic. They were hurt and angry. And while remaining for peace in general, students over the next few years became more militant in mood. The "economic miracle" brought new students into the universities who could not remember hardship, want, the horrors of violence, real fascism, or intimidation, and whose collective cocksureness was founded on material security taken for granted. And they were aggressively determined to be heard.

In 1965 the Free University of Berlin planned to commemorate the capitulation of Germany twenty years before, and the students, through the committee of their student council, asked that the journalist Erich Kuby be invited to give an address.

Years before, in 1958, Kuby had expressed a point of view on the naming of the Free University which at the time had offended not only the authorities but also the students, who had received his opinion with hisses and jeers. He had said that the name Free University expressed "an extreme degree of unfreedom" in that it was given to the new university deliberately to imply that the old Humboldt University, now in communist East Berlin, was not free. He said the name was therefore "a polemical reference to other state structures," which West Germany had avoided when it named itself the German Federal Republic (but which East Germany had not avoided when it called itself the German Democratic Republic). In other words, he was saying that the namers of the Free University were not only suggesting that their university allowed its students free access to ideas while the Humboldt no longer did so since falling into communist hands, but that the communist state which controlled the Humboldt was also not free. And further, that to believe such a fallacy was to have one's mind in some sort of propaganda vise.

Perhaps Kuby was only objecting that the naming of the new university was in deliberate aggravation of the Cold War, rather than saying that the communist states were free, and West Berlin unfree if it thought otherwise. But to his audience—most of whom seemed to have formed the firm opinion, on evidence which could not have been too difficult to unearth, that the Eastern bloc countries were indeed unfree and that the Humboldt University by no means allowed free access to ideas—Kuby's view was not merely exaggerated, or simply absurd, but offensive.

Yet now, in 1965, the students of the Free University wanted to hear Kuby say it all again. Clearly student opinion in West Berlin had swung leftward—perhaps because very few refugees from East Germany now swelled their numbers as they had done before the Wall was built. No longer did students cry "Away with Ulbricht and Mao" on the western side of the Brandenburg Gate. Perhaps the Wall itself was responsible for their softened feelings toward communism—cutting off their view so that they could begin to suspect that the grass might really be greener on the other side.

Certainly more students were leftist now, or sympathetic to the Left. And they may have reckoned that by simply asking for the man who had challenged the Free University with that view, they would force a confrontation with the university authorities. They did. The Rector—the head of the university—refused to entertain the suggestion that Kuby be invited, and so missed his opportunity to demonstrate that the university's name was fully justified by its policies. Indignation among the students flared.

The "Kuby affair" became a *cause célèbre* beyond the walls of the university, through the press and television. And the strikes, sit-ins, teach-ins, and other assorted forms of protest over this "free speech" issue were amplified to take in the Vietnam War, which was rapidly becoming the most popular cause for the New Left to champion all over the Western world, in this year of the United States military "escalation" in that small tragic country. Students felt themselves to be not only fellow sufferers with the victims of hardhearted and heavy-handed powers, but also their champions. "Amis [Americans, contemptuous] get out of Vietnam," and get out of the Dominican Republic too—and give us the right of self-determination. Down with the authoritarianism of the university—and of America.

A new Rector was routinely appointed, but changes in the administration were not significant enough to diminish the students' discontent. Through the rest of 1965 and all through 1966 the conflict between students and university authorities smoldered on.

The press in Berlin, almost monopolized by the Axel Springer organization, helped to keep public opinion irritable and biased against the students. Typical headlines and comments which annoyed them were such as *Die Welt's* "The Dream Dancers of West Berlin—Why Always Strikes at the Free University?"; or the *Berliner Morgenpost's* "The Clowns of West Berlin," the headline for an editorial on an anti-Vietnam demonstration by the student groups; or, in the *Berliner Zeitung*, on the same subject:

> Inspector says: A disgrace for our Berlin. Since last Saturday there has been a new situation in our city: a numerically small group of leftist radicals . . . have for some time now nursed fantasies of bringing about a "revolutionary situation." At the weekend they gave us a first taste: With communist slogans they went onto the streets. . . . Students who formerly no doubt put forward moving complaints against the abolition of milk subsidies, shied eggs against America House. Students who have the Americans to thank for their being able to study in peace in this city, violated the American flag! *Pfui Teufel!*

Pfui Teufel!—"Fie devil!"—is a common enough expression and was not aimed at any particular person. No one of that name had yet made himself conspicuous about the Free University. But, spoken of, he was bound to appear.

Early in 1966 police permission was obtained for a demonstration against the "dirty war in Vietnam," yet it brought students and police into angry clashes. The students sat down in front of America House. Eggs—but only five, the students claimed, from a pack of six bought at the Zoo Underground Station—were thrown (what happened to the sixth, one wonders; did someone keep it for his supper?) at the two rows of windows in the neat, modern, quite small cube-block building, with wide horizontal lines of blue and just a few thin stripes of red and a very few tiny white stars, and with a flag on a not very high pole in the grass of the curb outside its front door, easy for students to get at and tear down—which they did. And the facade was further insulted with the name of the Vietcong leader Ho Chi Minh, chanted as a war cry, and the singing of "The International."

It was to be a year of important developments. On the national scene the two biggest political parties, the Social Democrats (SPD) and the Christian Democrats (CDU), formed the Grand Coalition, and many ardent Leftists deserted the SPD. The world had seemed to them ready for radical change, the SPD had seemed the sort of party which might bring it about, and this compromise for the sake of power was "a sellout."

There were others who had a more cogent criticism: that here was a threat of one-party rule, which was just what East Germany suffered from.

And Fritz Teufel appeared.

He and Kommune I erupted onto the Berlin scene. They did not entirely change the mood or style of student politics, but they added their own, and in the early days were appreciated even where they were not imitated. The leftist SDS was enchanted with them at first, and before long twelve of its members decided to start a commune of their own. At the eleventh hour, however, the courage of five of them failed and only the remaining seven moved into a large apartment in the full risk of one another.

Many stories are told about the deeds of Kommune I and, especially, Fritz Teufel. No doubt a good many of them are distorted or entirely apocryphal. But some are essentially true: such as the one about Teufel breaking into the Rector's room, seizing his cigars and the seal of his office, donning his cap and gown and chain, and riding off on a small-wheeled bicycle with a horn instead of a bell, about the paths and roads between the university institutes and offices in the affluent suburb of Dahlem—some large old houses, some elegant made-to-measure modern buildings, parking lots, paved Japanese courtyards planted with slender silver birches and squat dark conifers—to the big, main, new, handsome Henry Ford building, where he rode right into the foyer, and on, claxing, into the Auditorium Maximum, down the ramp to the tiered platform where the microphones stuck out of their podium. Assembled students cheered. He leaped off his bike, lifted the velvet skirts of his gown to step onto the platform, and acknowledged their ovation with bashful and amiable smiles and waves. They elected him Rector, and at once he prohibited the presence of police on the campus and wrote out dismissals of all the professors the students didn't want, setting thereto the Rector's seal. He bowed to them, and they bowed to him and called him, with real enthusiasm in the satire, by the medieval title to which rectors still clung—"Magnificence!" Then the beaming player-Rector distributed his stolen cigars and finally had no choice but to step off the stage of the "Audi Max," unable to effect any new systems, redesign courses, abolish exams, or set everyone free of all rule and restriction so that the natural goodness of human nature could turn the Free University into paradise.

But the real Rector arranged to discuss the students' demands with them. Toward the end of 1966 he met them for an informal discussion in a lecture room of the Henry Ford building. He said he was there not in his official capacity but as a private person. For two hours they questioned him, and still he gave them what they called "evasive" answers. Then a group of students interrupted with loud complaints. They announced themselves as the "Provisional Committee for the Preparation of a Student-Help Organization," and one of their number proceeded to read aloud a pamphlet (produced the night before, if not out of prejudice then surely out of clairvoyance) to the Rector and the gathering: "We have nothing more to learn from this discussion. If we refuse to become specialist idiots by being trained by professorial specialist idiots, we shall have to pay with the risk of ending our studies without a proper exam."

The group, who had badges depicting Mao Tse-Tung pinned on their chests, advanced upon the Rector and pushed him forcibly from the microphone. He left the room at once.

Reprisals were threatened by a group of professors who decided to take the reference to "professorial specialist idiots" personally and to sue the authors of the pamphlet. But who were they?

They were, in fact, psychoanalytical drama amateurs from Kommune II, but the search carried investigators elsewhere, after Christmas was over and the new year had begun.

In the meantime the students had Vietnam to see to. The unpleasant outcome and dubious effectuality of earlier anti–Vietnam War demonstrations notwithstanding, December 3 to 10, 1966, was planned as a "Vietnam Week" by the SDS and other political groups, including the "Argument Club,"* which was far from being as Pickwickian as its name might arouse hopes of. Teach-ins (different from "lessons" in that they dwelt on one side only of the problem they were investigating) were followed by demonstrations. At the final assembly on the tenth, Rudi Dutschke, by this time well established as a student leader, called for the formation of an Extraparliamentary Opposition since there was none that voiced the radical viewpoint in the Bonn parliament itself. The protesters marched with placards through the streets:

> Christmas wishes on their way—
> Bombs made in the USA.

They came to America House chanting "Ho-ho-ho-Chi-Minh!" and "Amis get out of Vietnam!" and "John-son mur-derer!" and the surely expected clashes with the police came about. Some ninety people were arrested, with an indiscriminate conscientiousness on the part of the police which swept several of that long-suffering minority, innocent passersby, into a crowded prison for the night.

---

* Notes on this and subsequent statements and references in the chapters are given at the end of the book, beginning on p. 285.

That same evening outside the famous and elegant Café Kranzler on the Kurfürstendamm, the busiest and smartest shopping street in West Berlin, its name often shortened to Ku-Damm, Kommune I staged a "Christmas happening." They set up a Christmas tree, draped it with the flag of the United States of America, and a banner which read: "Bourgeois of all lands, unite!" Big carnival-type papier-mâché heads of the arch-villain, war-waging Lyndon B. Johnson, and, for balance, Walter Ulbricht, Chancellor of communist East Germany, were planted beside the tree. They tried to set fire to the figures and the tree, but only Johnson's gypsum hat caught alight. Onlookers stared from the tiered windows of the Kranzler. Passersby, ill-advisedly, stopped. There were cheers and jeers.

As if on cue, a few hundred policemen appeared with rubber truncheons. They put out the hat, confiscated the tree and the heads, arrested about sixty students and whatever innocent passersby were foolish enough to be wearing beards or long hair, or to be dressed too casually—in jeans perhaps, or without ties, or in hippy-fashionable mangy fur coats—or merely to be under thirty, or so foolhardy as to voice the opinion to the police that they were being unnecessarily rough.

The next day a brand-new mayor, Pastor Heinrich Albertz, exhibited his zeal, and proper prejudices, by saying that the students ought to be ashamed of themselves. But the students still felt themselves to be victims, innocent victims, although the old ideal of pacifism had been altered just a little—one should not say compromised—to a policy of "passive provocation." And now their blood was up. They planned another demonstration for December 17, of a kind which would make it hard for the police to charge at them with rubber truncheons or find excuses—if they needed any—to arrest them. The demonstration was of course about Vietnam, but the secondary motive was to use a new tactic against the police. It was to be a strollabout demonstration.

They would wander down the Ku-Damm with their banners, chanting their chants, but in small groups. If they saw the police coming they would fold their banners, hush their chanting, and break up quietly, then reassemble further on, unfurl their banners, and resume their chants against the Amis, against Johnson, for Ho Chi Minh—and against the police, thus:

> If the police come by
> We will pass them by;
> At the next corner then
> We'll go on with our game.

That it was a game was admitted only in song. But there they were, one week after the violent end to "Vietnam Week," making a new kind of demonstration for the good of the Vietnamese—repudiating any suggestion, then as always, that Vietnam was a pretext—and knowing quite well what the police reaction might be, and planning on it.

On the day of the strollabout demonstration the police, including a force of reserves of the Bereitschafts-Polizei, the "Bepo," no older than the students themselves, cordoned off the area in front of the Café Kranzler and, reaching further into the stream of the Ku-Damm, at its busiest on this pre-Christmas Saturday, caught some schoolchildren, more than the usual quota of innocent passersby—including a couple of journalists they would have thrown back if they'd known what they were—and seventy-four students. Patrols lingered about until late in the evening. Some of them had confetti and candy sprinkled over them and, after some hesitation, pronounced these sprinklings "technical assault" and grabbed the sprinklers. No fewer than four determined policemen swooped simultaneously upon Rudi Dutschke and arrested him, though he was at that moment, in the sight of all truthful witnesses, doing nothing more illegal or riotous than walking along the Ku-Damm with a Christmas parcel under his arm. And as this was the demonstration most obviously influenced by the anarchist-pacifist-dadaists of Kommune I, it is not surprising that the communards were scattered about in the Ku-Damm, or that Rainer Langhans, easy enough to spot even by artificial light with all that hair, was also snatched up by the police.

After this batch of arrests, another more sober way of fighting the police was tried. Early in the new year, about a month after the strollabout demonstration, a lawyer named Horst Mahler, the students' own legal champion and no mean demonstrator himself, demanded on behalf of twenty-five students that the state prosecutor of Berlin proceed against policemen who had acted against demonstrators exercising their rights of public protest on December 10 and 17.

Horst Mahler was thirty-one years old. With a pale round face, the square black-rimmed spectacles suggestive of the sensible man making a good income, and dark hair combed straight back, not long, but thinning a little in the middle of its high M above his convex forehead, he looked conventional, plump, professional, conservative in those days. The son of a dentist of right-wing persuasion, he had been brought to West Berlin in 1949 as a refugee from the Russian zone. As a student at the Free University in the mid-fifties, he had become a member of a dueling *Korps*. But in 1956 he had converted to the Left and joined both the Social

Democratic Party and the SDS. In 1964 he began practicing his profession. In 1966 he was the first German lawyer to lodge a complaint successfully with the European Commission for Human Rights and went on to show himself a keen defender of left activists.

Now on January 23, 1967—his thirty-first birthday—Mahler charged the Berlin police with committing punishable acts on December 10 and 17: with "depriving innocent people of their freedom," "using compulsion against peaceful citizens," "arresting the innocent," and "insulting behavior."

Undeterred, three days later the political police, "Popo," raided and searched the offices of the SDS on the Ku-Damm and took possession of the membership files. They were accompanied by news reporters. They claimed that they had warrants to search for proof of authorship of the libelous "professorial specialist idiots" pamphlets, read and distributed on the day that the Rector was shoved aside by aggressive students wearing Mao badges. Horst Mahler was summoned in a hurry. He insisted that the membership files should be sealed—which they were, before the police carted them off.

The next day there was a march to demonstrate against the high-handed and undemocratic action of the police. Horst Mahler marched with the students. So did other sympathizers from outside the university, including the writer Günter Grass. And the SDS decided that the policy of isolated protest actions was insufficiently effective and should be changed to one of "permanent university revolt." On the last day of January, the membership files were returned to the SDS with their seals unbroken, on a judge's order.

Easter came, bringing colored eggs to the facade of America House. As the permitted—and by now traditional—Easter march against the atom bomb proceeded down the Ku-Damm, some students, mostly members of the SDS, detoured to throw their "eggs"—plastic bags filled with paint—at the familiar windows and blue-painted brick. "Ho-ho-ho-Chi-Minh," they chorused, as the bags of paint were ritually hurled, first at America House and later at the police, who appeared with their truncheons to break up the unpermitted demonstration.

In April the United States Vice-President, Hubert Humphrey, was to visit Berlin. With antagonism to the United States government prevailing among militant students, there was reason to look for trouble; and the police discovered—and arrested—eleven young men and women students and members of Kommune I, Fritz Teufel not among them, concocting wicked things in the attic. The police later claimed that "they had come together in conspiratorial circumstances and had planned attempts against the life or health of the American Vice-President, Hubert Horatio Humphrey, by using bombs and plastic bags filled with unknown chemicals or with stones and other dangerous instruments."

Meanwhile the SDS were discussing the organization of a demonstration during the U.S. Vice-President's visit against his government's waging war in Vietnam, in their offices on the Ku-Damm. About eighty members were at the meeting, which was abruptly interrupted by some other members bursting in to announce that the offices were being observed from the street, where a collection of "apparently private cars with big antennas" were parked in front of the building. The eighty rushed out, broke off the antennas, and let the air out of the tires of the parked cars and painted them all over with swastikas. The "Popo," locked inside their cars, called for the "Schupo"—Schutzpolizei, town police—who came with five radio cars and two troop carriers full of men and arrested the SDS committee members. The others returned to their discussion.

The newspapers of Berlin were untroubled by the actions of the "Popo" but, led by the Springer publications, thrilled their readers imaginatively to the scandal of the bombs and unknown chemicals. Kommune I was renamed by its shocked critics the Horror Commune. "Mao's Embassy in East Berlin supplies bombs against Vice-President Humphrey." "Bomb assassination attempt against U.S. Vice-President Humphrey." "Bomb assassination attempt against U.S. Vice-President." "Murder attempt against Humphrey foiled by Kripo [the criminal police]. Free University students prepare bombs with explosive from Peking."

But before the burghers of Berlin had read these headlines over their morning coffee, it had already been proved to the Kripo by one of their own experts that the "explosive" was nothing but smoke candles, pudding (confections of flour and goo like comedy custard pies), yogurt, and—well tested against America House—harmless paint in plastic bags. The night before their arrest, the "conspirators" had tried out the messy qualities of their missiles against the budding trees of the Grunewald, the woody park on the posh side of West Berlin. Not a bang had been heard. The unharmed trees continued to sprout their sticky—perhaps a few abnormally sticky—buds. As the SDS pointed out, to suggest that such weapons would do harm to bulletproof cars was absurd.

Horst Mahler quickly petitioned against the false arrest of three of the accused, including Dieter Kunzelmann, one of the commune leaders, and the three were released the very next day, April 6, when Vice-President Humphrey flew into West Berlin's Tempelhof airport and was driven to the Town Hall, was welcomed by the President of the State

Parliament and by Mayor Albertz—whose stern demands for disciplinary action by the university authorities against student protesters were being well publicized—and inscribed himself in a "Golden Book."

That evening the three were able to join two thousand other demonstrators assembled in front of the Palace of Charlottenburg, where Humphrey was being entertained. As he arrived and departed, some threw eggs and flour bombs, many waved placards and chanted slogans. A pro-Humphrey demonstration popped up and contrary feelings were argued, as is their wont, with blows. Plainclothes police used a new "grab-troop" technique—pick out, pounce upon, and carry off known ringleaders. The residue of anti-Humphrey demonstrators moved on to the Springer publishing house where the Vice-President was to arrive at nine thirty. They chorused "Murderer!" and "Vice-Killer!" and waved flags of the Vietcong. And with Humphrey himself out of reach among the smiles of Axel Springer and other fans, the demonstrators vented their passion on the parked cars, so spoiling their sleekness with stones and bottles that a new fleet of limousines had to be summoned.

The police, of course, attacked with their rubber truncheons, the students replied with their stones, and twenty-four of them were arrested.

When all was still at last, the remaining eight "horror" communards were set free into the cold, crepuscular, empty streets. When the day was bright, they gave a press conference. They were only, they explained, intending to protest in the style of the Amsterdam "Provos" (provocationists), using pudding and smoke because such things were ridiculous, to provoke laughter, to tease, to humiliate, but not to hurt. One member admitted that "in view of the hysteria in West Berlin, one of the security officers might have started a shootout," but that, on the other hand, Provo actions were more effective than traditional forms of demonstration.

They had been let go because the investigating magistrate had refused to issue a warrant for their continued detention, since in his view smoke bombs, let alone cream cakes, could not be called dangerous weapons. But whether the Kripo removed the false accusations from its files was doubted by the APO, the "Extraparliamentary Opposition"—the student protesters and their allies. Few papers, and none of Axel Springer's, corrected the false information they had printed.

Still the unrepentant *Bild*—Springer's yellowest paper—stuck to its unfounded allegations: "After the assassination plan of the 'Mao' students," it crowed, "jubilation surrounds Humphrey—unprecedented police security." Its lead article fawned: "Berlin thanks Humphrey."

But even the Hamburg publication *Konkret*, a leftist paper largely by and for students (though it was too high-priced for most of them, and had at times so offended the political tastes of Berlin's university students that it had more than once been banned from sale on the campuses), was critical of the communards. Its columnist praised them for "preparing the pudding action" and being a "bourgeois scare," and pointed out that they were "most amusing" too, but complained that they did not exploit the limelight in the right way.

> They used their sudden publicity only for private exhibitionism; they snubbed not only interviewing journalists, but also their viewers and readers, and gave away the chance to mediate between their better knowledge of what was going on in Vietnam and a badly informed public.

Clearly the writer was a more serious-minded sort of critic, who perhaps missed the point of the satirical method and went on to show in what way the chance should have been exploited—by, for instance, challenging Humphrey's declaration in Berlin that the U.S. promise to maintain the freedom of the Vietnamese was to be kept as firmly as the same promise made to the West Berliners. She insisted that the Vietnamese had never asked for that promise, and the Berliners did not necessarily want it either. Her name was Ulrike Meinhof.

But uncrushed by the Springer papers, and not even sobered by the stern advice tempered with conscientious amusement meted out by the half-approving columnist of *Konkret*, the communards continued to clown obligingly for television and the newspapers. Far from snubbing journalists, they granted interviews with enthusiasm. They found them rewarding in terms of hard cash.

But news crowded news out. Another war was looming in the Middle East. And besides, the Berlin papers had some specially titillating items to fill themselves out with. In a few weeks there was to be nothing less than a royal visit to the city-state, by the Shah of Iran and his wife. Popular papers which like to satisfy the curiosity of an obscure majority of their readers concerning the intimate lives, problems, and tastes of well-known persons, especially those of enormous wealth and power and unlimited leisure, turned with relish to the Shah: his riches, his palaces, his peacock throne, his wife, his fabulous this and that, and best of all the "confessions," factual or fictitious, of his ex-wife, Soraya.

Not that the communards would let themselves be forgotten entirely. Dieter Kunzelmann of Kommune I raised his voice and announced to reporters:

"I do not study, I do not work, I have trouble with my orgasm, and I wish the public to be informed of this."

The public was. No doubt a part of it laid down the confessions of ex-Queen Soraya long enough to express its disgust.

2

A Night at the Opera

The Empress Farah Diba herself contributed an account of her family's life to the *Neue Revue,* a glossy weekly. *Konkret* of May 28, 1967, informed its readers of the realities of the Shah's regime with "An Open Letter to Farah Diba":

> You say: "Summers are very hot in Iran, and like most Persians I and my family travel to the Persian Riviera on the Caspian Sea."
>
> Like most Persians—isn't that somewhat exaggerated? . . . Most Persians are peasants with an annual income of less than $100. And for most Persian women every second child dies—50 out of 100—of starvation, poverty, and disease. And the children too, those that knot carpets in their fourteen-hour day—do they too, most of them, travel to the Persian Riviera at the Caspian Sea in summer?
>
> You write: "In this respect the Persian constitution is very strict. The Shah of Persia must have a son."
>
> Strange, that otherwise the Shah does not care two hoots for the constitution, so that not one uncensored line can be published in Persia, so that no more than three students may at any time be standing together in the grounds of the University of Teheran, so that Mossadech's Minister of Justice had his eyes torn out, so that trials take place from which the public is excluded, so that torture is an everyday event of Persian justice.

The open letter goes on to describe an example of tortures by an examining magistrate, including burning by means of a hot plate pressed against the body of the victim and beatings with a truncheon dipped in acid. It ends:

We do not want to insult you. But we also do not wish to see the German public insulted by contributions like yours to the *Neue Revue.*

Respectfully,
Ulrike Meinhof

The issue of *Konkret* was held up by an injunction taken out against it by *Der Spiegel*, because it was imitating its famous red-framed cover. But the open letter was printed separately and distributed as a pamphlet. So even before *Der Spiegel* withdrew its objection and *Konkret* went onto the newsstands, Ulrike Meinhof's message may have reached some five hundred students of the Free University of Berlin.

It was not, however, by means of the pamphlet that most of them were informed about the situation in Iran. Some three days before the state visit, posters appeared all over the city, "Wanted for Murder" notices, with a picture of the Shah and a list of accusations against him, put out by an organization calling itself the International Freedom Front, with an address in Vienna. And at about the same time the agitating news spread that the State of Bavaria was compelling 107 Iranian students to leave Munich and stay in rural parts for about four days, reporting daily to the police, under threat of a year's imprisonment if they disobeyed, until the Shah's visit was over, as they "constituted a danger to the Shah," and Munich students were marching in protest.

On June 1, the eve of the visit, the University Students' Council (to which leftist officers had been elected, and which was therefore not nearly as nonpolitical as in theory it should have been) held a teach-in in the Audi Max on the theme "Persia—Model of a Developing Society." The chief speaker was an Iranian writer in exile, Dr. Bahman Nirumand. He presented the case against the Shah, and the students were horrified by that foreign autocrat and his heartless wielding of power. Another speaker was a lawyer of unquestionable integrity named Hans Heinz Heldmann, who had been an observer of political trials in Iran for Amnesty International in 1965. Kommune I contributed its own kind of comment by offering for sale "Shah and Farah masks," with eye slits, to protect demonstrators from recognition by the police. There was also a paper for sale with the headline "The Shah Is Dead—Farah Ravished."

On June 2 the Shah was officially welcomed to Berlin. A few thousand Shah-loyal Persians had asked to be allowed to greet their emperor at the Tempelhof airport with banners and jubilant cries but had not been permitted that privilege. Instead they were granted the best viewing places at all vantage points, having special areas marked off for them, to which they were whisked in buses. By 2:30 P.M., when the royal couple stood on the steps of Schöneberg Council House to smile and wave, the fans and protesters were thickly assembled on the *Platz*.

Already the fans, armed with small weapons to hit with, like truncheons, had skirmished with some of the protesters. But some protesters, who were armed with small things to throw, like eggs, had waited for this moment. No egg actually struck the Shah or Farah Diba, but one did hit a bodyguard and splattered his trouser leg and shoe. The Shah, however, could not fail to notice that some of the Berlin crowd were hostile to him.

At eight o'clock that evening he and his wife were to be driven in a motorcade to the Opera House along the wide, grand Bismarckstrasse, with Federal Republic President and Frau Lübke, and other dignitaries, among them Willy Brandt, then Vice-Chancellor and Minister of Foreign Affairs, to attend a command performance of *The Magic Flute*.

The buses pulled up in good time for the loyal Persians to assemble in their reserved places directly opposite the Opera House. Their gay and friendly banners were ready to be hoisted on good stout staves, the kind known in England from many a street riot as two-by-ones, that being the measurement in inches of their width and thickness. Fritz Teufel too arrived early, on this fine Friday evening, and seated himself on the edge of the street, behind the police barriers, next to the loyalists: "Jubilation Persians," he called them. Some of the police claimed afterward to have remarked a potential danger in the alien groups' being separated from each other only by "Hamburg barriers," which were effective for demarcation but not at all as shields.

Soon students were very thick on the scene. And all the police were there: Kripo, Schupo, Popo, and Bepo—the anti-Marx brothers.

Certain of the rightness of their cause, the students were in a mood of intense hostility. The police were ready for aggression from the students. The students were ready for violence from the police. Intent on using their new prevention tactics, the police looked about for known ringleaders. There, sitting stubbornly in the most obvious place, was Fritz Teufel. They grabbed him, arrested him, and bore him off some half hour before the Shah arrived and the opera began.

The students and the police continued to feel the threat of each other. Both sides stuck grimly to their mission as they saw it: the students to protest, the police to protect. There was some shoving and shouting, hurling of invective, cheers from the Jubilation Persians. (A senator watching from his own apartment overlooking the scene was to insist afterward that it was the Persians with their staves who made the first violent attacks.) And then there was a rumor that students had stabbed policemen. Some say it was started deliberately by unidentified malicious persons, others that an accidentally misinformed or genuinely mistaken radio announcer had announced it in good faith. However it was started, by the time it reached the Opera House it was all that was needed to unleash violence among the police. Whether in some section of the crowd stones, eggs, and tomatoes were in fact hurled before the police charged, or whether the police charged first, nobody could ever be sure, but the police did charge, stones and other things were hurled, staves were wielded, batons were swung, arrests were made. Many tried to escape, but there were police blocking them off, using a prepared and rehearsed "liver-sausage" tactic—seal both ends and attack them as they burst out of the center.

"Never," a watching television reporter commented, "have individual police been so brutal." (He was, of course, a young man.)

Water cannon were turned on the students as many of them tried to flee down a side street called the Krumme Strasse. They spread out, some turning aside to run into the driveway of an apartment-building courtyard, and there, where cars were parked along the low street wall, and apartment-building walls enclosed it at the back and side, they realized too late that they had rushed into a trap. The police were hard behind them. Several students were knocked down in the rush, or by the enemy falling on their backs with rubber truncheons. Those who could, picked themselves up again. Plainclothes sergeant Karl-Heinz Kurras of the Kripo had his gun out. He aimed and fired, and a man fell. A fellow officer looked to see who had shot, saw the gun in Kurras' hand, and could think of nothing better to do than take the gun away from him. A group gathered around the fallen man. Then a space was cleared around him, and photographs were taken for the newspapers. He had short dark hair and a moustache like a bow.

Late that night a doctor telephoned the SDS offices from the hospital to tell them that the man had been shot in the back of the head and had died soon after 11 P.M., about two hours after reaching the hospital. His name was Benno Ohnesorg. He was a twenty-six-year-old Protestant student from Hanover. Soon it was also known that he had come to participate in his first big demonstration and had hitherto taken no part in political activities, that he was married, and that his wife was pregnant.

The Springer papers made their own fictions out of the event. *Welt am Sonntag* alleged:

First they were kicking, then they pulled out their knives.
. . . They pushed him [the Kripo officer] into a yard, surrounded
him, and kicked him down. When they pulled out their knives, the
Kripo officer pulled out his police gun. . . . Teufel functioned as
the leader of a group which threw stones at policemen, in which
action two officers were wounded.

Scores of people had been hurt in the riot.

The Mayor of Berlin, Pastor Heinrich Albertz of the SPD, was asked
in a television interview why the public were informed that the police
had in fact used guns only when it was revealed that gunshot wounds had
been found.

Albertz replied, "One should perhaps have informed the press some-
what more centrally on the whole course of the Shah's visit. I myself
have the impression that the reporters·of the various papers picked up the
information from their own observations. I would imagine that the reporters knew that shots were fired, if only into the air, as it appeared at
first. Whether information was given or not given on that, I do not know.
It would not have been my job to do so."

The reporter, more placating than aggressive, said, "A speaker of the
senate has said that it was a ricochet. Can you confirm this?"

But Albertz did not seize that rumor as an excuse. "No," he said, "it
was no ricochet. From the deformation of the bullet it can be confirmed
that it was not."

The reporter tried again: "What about self-defense in such situations?"

On this point Albertz was sure. "One can only see it in that light,"
he said, "since an order for the use of firearms was not given. We have
no doubt about its being self-defense. There is no statement and no circumstance which makes the self-defense statement of the officer appear
untrue."

On the Saturday and Sunday following the riot, students brought
flowers to the spot where Benno Ohnesorg had been killed. Official permission for a memorial cross to be erected there was refused.

There were student meetings all through the day and the night of
June 3, and again on June 4, and for many days and nights after that: at
the headquarters of all the parties, in the Audi Max, in the AStA offices,
on the campus, in communes, in the Protestant hostel, in private houses
and apartments. Excitement ran high, not only in Berlin but in all the
universities in the Federal Republic. The shooting of Benno Ohnesorg
stimulated students in other countries: in France, Holland, Britain, and

the United States, wherever in the Western world they were already militant (though the Western world as a whole may have been taking more notice of the war in the Middle East). Günter Grass said that the killing of Ohnesorg was "the first political murder in the Federal Republic."

At a meeting in the SDS offices on the night of June 3, a tall blonde named Gudrun Ensslin protested shrilly that the "fascist state" was out to kill them all, that they must organize for resistance, that they could only answer violence with violence. "It's the generation of Auschwitz—you cannot argue with them!" she cried, reaching a pitch of hysteria and weeping uncontrollably, the black makeup around her eyes running down her cheeks and smeared about her temples. Some were intoxicated with the new strong reality of a battle the students had been spoiling for, more than half pretending to, and now surely had upon them, hard and bloody. Perhaps some felt grief, some fury, but others felt strangely exalted. Grief, fury, or exaltation might have been the emotion which overwhelmed the hysterical blonde. But in the light of subsequent events, it may seem possible that her tears that night were shed in frustration at that being done which she had never yet permitted herself to do—the extreme and violent act.

3

Martyrs and Scapegoats

Some eight thousand students followed the coffin of Benno Ohnesorg on June 8, from the Audi Max of the Free University, where they had assembled at 1 P.M. to hear funeral orations from a student leader and a professor, to a venue near the border of East Germany, where another, short valediction was spoken by Professor-and-Pastor Helmut Gollwitzer to a crowd of about fifteen thousand, and then the motor-borne cortège—one hundred and fifty vehicles—drove on through the DDR, where no mourners lined the route to the border, and so to Hanover in West Germany, where the next day thousands again—twelve thousand, it has been estimated—paid homage to the first martyr of the cause: of—what exactly? University reform? The right to protest? Extraparliamentary oppositionism? Anti-Iranian autocracy? Anti-Western power elites in general? Or what some called "antifascism" and others more credibly "antiauthoritarianism"? Rudi Dutschke expressed the view on television that the state was not yet fascist but was "tending toward fascism."

The funeral of Ohnesorg was marked by a congress held at the University of Hanover, with the theme "University and Democracy." The speeches were published in Number 12 of a series called "Voltaire Pamphlets," edited by one Bernward Vesper, with the title "The Conditions and Organization of the Resistance—the Congress in Hanover." Vesper was the lover or "fiancé" of Gudrun Ensslin, the impassioned prophetess who had cried out against the "generation of Auschwitz" the night after the shooting of Ohnesorg. "Resistance" was the word for the mood of the congress, rousing as a battle cry: "resistance" being the strong reaction of victims, or of those threatened with victimization.

Yet it was just there and then, when the students felt most that their cause was just, with the corpse of Benno Ohnesorg and the fatal wound in the back of his head from a police bullet to prove it, when their official emotion was "righteous indignation," that a warning came from one of the least expected sources that it was they themselves, the students, who were showing tendencies to fascism. The danger of a development in the student movement of a "fascism of the Left" was pointed out by Professor Jürgen Habermas, famous supporter of the cause of university reform, one of the teachers most admired by students, and one of their favorite philosophers—associated with the Marxist "Frankfurt School," to which also belonged Theodor W. Adorno and Herbert Marcuse. At the congress, where officially the discussion was on "university and democracy," Habermas listened to the inflammatory speeches of some of the student leaders, particularly Rudi Dutschke, and then he said, in part:

> The meaning of "provocation" was to be settled tonight so that we do not all talk past each other. In so far as you mean by "provocation" the practice of demonstrational force, it is entirely legitimate. Demonstrational force is that with which we force attention to arguments and so establish conditions for a discussion where it is needed. But if I am to understand provocation in the sense of provoking violence hidden in the institutions into declared and manifest violence, then systematically undertaken provocation by students is a game with terror (with fascistic implications).

The students were affronted, and many other adherents of the Left were disturbed by Habermas' accusation. But Habermas maintained that it was a justified warning, and one that must stand and should be heeded.

But—another surprise for the students—one of their leading antagonists came over to their side. Mayor Albertz announced that the students were right after all. He did not stay in office long after that, being ousted not, it seems, because he was picked as scapegoat by the Berlin authorities but because of his sudden difference of opinion with most of his fellow politicians.

A scapegoat of a kind was, however, supplied: Fritz Teufel. He was held in custody and was not to be let out while awaiting trial, as he was suspected of a "severe breach of the peace": by plotting violence against the American Vice-President, by throwing a stone at a policeman on June 2, and by inciting arson.

The Kripo sergeant Karl-Heinz Kurras, on the other hand, was allowed his freedom while awaiting trial, because he was only to be charged with "careless manslaughter," which, if proved, would carry a lighter sentence.

The Shah, on his part, was also full of righteous indignation. He had driven in his bulletproof car, with the President's wife, Frau Lübke, at his side, to the chunky cubic opera house and alighted to the cheers of the Jubilation Persians and assorted Berliners come to assess his sex appeal with their own eyes; and President Lübke and Farah Diba emerged from their own bulletproof car to the cheers and the personal assessments of those same few eyes which could actually see them in that small space and those few seconds before they disappeared in a lightning of flashbulbs into the building. They could have known little enough of the tumult. At most the Shah could have seen a few antagonistic placards and angry faces, as he sailed down the Bismarckstrasse. But he had seen the placards, heard the catcalls, narrowly escaped the egg earlier in the day. He demanded that the government take action against the demonstrators.

When the demonstrators knew of the demand, they chose a Teufel-like form of resistance. On August 3 they reported by the thousand at police stations and accused themselves of having demonstrated against the Shah. There were far too many for the police to arrest, the prisons to hold, or the courts to deal with, so that round was won by the students.

It could only seem to Teufel's friends and well-wishers that Berlin was lusting for the blood of the poor Devil. But they did not desert him. A hundred students went on a hunger strike in the hostel of the Berlin Protestant Students' Union to protest against his being held in custody.

In August a complaint was lodged with the state court, and he was released. He was told he must hand in his legitimation card and passport to the police. He refused. Instead he went back to the Moabit prison and demanded to be let in again. But without a court order or the agreement of the arresting board, which was not in session, no one could oblige him by locking him up. On September 15 he staged a "go-in" to the Berlin State Parliament with a following of witnesses and disciples, and so achieved rearrest and reincarceration.

The charge of incitement to arson was laid by a Free University student because of a leaflet distributed by Kommune I. When the defense asked the chief prosecutor why he had not charged all the members of Kommune I, as by law he was obliged to prosecute all offenders, the reply was that all the members had been required to attend interrogations, but had not appeared, so they had charged only Fritz Teufel and Rainer Langhans: perhaps because they looked like rebels against law and order, Teufel with a beard, and Langhans with his Struwwelpeter mop. Of course they were guilty. If nothing else, they were guilty of hair.

On November 23, 1967, Detective Sergeant Karl-Heinz Kurras—whose hobby, it transpired, was collecting firearms—was found not guilty of the manslaughter of Benno Ohnesorg on the ground that in the heat of the events of that hour on June 2 he had not been able to think calmly and collectedly before acting. It was a whitewash. It was not explained why, if some policemen had been armed in case of the need to protect the royal guests and the officers of state from violence, orders concerning the use of such arms should have been so unspecific as to permit the aiming of a gun at the back of a man who was trying to flee in the opposite direction.

When the trial of Teufel and Langhans opened on November 28, a thousand students came out to demonstrate for them with red flags outside the Moabit prison and were dispersed with horses and hoses. Rudi Dutschke escaped arrest by fleeing into an architect's office and hiding under the desk, but he had been spotted, and next day a Berlin senator laid charges against him for his part in the unpermitted demonstration.

On appearing in the dock, wearing an open-necked violet shirt under an anorak, Fritz Teufel waved amiably to his audience—the public and the court—before he sat down to hear the proceedings.

"Will you stand up, please," the judge ordered on one occasion.

"Certainly," he replied, "if it will help to uncover the truth."

When a previous conviction was brought up, Teufel explained the theft by naming it a "Mammon-possession-equalizing experiment." He had taken what he needed without paying for it because he considered that "with the present system of utilizing the means of production, it was the right thing to do."

He called the Shah "an operetta gangster from Teheran" and deplored that "the population was degraded into a theater audience with this ham performance."

And of President Lübke: "Some people are puzzling. Take Heinrich Lübke, for instance. One would never believe that he had once designed concentration camps. At most one might expect him to have been a headwaiter at the Führer's headquarters."

And of his own father, who was in court, he said, "My father was anything but a Nazi. He was also no resistance fighter. He was a loyal citizen, sometimes against the church and government, but paying his taxes and church taxes regularly all the same." (He did not remark that it would have been especially curious if he had not, as Teufel Senior was a tax adviser by profession.)

In the world outside, the campaign to free Teufel went on. In the middle of a Berlin concert conducted for the British Broadcasting Corporation by Pierre Boulez, students paraded about with placards demanding "Freedom for Teufel." The BBC announcer asked Boulez if he did not think that the concert atmosphere was too sacred for such actions.

"No, no," the conductor replied. "On the contrary, I am absolutely for doing something under these circumstances. It is very good if some pepper gets into the concert hall."

Teufel was at last let out of the grim brick-and-bar fortress of the Moabit prison in early December 1967, at the end of the first week of his trial, though he was not yet acquitted of all charges. He was met by friends who crowned him with a bulky wreath of fir and presented him with a bouquet of white carnations. Looking like a fancy-dress Spirit of Christmas, he smiled shyly for the press cameras.

The charge of having conspired to bomb Humphrey had been dropped in October, and the judgment on the stone throwing was deferred to January. But early in that month an unrepentant Teufel was offending authority again. He came into court, distributed pamphlets, and set off some firecrackers. So a new charge was brought against him, and on February 23 he was sentenced to two months' imprisonment for distributing pamphlets, insulting behavior, and setting off firecrackers in court. He had still to be judged on the charge of incitement to arson. But as he had been in prison for most of the second half of 1967, there were a number of violent events for which he could not be held responsible.

There had been the August military parade of the Americans, which students in pursuance of their policy of "resistance" had turned out to counter with a parade of their own in support of the Vietcong, waving red flags, and shouting "Ho-ho-ho-Chi-Minh." They were set upon and beaten up by exasperated citizens.

In December a demonstration against the junta in Greece went on from the Greek military mission to take in America House as usual: Ho-ho-ho and the eggs and the paint.

And to round off the year with a joyful noise, students clashed with churchgoers in front of the Gedächtnis Church, an artistic ruin preserved and floodlit at one end of the Ku-Damm as a memorial of 1945 when total war came home to Berlin and bombed it into rubble.

On February 6 the first anti–Vietnam War demonstration of the new year took place, past America House: Ho-ho-ho. And on February 17 and 18 there was a Vietnam congress at the Technical University, from which a protest march set forth, the marchers numbering as many as forty thousand, some have reckoned. They were not only students but many supporters of the Extraparliamentary Opposition (APO)—a community of political opinion rather than an organization. Left-wingers of all shades numbered themselves among its adherents: members of the Argument Club, the Republican Club, the avant-garde of the intellectuals, younger and enlightened academics, communards. But the editor of *Konkret*, Klaus Rainer Röhl, was disgusted to see, as he marched, some seven members of Kommune I—not including Teufel himself— sitting on a balcony overlooking the route, displaying placards which mocked the demonstration and the antiwar enthusiasm, laughing down on the marchers as they calmly smoked their hash pipes.

The communards, it seemed, were beginning to divide, into those who believed in protest and those who believed in hashish. And Dieter Kunzelmann declared his own cause: "I don't care about Vietnam, I care about my orgasm."

On went the demonstration, its voice raised in the chorus of "The International" and the name of Ho Chi Minh. One intrepid enthusiast climbed a crane on a building site to fly the Vietcong flag hundreds of feet up in the air, where, however, it waved in triumph for only a few minutes, because some irritated workmen on the site climbed up and tore it down.

The protest march was considered a great success, sneer though the hash-hippies might: so successful, indeed, that the Berlin senate, the political parties, and the trade unions organized a counter demonstration of their own. A large number of irate citizens marched against students and anarchy on February 21. Anyone who looked as if he might be a student was under threat, and quite a few young or hairy people were beaten up.

This unpleasantness may have influenced the APO to calmer counsels. It established a system of monitors for demonstrations to identify troublemakers and hand them over to the police. The result was that Vietnam demonstrations in March went off without incidents of violence. Ho-ho-ho and "The International" were chorused as lustily as ever, but the messy missiles were not thrown.

But those who were against the protesters were not so easily to be mollified. It was the duty of all good citizens to come to the aid of law and order, as the Berlin press had often enough made clear:

STOP THE TERROR OF THE YOUNG REDS NOW!
Confronted with what is happening today [a list of violent actions by students in many centers of West Germany supplied] one cannot simply go about one's daily business, nor should one leave all the dirty work to the police and their water cannon.
Are our judges asleep? Are our politicians asleep? How long

are they going to permit our young people to be incited by red agitators and our laws to be called into question, made hollow, and disregarded?

Are we a banana republic in which one can trample underfoot justice and law, authority and order with the flimsiest of pretexts; make a fool of the law-abiding citizen and a hero out of the lawbreaker; and in which one can with impunity smash the windows of the Americans, those same Americans who protect us militarily—a protection which is a precondition of being able to demonstrate in freedom in our country?

So blustered the *Bild* on February 12, beside a picture of Dutschke captioned: "SDS—Dutschke: 'Our Vietnam is here in Europe.'"

It was as if in obedience to the prompting of such press items that a twenty-four-year-old housepainter from Munich by the name of Josef Erwin Bachmann went in search of Rudi Dutschke with a loaded gun in his pocket on April 11, 1968, the Thursday before Easter. He inquired for him at the SDS offices and was told he was not there but was likely to be in later.

Dutschke was with a couple of friends, one of them Stefan Aust, who worked on *Konkret*. He parted from them to go and pick up some nose drops for his son, Hosea Che. When Dutschke came riding along the Ku-Damm on his bicycle, the would-be assassin was waiting on the sidewalk outside the SDS offices. Bachmann recognized him, took out his gun, and shot him three times, in the head, throat, and chest. Dutschke fell a few yards from the door of the SDS.

He was taken to the Westend Hospital, unconscious but alive. Photographers arrived to take pictures of his bicycle and his shoes lying in the street. He was operated on that evening. Two days later the chief neurosurgeon at the University Clinic of the hospital was able to report that he no longer had fever, and that there was no fear of paralysis as a consequence of the damage done to his brain.

Bachmann was arrested and interrogated. He said he had done it because he just couldn't abide Communists; that he had been inspired to make his attack by the assassination (on April 4) of Martin Luther King; that he had planned and carried out the deed alone and belonged to no political party. It was found that he had a criminal record and was mentally subnormal. He was held in custody for many months, tried in 1969, and sentenced to seven years' hard labor. In 1970 he committed suicide. It was said that he had tried to kill himself twice before he tried to kill Dutschke.

Whether Bachmann had in fact been inspired to his deed by Axel Springer publications, no one could ascertain. It was soon accepted even by the students who were furiously crying vengeance that he was an unworthy target since he was soft in the head. And whether this made him a typical Springer-paper reader was a question only prejudice could decide. But hours before the identity of the attacker had been found out, reprisals against Springer were under way.

The SDS issued a bulletin:

Friends and Comrades,

This afternoon Comrade Rudi Dutschke was attacked by a youth with three mortally dangerous pistol shots. . . . Irrespective of whether Rudi was the victim of a political conspiracy, one can now positively assert that this crime was plainly the consequence of systematic incitement, mounted by the Springer company and the Senate in ever-increasing measure against democratic rights in this city. We call upon the Extraparliamentary Opposition to come to the Audi Max of the TU [Technical University] at eight o'clock.

From the TU that evening a few thousand demonstrators, chorusing "Spring-er mur-derer!" and "*Bild* shoots too!" and "Burn, Springer, burn!" set out for the Springer building.

"Violence against property but not people," many propounded. Others saw no reason why they should be tender of persons when their own kind were assaulted, arrested, beaten, hosed, and shot.

When the avengers reached the Springer building, they found it protected by armed security guards of the Springer company, police cordons, and water cannon. They smashed the glass front of the entrance hall, set fire to five cars parked in the drive, and badly damaged fourteen others.

Over the Easter weekend there were demonstrations all over West Germany. "Bloody Easter," the newspapers called it. The outbreak of mass violence brought the Minister of the Interior, Gustav Heinemann, to the nation's television screens, to caution that when such a thing as the attempted assassination of Rudi Dutschke happened, it was time for everyone to pause and examine his own conscience, and ask himself how much he personally had contributed to making a climate of opinion in which such a deed was possible, before he accused anyone else.

But the students had made their accusation, and in Bremen, Essen, Esslinger, Hanover, Karlsruhe, Cologne, Bonn, Dortmund, Stuttgart, Freiburg, Ulm, Hamburg, they rioted and went after whatever was Springer-owned and destructible. In Frankfurt the SDS declared that "the

uncontrolled hate campaign of the Berlin Senate and Springer Press
against the minority had turned all who opposed them into fair game for
hunting down," and they marched against Springer's Frankfurt offices
chorusing:

> "Two, three, Vietnam,
> We will catch that Springer man."

Axel Springer returned hurriedly from a visit to America to confer
with Mayor Schütz, successor to Albertz, at the northern seaside resort of
Sylt.

The anti-Springer, pro-Dutschke enthusiasm spread far and wide.
Students in other countries seized upon the issue. Offices of the Springer
organization or, failing them, German embassies, were attacked or
abused by voice and placard in Washington, New York, London, Amsterdam, Brussels, Paris, Milan, Belgrade, Tel Aviv, Vienna, and Prague
(where Dutschke had paid a visit not long before he was shot). In Rome
police dispersed rioters who were setting off giant firecrackers in front of
the German embassy. In Oslo the embassy was painted with black swastikas.

In Munich (where the SDS had declared earlier in the month, some
six days before the shooting, "We intend from now on to use violence
against property, and also to transgress the laws"), demonstrating, resist-
ing, righteously indignant students attacked with stones, which struck an
Associated Press photographer so hard upon the head that he was carried
off to the hospital unconscious and died some days later. A student also
was stoned to death. The students blamed Springer and the police and
the authorities generally.

The AStA (Students' Council) of Munich University, however, rejected all violence. They maintained that the two dead were victims of
the demonstrators. And the Student Liberal Party (LSD) spoke out
clearly: "We accept our share of the responsibility for the deaths of these
two people."

In Berlin the violence went on and on, and the APO announced
that it would go on demonstrating until, and through, May 1. A bishop
of Berlin offered to arbitrate, but was turned down. Groups of the SPD
and the Liberal Party offered to arbitrate, but were also turned down. And
ex-Mayor Albertz offered too, but got no further than the others.

On the day that Dutschke was shot, Stefan Aust, the friend he had
parted from shortly before, came looking for him in the later afternoon.
He found Dutschke's shoes still lying in the street, and the abandoned

bicycle. He also found *Konkret* columnist Ulrike Meinhof—his colleague and erstwhile editor in chief—piling up stones outside the door of the SDS. She told him she didn't think she'd be able to throw them; she was too afraid, she said. But it was expected of her that she do something. The two got into her blue Renault and drove to a spot not far from the Springer truck yard.

The car was parked, so it seemed to the police, precisely for the purpose of blocking the egress of Springer vehicles. Ulrike Meinhof was charged and tried, as were others, including Horst Mahler, for their share in the riots and the damaging of property. Mahler was found guilty, ordered to pay damages amounting to DM 76,000 (about $20,000), and sentenced to two years' imprisonment, suspended. Ulrike Meinhof was luckier: Stefan Aust, being a kind and sensible friend, explained to the court that she had parked extremely badly. Her defending lawyer, one Kurt Groenewold, wanted to make political capital out of the trial by stressing the political justification for the attack. His address to the court could have amounted to a confession of aggressive intent. But the court had already accepted Stefan Aust's story, and Ulrike Meinhof was acquitted. It was true she had thought of throwing stones, but hadn't brought herself to do so. She had thought of helping to make a barricade with her car, and regretted it. She was not quite ready to be a political martyr. Not yet.

4

For Theoretical Consideration Only

Student revolt began to cool after the middle of 1968.

Many of the nonaligned students—always the majority—who had been shocked by the shooting of Benno Ohnesorg into supporting the SDS or, more broadly, the APO, were helped back to detachment by the politicos themselves, who, for weeks after June 2, 1967, would interrupt lectures and demand that everyone stop and discuss "the political struggle," to the increasing annoyance of those who wanted to qualify. Furthermore, students who were by no means right-wingers or even staidly conservative, often found the methods of the Leftists unacceptable. There was, for instance, the SDS action in Frankfurt in September 1967, where they were holding their national congress. A group broke into the Frankfurt America House and busted up a debate on the Vietnam War in which, and because, different opinions were being freely expressed.

Those who remained in the protest movement now advocated taking the initiative of attack, though a last fingernail-hold on the old principle of pacifism was maintained with the argument that the state, the police, the power wielders of the Western world were violent (vide Vietnam) and therefore they were still only defending themselves by attacking. When Horst Mahler's colleagues were sitting in deliberation over the question of his disbarment after the Springer riots, a group of his student supporters demonstrated for him by making a planned attack. There had been a meeting at the Republican Club, and the two factions of the SDS could not agree. The discipline-minded socialists wanted to wait and see what the outcome of the hearing would be, but the anarchists, the "wild ones," wanted action. They marched to the Administrative Court ready-armed with stones, and as soon as they saw policemen they attacked them. As it turned out, Mahler was let off by his fellow lawyers; but still his student supporters held that they had been "acting defensively against fascism." In their own view they remained victims and the champions of victims.

The phase of riot and disruption was put an end to at last by the reform of authoritarian and unadaptable systems in the universities. In 1969 they were granted new constitutions. Students were represented directly on the governing bodies, in some cases to the extent of composing a third of the council, the other two thirds being composed equally of the senior and junior teachers. The SDS, torn apart by internal strife, dissolved itself in 1970. The public protest demonstrations, which had become a feature of the sixties, became rarer and more local and immediate in aim. The Vietnam War, however, continued for another five years.

But there were some students who did not easily find their way back to normal life after the excitement of the demonstration years; and a few did not find their way back at all.

In 1969, while overt protest was on the decline, there were forty-eight mysterious bomb attacks directed against "things and not people." The government gave its opinion that those who were responsible were "isolated individuals and small militant groups on the fringes of the New Left." And a number of Leftists gave it as theirs that the bombs were planted by the police to create a fear of terrorism which would justify repressive measures on their part—such as the implementation of the "emergency laws" which were finally passed in the late sixties after ten years of parliamentary debate, several of intense APO protest, and which have never yet been applied.

But many believed, not implausibly, that an underground resistance movement was forming. The guess was made that those behind the bombings were no other than that group which had been suspected of plotting such things before now: Kommune I.

After it had broken apart, some members stayed in Berlin, while others went south to Munich. Rainer Langhans showed up in Munich as manager and lover of the glossiest of fashion models. There he lived the chic life, but that by no means required the sacrifice of leftist sentiments. On the contrary, many of the most fashionable and affluent of the Western world were part of what was called the Chic Left—the "Schili" in Germany (from *schick* meaning chic and *die Linke* meaning the Left, a term originating in Hamburg, probably in *Konkret* circles)—and Langhans could not have found it hard to fit in with them nicely.

But not so the nation's favorite scapegoat, Fritz Teufel. To stay outside of society was the only right way for those, no longer students, who wished, as Teufel did, still to be the champions of the victims of fascism, capitalism, and the imperialist exploiters: and to avoid becoming too obviously sufferers from prosperity themselves. He too went to Munich, but made no compromise with law and order. In 1970 he got into trouble for putting little bombs into a courtroom. (An amnesty for students kept him willy-nilly out of jail for a time.) But meanwhile his past deeds—or his alleged deeds—had begun to have great consequences.

For something else happened in 1968 for which it was thought Teufel might be to blame, though in fact he was positively acquitted of the charge which might have connected him to the event.

It was that "incitement to arson" of which he and Langhans had been accused. And the event, which happened eleven days after Teufel and Langhans had been acquitted of inciting arson, was arson. And to know how they came to be charged with the crime at all, the story has to be traced back even further, to May 22, 1967, between the Humphrey visit and the shooting of Benno Ohnesorg.

On that date a terrible fire spread through a department store called A l'Innovation in Brussels. On May 24 four pamphlets were distributed at the Free University by Kommune I, signed with its own name. One of them tells a story of how the fire came about, claiming to have got the information from a member of a pro-Chinese group, "Action for Peace and Friendship among the People":

NEW FORMS OF DEMONSTRATION TRIED
FOR THE FIRST TIME IN BRUSSELS

In a superscale happening, Vietnam demonstrators created warlike conditions for half a day in the center of Brussels.

This largest fire catastrophe in Belgium for many years had a prelude. At the time of the fire, an exhibition of American goods was being held at the large store "A l'Innovation" to increase the sale of American goods. A group of anti-Vietnam demonstrators took advantage of the occasion to give emphasis to their protests against the American Vietnam policy. . . . "We decided on this form of happening, which was to help remove the difficulty of imagining the conditions in Hanoi during an American bomb attack" [said the activist "for Peace and Friendship"].

The course of the happening speaks for careful planning: for days before, smaller demonstrations of the same kind had taken place in front of the store with placards and speech choruses, and in the store itself firecrackers were set off between the counters. The personnel were therefore accustomed to such noises and disruptions. The significance of these preparations showed themselves when the fire broke out, when the personnel in the first instance reacted neither to the explosions nor to the shouts and the sounding of the alarm bells. . . . The fire very quickly took hold of the upper floors and spread to the surrounding stores and businesses as the streets in this area were very narrow for the approaching fire brigade. . . In all, about four thousand shoppers and employees must have been involved in the catastrophe. The store was one ocean of flames and smoke. Panic broke out among the people, many of whom were trampled underfoot. Some fell like burning torches from the windows. Others lost their heads and jumped into the street and were smashed to pieces. Eyewitnesses report: "It was a picture of the Apocalypse"; many, screaming for help, died of suffocation. A huge task force of firemen and police was extremely hampered in its operations because of the crowd of curious onlookers and the unfavorable location. Their vehicles were themselves several times endangered by the flames. . . .

Only after seven hours was the huge conflagration under control. The damage is estimated at about DM 180 million ($45 million).

The next two pamphlets offered "King Customer" the experience of burning as a novelty for sale: "revolution in rose, propane gas in red" and "a prickling Vietnam feeling." They were written in the extravagant language of advertising, and as though American business interests had been behind the "Apocalypse of Brussels" out of heartless commercialism, as, the satirists implied, they were behind the Vietnam War.

But it was the last pamphlet that seemed to many readers, including the state prosecutor, to urge the committing of similar atrocities.

WHEN WILL THE BERLIN STORES BURN?

Until now it has been the Amis who have had to pay the supreme price for the sake of Berlin. We regretted that these poor pigs had to splash their Coca-Cola blood in the jungles of Vietnam. So at first, we shambled with placards through empty streets, once in a while threw eggs at America House, and finally would have liked to see H.H.H. smother in pudding. We may piss on the Shah when we storm the Hilton, and maybe he'll also find out how beneficial a castration is if there's anything at all still hanging there . . . one hears such naughty stories.

Things can be thrown at facades, representatives [e.g., of America] can be made to look ridiculous, but the only way the population can get to participate is through exciting press reports. Our Belgian friends have now discovered the trick of how to let the population take a real personal interest in the merry goings-on in Vietnam: they set fire to a store, three hundred satiated citizens and their exciting lives come to an end, and Brussels becomes Hanoi. Now no one needs to shed tears for the poor Vietnamese people over his breakfast paper. As from today he can simply walk into the made-to-measure department of KaDeWe, Hertie, Woolworth, Bilka, or Neckermann and discreetly light a cigarette in the dressing room. . . .

If there's a fire somewhere in the near future, if an army barracks goes up into the air, if in some stadium a stand collapses, be little surprised. Just as little as when the Amis transgress the demarcation line, or bomb the city center of Hanoi, or send marines marching into China.

Burn, warehouse, burn.

The mixture of callousness or even outright sadism in the attitude expressed toward the sufferings of shoppers and the workers in the store, with a "humaner-than-thou" attitude toward the victims of war, was not only the result of a pious belief that people who go about shopping in Western Europe deserve to be punished for their presumed indifference to the war in Indochina, but a more general conviction too: that buying things from department stores is fraught with hidden political danger and, indeed, that department stores themselves are evil. They are the temples and the poison wells of the consumer society. And the consumer society is one in which certain power elites, such as big business and the American government (the latter so propped up by the former as to be virtually indistinguishable from it), keep the mass of the people subjected to them, unable to rise against their subjugation because they are placated into an illusion of contentment by the material plenty which the rulers make available to them. Thus one side of the picture is material plenty and "choice," with all the illusion of freedom that that conjures up, and the other side is the war in Vietnam, the black slums of the United States, the wretchedness of the peasants of Bolivia and Uruguay. These implications were often summed up in the expression "consumption terror" (or "consumption fascism"), which emphasized the connection between oppression and the goods for sale in the stores of developed nations.

It was a point of view expressed in works of the Frankfurt School philosophers, most famously in Herbert Marcuse's *One-dimensional Man*, published in 1964. It was not that such a philosophy inspired those students of North America and Europe who threw themselves into the emotionally energetic riots of the sixties, but it confirmed and justified some of their existing attitudes.

Marcuse held that workers in the prosperous, technologically advanced countries now have their needs satisfied beyond sufficiency to superfluity by the power elites and that much of what they get is in satisfaction of false needs, while their true needs remain undiscoverable by themselves.

What was wrong was not that power elites were manipulating the irresponsible masses, but that they were the wrong power elites—an idea by no means new. Nor was the lament that man is threatened by his own technology a new one. Others had admonished man about that too. But the idea that provision in surfeit for material and immaterial needs made for a new "opium of the people" gained much currency not only among the children of Germany's economic miracle, and not only among students (whose material needs are in any case fewer than their elders'), but generally among that dispersion of leftist sentiment known as the Schili; so it was mostly members of the upper and middle classes who, being the most amply provided for, took up this fierceness against the amenities.

Marcuse despaired of the workers as a potential revolutionary force, because they think they're happy.

" 'The people,' previously the ferment of social change, have moved up to become the ferment [sic!—one might suggest "cement"] of social cohesion. . . ."

For the necessary dissatisfaction, he looked elsewhere: "Underneath the conservative popular base is the substratum of the outcasts and outsiders, the exploited and persecuted of other races and other colors, the unemployed and the unemployable. They exist outside the democratic process. . . . Thus their opposition is revolutionary even if their consciousness is not."

In Marcuse's terms, the students might see themselves as representing "the most advanced consciousness of humanity," whose mission it is to lead the "substratum" of society, its "most exploited force" too ignorant and powerless to be effective by itself, in revolutionary uprising. The enemy is the established order of all or any of the advanced industrial societies. The leaders who "without hope . . . give themselves to the Great Refusal" must not be committed to the society whose interests require the peaceful continuance of its ways, because they must be willing to try illegal means when the legal ones do not answer. The students were such a group, and found "the most advanced consciousness of humanity" a description aptly applicable to themselves.

But Marcuse gave them something even better than that: a justification for their aggression. He told them that they were quite as subjugated as those who lived in the politically totalitarian states on the other side of the Berlin Wall—by being forced to endure the tolerable and rewarding and comfortable, to suffer food and clothing and lodging beyond bare necessity, to have many varieties of luxury foisted on them, and to be conned into the illusion that they were free.

In their insistence that authorities of all kinds were "fascist" or "tending toward fascism" was a desire to fight a battle a generation too late (while at the same time, critics pointed out, taking advantage of the actual freedom which democracy and its liberal institutions gave them in order to abuse democracy and freedom). It was a youthful ambition to be heroic—to be the heroes their fathers had failed to be. At the same time there was another desire, to identify themselves with victims. Often in the late sixties students were heard to say, "We are the Jews of today." The recent victims had become hero-martyrs, and the children of the martyr-makers felt an envy of suffering—in German, more neatly, *Leidensneid*. This was not an assumption of guilt, but a repudiation of it.

The American "denazification" plan had educated this postwar generation to values by which America's war in Vietnam could only place the white, Western affluent classes in the invidious position of being the guilty. But though they were white, middle-class, and lived in the prosperous West, none of this was by their own choice. It was their elders who made the war, not they. So they took refuge in "belonging to a generation" which disclaimed the guilt for what their fathers were doing, whether making war in Vietnam, exploiting the South American peasants and the North American blacks, or ordering the police action in West Germany; and, as they were the victims of the last, they had a right to identify themselves with, and champion, the victims of the distant wars and exploitations. It was a "Don't blame me!" cry that had to overprove itself with emotional aggression and exaggerated accusations. The whole of the older generation was "fascist," by default if nothing else, unless an individual member of it could prove himself otherwise. (Fritz Teufel's accusations against his father in court exemplified this attitude.) But once having put themselves on the side of the oppressed and downtrodden, they preferred to call their movement a "class struggle" rather than a generational one. The oppressors, the warmongers, the exploiters, the older lot were "the bourgeoisie." And scorn of the "bourgeois" forced the young to define that contemptible being not in terms of income, occupation, job status, descent, or education, but, to let themselves out of the category, by opinion merely. He ceased to be bourgeois who scorned the bourgeoisie. Only a few were troubled by an inconsistency, which many marked in their parents, between views held and the values a way of life reflected. Some of those few felt they must prove their sincerity by living differently—in communes, for instance—and doing something to change the way things were.

Since the war many parents had raised their children with liberal-leftist ideas, and the "rebellion" of their sons and daughters was not against the ideas but against the hypocrisy they saw in those who taught and did not live by them. Big Daddy America too had set himself up as a good guy and yet had dropped atom bombs on Japan, and now he was bullying Vietnam. They repudiated what their elders did, and claimed to want no part of the world they had made. And yet, at the same time, they did not really want to be poor, or to have any less than they had, materially or immaterially.

To pretend to be victims was one thing, to become victims another. It was the conscience of the rich they were displaying, and accusing those whom they really trusted of vicious intent was a luxurious game of revolt (which was why the shooting of Benno Ohnesorg came as a real shock to many of them—though for some it was a starting pistol, providing a better excuse than Vietnam for making terror).

They have been called the "fatherless generation," not only because of the numbers of men who died in the Second World War but because the fathers were preoccupied with making the "economic miracle." But more importantly, the authority of the fathers had been weakened by a police state. The expropriation of individual moral responsibility by an authoritarian regime may have done damage that was harder to repair than material ruin. Then the demoralization was intensified by defeat. And outlasting that by far was their stigmatization in the eyes of their children of having been inarguably and terribly in the wrong.

But some call them the spoiled children of the economic miracle, who, never having known want and oppression, were simply incapable of appreciating what their fathers bestowed upon them. To be privileged, free, indulged, well fed, well housed, well clothed, was to stand accused! Except that Herbert Marcuse came to their rescue. He placated their *Leidensneid.* He told them that they were in fact oppressed and subjugated by the very plenty and comfort and tolerance which they enjoyed.

The subtly oppressive power elites who were inflicting material plenty and ambivalent liberty upon them had to be overthrown. And when the students went out into the streets and used violence to resist the fascist or tending-toward-fascist government and its police forces, they were doing no more than Marcuse and others of their prophets, such as Adorno, explicitly advocated. However, they were in for a surprise which left some of the disciples with a sense of actual betrayal.

In July 1967 Dr. Herbert Marcuse arrived in Berlin to lecture to the students at the Free University, some of whom met him at the airport and drove him first to the courtyard where Benno Ohnesorg had been shot a little over a month before. Marcuse commented sympathetically that they should never have allowed themselves to be driven into such an obvious trap.

He was received at the Free University (of which he was an honorary professor) with huge enthusiasm. He paid a visit to Kommune I, where he did not find Fritz Teufel, who was in custody in the Moabit prison suspected of conspiring to bomb Humphrey, throw stones, and incite arson.

The students swarmed to hear him. But he left having lost much of his popularity with them. They said that his talk was "superficial" and "thesislike."

However, he returned on May 13, 1968. It was the day of the great march of students and workers in Paris, under the red flags of communism and the black flags of anarchism, a day of euphoria and conviction that at last student leadership, or at least cooperation, was to be accepted by workers, and a real revolution was to begin (an event which was, in fact, to prove not the dawn of revolution but the high noon of the student protest movement in France).

The Audi Max and a nearby lecture hall into which Marcuse's voice was carried by loudspeakers were both packed full.

He told his large audience that he had come to Berlin to visit Rudi Dutschke in hospital, who was, he assured them, getting along nicely, and almost his old self again.

In the course of his lectures he said, more than once, in different words but with the same implication, that the "liberation of consciousness means demonstrations, in the literal sense."

When he was done, discussion was invited.

There was a noisy outburst of heckling. Some wanted to talk about the events in France, the siege of the Sorbonne, the big march. Others shouted that there was no need for talk any more, that there had been more than enough talk, that if Marcuse meant what he had written and said he should be participating in the practice ("praxis" was the word they used, which has become a jargon word of the New Left, even among English speakers) of revolution.

Professor-and-Pastor Helmut Gollwitzer, who had delivered a funeral oration for Benno Ohnesorg, said, "Anyone who is not interested in theory should stop calling himself a socialist." The rowdy objections grew rowdier. "Do we," the Professor asked, "want to carry on with a discussion at all?" Incoherent voices answered him. He asked several times, and the answer was clear enough, however inarticulate. So Dr. Marcuse decided to leave earlier than he had planned.

He paused to give his curtain line:

"Those who are for 'praxis,' " he said, "and against theory, are nevertheless the ones who have talked most here today."

The guest departed, and for some the sport had ended too soon. Members of Kommune I opened the sliding doors behind the lecture podium, lifted the emblem of the university out of its slots, kicked out the wooden motto, *Libertas*, took it outside the Henry Ford building, and set fire to it. (Passersby paused to watch, and one shouted out to Dieter Kunzelmann, "Ach so, that's the way you manage to get your orgasm!")

However, Marcuse was never entirely rejected by his fans. He lost popularity less than his Frankfurt School colleague "Teddy" Adorno, who was so abused by his Frankfurt students that some say he died of it. In 1969 at Frankfurt University, girls bared their breasts in his lectures— the "praxis" of that sexual liberation which was part of the Frankfurt School philosophy. Adorno found "the malicious enjoyment of the conservatives over the lecture room striptease the most disgusting part of the whole disgusting business." But he firmly maintained, "In my writing I have never provided a model for any sort of action or campaign. I am a theoretical person."

In 1967 students of the Free University of Berlin had presented him with a small red rubber teddy bear, symbolically and contemptuously. Marcuse at least got red carnations. But the radical students could not forgive either of them for refusing to support them in the actual event of their forcing violent confrontation.

Some say that on one occasion a satirical comment was made on Marcuse's adherence to his position as theorist, when someone in his audience began to accompany his familiar phrases with a little tune on a recorder. Fritz Teufel was, of course, given the credit or the blame by some. But it may have been one of the things Fritz Teufel didn't do: like, the court decided at last, the incitement he had been accused of.

The words of the pamphlets about the Brussels fire were studied long and carefully by literary pundits and psychiatrists, who had been called in as expert witnesses, and who testified that Fritz Teufel and Kommune I were—and showed in their writing that they were—essentially nonviolent.

Readers of Springer's *Bild-Zeitung* might not agree. They might be convinced that students and other reds, sitting on the floors of their rooms in the communes, under the posters of Che Guevara, where sex and germs abounded, would lay down their hash pipes and guitars to read the pamphlets, and leap up to go and commit arson in German department stores. Not that they in their turn failed to believe that apparently inciting words might be quite honestly for theoretical consideration only—as in the case of the *Bild* articles which were falsely and unjustly blamed for Bachmann's attack on Dutschke—but in the pamphlets criminal action was obviously being incited.

No, the experts and the judges concluded, it was not; the pamphlets were literary compositions, not to be acted on but for theoretical consideration only.

So Fritz Teufel and Rainer Langhans were acquitted of incitement to arson on March 24, 1968.

Eleven days later arson was committed: in order, it transpired, to bring the Vietnam War home to Europeans lulled into euphoric contentment by the "consumption terror." And it was only a beginning, for the arsonists were later to claim that their deed with fire bombs was the first battle in what they called the People's War—*der Volkskrieg*—the first shot of which, however, had not been fired by them, so they would maintain, but by Detective Sergeant Karl-Heinz Kurras on June 2, 1967.

PART TWO
BURN, WAREHOUSE, BURN

5

Momma's Boy and the Parson's Daughter

The arson—or the first battle in the *Volkskrieg* against the "consumption terror"—took place in Frankfurt on the night of April 2–3, 1968, when two department stores, the Kaufhof and Schneider, were deliberately set on fire by means of fire bombs.

On April 4, four people were arrested and charged with the crime. Three of the four had recently come from Berlin. Two of the three had been students at the Free University. One of the two had been a vociferous member of the SDS; that one was Gudrun Ensslin, who had been so inflamed by the killing of Benno Ohnesorg. The others were Andreas Baader, Thorwald Proll, and Horst Söhnlein. They all denied having had anything at all to do with the fires. Later two of them confessed. They claimed a high moral motive: "to light a torch for Vietnam."

Thorwald Konrad Proll was born in Kassel in 1941, the son of an architect. He passed his *Abitur*—the final school examination—in 1962, at a school of high academic standards, his own attainment, however, being an average of "just under Satisfactory." The year before he finished his schooling, his parents were divorced. His father undertook the care of Thorwald and his sister, Astrid (since their mother who had left them all "did not properly attend to her parental duties," as the court put it). Thorwald went to Berlin to study art at the Free University, but gave it up, perhaps because he found academic study too hard or perhaps because he believed that one should work with one's hands and become "a member of the *Lumpenproletariat*"—to which status he laid claim in court when asked his occupation. He did not have regular employment in this capacity and found time to attend anti-Vietnam demonstrations and congresses—also to sit and drink in a local dive, where he encountered Andreas Baader. He was also seen often in the communes of Berlin.

He had married, but was separated from his wife. And he was out of work and out of funds.

Hubert Hartmut Horst Söhnlein was born in 1942 in Thuringia, which became part of East Germany after the war. His parents brought him to West Germany. There his father worked as a factory engineer and a head of a department. In 1961 Horst found himself a pad in Munich and started the "action theater" in which he also performed as an actor. The venture was not a financial success. He too had married and separated from his wife. He and Thorwald Proll were described in court as "comrades in faith" with each other and with the other two accused.

Gudrun Ensslin was born on August 15, 1940, in Bartolomä, a tiny hamlet in Swabia, north of Stuttgart. She was the fourth of seven children. Two of the children were mentally defective. Their father, Helmut Ensslin, who openly confessed to a descent from Hegel, was a pastor of the "Evangelical Church in Germany."

"A parson's daughter!" many exclaimed when the deeds of Gudrun Ensslin made newspaper headlines, as surprised as if Christianity and violence have always been antithetical, or ideals of peace incompatible with acts of war.

Certainly the church to which the father, Helmut Ensslin, belonged had a significant influence on the opinions by which, and to which, his daughter was raised.

The Evangelical Church in Germany, the EKD, put much stress on the examination of conscience. An organization formed in 1945, the year of Germany's defeat and Hitler's downfall, it claimed its origin in the "Confessing Church" which had been formed shortly after Hitler's rise to power in opposition to his *Reichskirche*, in which he unified the twenty-nine German Protestant churches. Soon after its postwar inception, the EKD announced that it was against blind obedience to authority and with this in view would promote education in political, social, and international realities. It concerned itself deeply with the problem of the reunification of Germany, since nearly half the German Protestants were in the eastern communist republic, and many of its members held strong views against rearmament.

The theologian whom Pastor Ensslin most admired was Karl Barth, spiritual leader of the Confessing Church, who had refused to swear an oath of loyalty to Hitler and had moved to Switzerland. Barth rejected what he called the "Neo-Protestant doctrine of the revelation of God in history," so a sharer of his views might be expected to reject Hegel's "justification of God in history" and the Marxist view of history as an arbiter;

but Helmut Ensslin, disgusted with what he called the "present capitalist bourgeois climate," was less out of tune with Marxist views.

He denied that he withdrew much to search his conscience—"a cliché about parsons," he said—but did withdraw into his study to sketch and paint. He liked to do portraits of members of his family, sentimental pictures generally, during the forties and fifties. Later his work was non-figurative. His "two callings," he said, were "jealous of each other." Small and lean, morose and uneasy, simultaneously forbidding and timid, alternately offering and refusing to explain himself, he had chosen two callings which together expressed a conflict between desiring involvement in the world at large, and grudging it any attention beyond scorn. Events in the family had been painful enough to make him and his wife, Ilse, become touchy, bitter, and aggressive. But even in their youth they had both been attracted to circles which despised society and sought romantically to escape from it. Both of them had belonged to the Wandervögel—"wandering birds," a movement which started before the First World War—a rucksack, campfire, and moral-purity movement which involved rejection of city life as degenerate and overrefined and the revival of old soldier-of-fortune songs. It was escapist and elitist. After the First World War the Wandervögel believed that the Allies had imposed democracy and parliamentarianism on Germany against its natural inclinations. The West they regarded as superficial, brittle, brash.

The youth associations which came after the Wandervögel took much of their ideology from them: the joining of a socialistic community, obedience to a leader, a damp cult of comradeship, a sentimentality over old national customs, back-to-nature health cults, a mystical idea of the German nation; they added self-sacrifice and the romantic idealization of violence, death, and Wagnerian disaster. A youth who could like or even swallow all that needed no great powers of adaptation to move on to the Hitler Youth. The Wandervögel had not been exactly like the Hitler Youth, but they prepared a useful state of mind for it.

In addition to all this or underlying it as a cause was the generally censorious atmosphere of traditional Swabian Pietism, in which Ilse Ensslin had been raised. (Pietism is an extreme form of puritan Protestantism which only in Swabia was allied with the established church.) It was all very serious.

Gudrun was educated in political, social, and international realities: to be against rearmament and for reunification, and concerned generally with social problems, especially those of developing countries. She learned of the great wrongs and injustices: the sufferings of the Third

World, the cold war between the two armed camps, the horrors of war and the atom bomb; she acquired a trust in the efficacy of unilateral disarmament and a contempt for the base materialistic greed of bourgeois society.

In 1950 she left the elementary school and started at the Tuttlingen *Gymnasium*. The blond schoolgirl had strong, distinct features even in the soft flesh of childhood—straight nose and firm jaw. She uttered radical and extreme views, learned at home and heated up with adolescent emotionality. The injunction against making peace with her own conscience did not aid tolerance of others. But she did her duty by them, laid her care and consideration upon them, attended the gatherings of Protestant youth in the parish or further abroad, joining in the songfests to the accompaniment of guitars. Plainly dressed, and with her hair tied up in a pair of pigtails, she would belt out the folk songs and the Lutheran hymns and traditional songs—as later she would the anti-bomb songs, peace songs, protest songs. At home there was many a family concert. Frau Ensslin—who had played the church organ while her husband was at the war—would be at the piano, one of the boys played the cello, and Gudrun the violin.

Gudrun helped her mother, worked hard at school, got good grades, took the Bible-instruction class, and scraped away yet again at, or joined in another chorus of, "At All Times Sing Hallelujah!" or "Is Your Life Full of Guilt?" or "Must I Then, Must I Then from the Little Town Depart?" It was decided early that she was going to be a teacher. In June 1958, under a scheme of the International Christian Youth Exchange, Gudrun went for a year to Warren, Pennsylvania, where she attended the local high school. She lived in the Methodist parish with temporary foster parents and fell in love with an American boy. But she said later that she was "horrified by the political naiveté of the Americans." She found much fault with America, its social injustice, its material inequality. But she had not arrived innocent of all prejudgment of the country, so this was not a case of an eye-opener or an education in social realities. She found what she looked for, and what was certainly there to find.

She returned to the new family home at Bad Cannstatt in Stuttgart, where her father had meanwhile transferred to become vicar of the Martin Luther Church. The school she attended was the Königin-Katharina-Stift, where she won a prize, donated by the rich father of a fellow pupil who had died, for "social engagement in pupil-codetermination." In March 1960 she took her *Abitur*. Her average mark was a little under "Good" (that is, just under two in a descending six-level grading system). She applied for the coveted and generous grant awarded by the Study

Foundation of the German People, but her grades had not been quite good enough. However, she went on, that summer, to the University of Tübingen, to read Philosophy and two subjects formidably designated Anglistics and Germanistics.

She lived at first with a strict spinster aunt who "horrified" her. And when the aunt found her smoking a cigarette and presented her with an ultimatum, "Stay and do not smoke or smoke and go," she went.

She took a small furnished room near the university, where she attended lectures on Goethe's novels, Shakespeare's dramatic art, the poetry of Hölderlin, the work of modern philosophers, including Sartre.

In her fourth semester she met a fellow student of Germanistics named Bernward Vesper, the editor-to-be of the "Voltaire pamphlets."

Bernward (a medieval German name such as appealed to romantics of his father's generation) was the son of Will Vesper, a writer of the "Blubo" (Blut und Boden—Blood and Soil) school of emotional-mystical-nationalist literature much favored by the Nazis. Will Vesper had been at it for some time before the Nazis came along. In 1908, when he was twenty-six, his book of poems The Harvest had been a success. His first wife was an artist who drew the decorations for his book. She bore him four children and they had a long and happy marriage. But then he met a very rich young lady, and he divorced his wife so that he could marry her. They lived on a farm. "Earthy is everything true," he wrote in the front of one of his own volumes for a friend, "and this alone endures." His second wife bore him two children; the younger was Bernward.

The Nazis liked Will Vesper, and he apparently liked them:

> My Führer, at every hour,
> Germany, Germany, knows what a weight
> You bear, and how at your heart's core
> You fight and win the burdensome battle of fate.

He did not believe in education for girls. His daughters did, and resented being relegated to sewing and such occupations as their father judged aesthetically suitable for them. But Bernward was to have lots of it. His mother was very ambitious for him. He went to Tübingen University, rebelled against his father, became an ardent Leftist, and engaged in the antibomb movement. But he had an "inner gentleness," according to his half-sister Marlene, and was "not a dynamic personality." His father died in 1962. In the summer of that year he met Gudrun.

They went off together to Spain and hid in the Alhambra so as to be locked in for a night. And there they consummated their love.

Marlene Vesper remembered Gudrun in her Tübingen days with

Bernward as "so quiet, she seemed to hang on his lips, you didn't even know she had an opinion of her own until you got her alone without him." Idealistic and intellectual, he was everything Gudrun could approve of. He read his Marx, his Marcuse, and his Mao. She too committed herself passionately to opposing the atom bomb and to pacifism in general, though she was not a peaceful soul. With two other students, a French girl and an American boy, they started a small publishing venture, Studio Neue Literatur. From several writers, among them Heinrich Böll, they requested and received contributions to an anthology which they published in 1964: *Against Death—Voices Against the Atom Bomb.*

In 1963 Gudrun left Tübingen and attended the College of Education in Swäbish Gmünd, where in the spring of 1964 she took her first exam to qualify as a primary school teacher. Her average mark was Satisfactory. She was judged to be Good in sociology and philosophy, but her teaching ability was assessed as only Adequate.

She then changed her mind about becoming a teacher and started to work on a doctorate on the poet Hans Henry Jahn.

The publishing business was not flourishing. Studio Neue Literatur began to put out Will Vesper's unpublished works. They advertised them in the *Deutsche National- und Soldatenzeitung* ("German National and Soldier's Paper"), an organ of the extreme right NPD, successor to Hitler's NSDAP.

They also, however, approached leftist writers for new work to publish. One was a young poet who married Gudrun's younger sister Johanna in 1965 (they were divorced in 1969). Also in 1965 Gudrun and Bernward announced their engagement. Gudrun's parents had not been happy about their sexual cohabitation in the parsonage without marriage even in prospect, so perhaps there was truth in their later claim that this was a sop to the bourgeois morals of their parents; but it was a very stylish and thorough sop. Invitations went out, on huge pieces of red cardboard with the words printed in tiny letters around the edge, to a party at the spa house of Bad Cannstatt.

The Vespers, several of them writers or artists, and bohemian in outlook, thought the Ensslins all dressed in their dark suits or lady's equivalents very conventional and bourgeois. They did not have the sort of morals which needed to be given sops.

In the summer of 1965 the engaged couple went to Berlin. Vesper started work as editor of the Voltaire Pamphlets, and Gudrun enrolled at the Free University. She was to study German as her main subject and

English as a subsidiary. In that year she was at last granted the scholarship of the Study Foundation of the German People, helped by a testimonial from a Berlin Professor Dr. Ernst Heinitz, erstwhile Rector Magnificus, who has said of her, "In the fifty-two years I have been associated with students, I have never made the acquaintance of such an extraordinary girl." Others of her professors were differently impressed, some by her clothes, which were deliberately unsmart—such as most students everywhere were wearing at that time, but rather more eccentric—and by her appearance in general, bizarre though not uniquely so, with her deep eyes blackly outlined in her sharp white face. (And she had an inch-long scar above her right eyebrow, from splitting her forehead against a wall she had run into on a toboggan as a child.)

In her application for the grant, she stated that she wanted to work for her doctorate and thereafter to work in publishing. Meanwhile her ambitions had become literary. She and Vesper submitted poems to *Konkret*, but the editors, Klaus Rainer Röhl and Ulrike Meinhof, returned them, dismissing them as "hysterical."

As members of the SPD, Gudrun and Bernward worked in the office set up by a number of writers to support the party in its election campaign. Bernward, with fourteen others, wrote speeches for Karl Schiller, then Berlin Interior Senator, soon to become Minister of Economics. Both were energetic in the cause, working at times almost around the clock. The ardor of their concern that the Social Democrats should win the 1966 elections was obvious to everyone they worked with.

But when the election came in 1966, the Social Democrats failed to get their majority. They formed the Grand Coalition with the conservative Christian Democrats, with Kiesinger as Chancellor. And Gudrun Ensslin, for one, could not forgive them. She saw it as a betrayal of the Left. To join with the party of Franz Josef Strauss! Her hopes for radical political change were dashed, and her disgust was strong. She left the SPD and shifted her support to the SDS. She and Vesper demonstrated against the war in Vietnam, against the emergency laws, with red flags—Gudrun singing "The International" now instead of "At All Times Sing Hallelujah!"

In the autumn of 1966 the couple received a contract to write for a publisher. By way of celebration they decided to conceive a child. He was born in May 1967; they named him Felix Robert and told their friends that he was a "wish child." His life as a demonstrator started early. He was pushed along in his baby carriage to Ho-ho-ho and "The International" but no doubt slept on, too young to be disturbed by the noises of defiance or by the gruesome lullabies of the antibomb campaign, concerning such things as crows on cradles prophesying doom. At an American armaments exhibition Bernward carried a stern poster with pictures of shot-up, burned, or blown corpses: "Tell your children what you have learned: Weapons are not toys." And on a placard attached to the handle of the baby carriage: "When I am big I'll carry my machine gun with me always. Use your head!" Little Felix was to be raised rigorously in love, with the cause of peace brandished ever before him.

But shortly before the advent of Felix Robert, his parents fell out, or at least his mother fell out of love with his father. They continued to live together for the first seven or eight months of the child's life. Gudrun took a leading part in a short porno film called *Das Abonnement*. She seemed to be in a fevered state of mind. She read Marcuse; wrestled with James Joyce's *Finnegan's Wake* and lost; attended demonstrations; got into trouble with the police by distributing defamatory pamphlets against the Berlin state prosecutor; helped to put pepper in the concert hall during the performance conducted by Pierre Boulez for the BBC, over the Teufel cause.

It was very soon after Felix was born that Benno Ohnesorg was shot. The birth may well have had something to do with Gudrun's tearful reaction. "She was too hysterical," one of the SDS leaders recalled, "to help us in an analysis of the event for a pamphlet we were going to put out about it. She was making very emotional speeches. She was saying, more or less, 'They'll kill us all—you know what kind of pigs we're up against—that is the generation of Auschwitz we've got against us—you can't argue with the people who made Auschwitz. They have weapons and we haven't. We must arm ourselves.' Her words had a big effect on many students. Suddenly she seemed to be speaking for an entire faction. She seemed to be expressing a reaction that many of them had to police brutality. It was as if the event had brought some sort of revelation to Ensslin: 'Now that I have experienced reality I cannot be a pacifist any longer.' At times on the night after Benno Ohnesorg was shot she was crying so much we thought we'd have to lock her up. Later her view seemed to represent that of many of the 'peaceful' antibomb faction—who were all for fighting it out on the *Platz*. A few of us, highly trained political theoreticians, would try to educate them to the right way. We would say that we—the SDS—must get organized in a rational way, that the struggle would take twenty years or more. We believed in day-by-day analyses, discussion of the power question, the national identity question, and after analysis then the putting into practice. That is a central point of Marixt theory."

So Gudrun Ensslin was one of those who turned against analysis after June 2 and wanted to "fight it out on the *Platz*."

Bernward Vesper said, "The reaction of the politicians to the Berlin event has destroyed our last illusions about the system."

Then one must work outside the system. The system was the enemy. Now that the first shot had been fired, why did not the students rise in armed rebellion, and the workers follow them? The enemy had started it. Their own action would be resistance, not attack. The only way to resist violence was with violence. Gudrun's friends, she accused them, did nothing but talk or write, endlessly go on about it all in theory, and do nothing. She did not want to hear about waiting, about planning, about discussing, about moderation. Günter Grass, who knew her in Berlin, said, "She was idealistic, with an inborn loathing of any compromise. She had a yearning for the Absolute, the perfect solution."

Gudrun took part in the protest demonstrations through the rest of 1967, but was unable to content herself with the political activities of the SDS and the unachieving student movement, unable to sit at home and look after Felix and talk to friends about the issues that she burned to do something about. She could not accuse Bernward of doing nothing; he edited the Voltaire pamphlets and wrote the introduction to No. 12, which advocated "resistance." But at last she repudiated them all: Vesper, the SDS, the friends, and, after a while, her wishes having changed, baby Felix too. Motherhood had "felt like a trap" to her, and as soon as she had somewhere to go, she went. (Ilse Ensslin later commented that she could not understand why people said that Gudrun had abandoned her child. "She looked after him for eleven months." In fact it could not have been as much as eleven months, but reducing the time does not affect the force of this argument.)

Bernward Vesper was to explain at the arson trial that their estrangement was only an expression of "the inner contradictions in society."

Not only. It was also an expression of her shift of interest and desire from one man to another.

For this new sort of man she had been amply prepared not only by her boredom with Vesper and the child, or suddenly by her taste of violence, but by nature and by nurture, through all the long years in the parsonage, the long restraint in a vise of moral scruple.

Andreas Baader was swarthy as a gypsy. He swaggered. He was quite free of moral conflict, immune to all kinds of scruple. He hadn't read Marx or Marcuse or Mao. He hadn't read anything at all. He had had nothing to do with politics. It was all "shit." He liked to defy for the sake of defying, so he had taken part in protest demonstrations, favoring the

forbidden ones. When Gudrun talked about the "fascist state" and ratio-
nalized her desire to attack it, he replied that the state wasn't worth thinking about at all, it was just a "shat-in shithouse." The police were "bulls"
or "pigs." He showed her how to break into locked cars and start them
without an ignition key. "Oh," she said, he was more "refreshingly close
to reality" than anyone else she'd known. When she wondered what she
should do about it all, he said, "Do anything, it doesn't matter what, everything's just shit anyway." Such was the pure simplicity of Baader.

Bernd Andreas Baader was born in Munich on May 6, 1943. His father, Dr. Berndt Philipp Baader, was a historian employed from 1941 as
archivist by the state of Bavaria, but was in the army and was killed on
the Russian front in 1945. Anneliese Baader, his widow, did not remarry.
She worked as a typist to bring up little Andy and provide him with everything a boy should have. Andy's mother and several other women relatives (other men of the family had also died in the war) doted on the
pretty boy. He really was very pretty indeed, with long black eyelashes
and blue, mischievous eyes.

First he went to some state schools: a *Gymnasium*, and another, and
another. And still the teachers failed to be delighted with him, although
his devoted relatives continued to assure each other that Andreas was really an intelligent little boy, of that special kind of intelligence which is
best proved to fond parents by their child's inability to pass exams. He
was not liked by his schoolfellows any more than by his teachers. He was
a bully who liked to use his fists. He wanted to be a gang leader, and if a
boy did not wish to follow Andy, he could expect a bloody nose. If it was
Andy who got the bloody nose, he would sulk—though to those who
loved him this was the sensitivity of the misunderstood. Some who observed Andy without initial prejudice in his childhood and adolescence
were left with a general impression that he was sulky and lazy. Even his
own grandmother said that he had no backbone. His mother decided
that, the ordinary schools having failed to develop her son's latent intellectual gifts, she would send him to a private tutoring establishment—the
sort that is called a crammer by those who don't need it—at not inconsid-
erable expense to herself. But Andreas' gifts remained hidden. Even the
"talent" for German which his mother and aunts had detected did not
flower under the heat and pressure. He never got his *Abitur*. Still, they
thought he could put his "talent" to use as a writer. Perhaps he could
even make a living as one—a journalist, say. Or perhaps he could fall
back on art. But he had always liked to defy. Once when Anneliese took
her little son boating on the Starnbergersee, she called out, always
thoughtful of his safety, always taking the greatest care of him, "Mind

you don't fall into the water!" and Andy jumped in at once, clothes, shoes, and all, and swam along behind the boat, smirking. It was hard to scold such a lovely little fellow. His willfulness and refusal to take orders, or even advice, hardened.

Andreas did not want to learn anything or work at anything. He preferred to scorn what he had heard called the "performance society," but as he had reached an age when it was no longer feasible to lie back in the little world his mother had upholstered for him, he agreed to take up pottery at a Munich art school. But he made no great effort at it.

To quicken more interest in his contemporaries, the almost-adult Andreas made up a melodramatic lung cancer of which he was bravely dying. For weeks he coughed pathetically in public, but failed to excite envy, admiration, or concern in the boys or even the girls.

When he was twenty, he went to Berlin, where young men were exempted from national service. Ostensibly he was to study art or work as a journalist. He did in fact take a job with the Springer-owned *Bild-Zeitung* for about three weeks. Later the *Bild-Zeitung* preferred to forget that Andreas Baader had ever worked for them, but Andreas did not deny his days with the *Bild-Zeitung*. Having nothing to do and no money, he became more and more sure that the way society was run was profoundly wrong. Here was he, penniless, while others less worthy were driving about in big, fast, expensive cars. It sickened him, the rat race, the consumer society, the social injustice. But there were people who could recognize Andy's worth. Some women did. His talent was his virility, after all.

He went to live with—and on—Ellinor Michel, an action painter, in her commodious apartment and studio. She was married to another artist, who stayed on for some time after Andreas moved in. It was more than a *ménage à trois*, however, as others were there too, hangers-on of Baader's, sleeping overnight or staying awhile, having nowhere else to go; and, having no job, often borrowing money from the action painter. She would set up her canvases between loudspeakers blaring the emotionally incontinent music which was the height of fashion, American rock and English pop. She sold her large, vivid pictures for respectable sums. A gregarious and generous person was Elly Michel, and her apartment was a haven for refugees from the consumption terror, visionaries who refused on principle to take part in the rat race, brave men who had made what Marcuse called the Great Refusal. Andreas begot a daughter upon her, named Suse, who was born in 1965. He was her mate, but not boringly faithful to her in the narrow bourgeois sense of the word.

He was desired by women, and he gave himself to them. His blue long-lashed bedroom eyes he could depend upon, his black hair, the manly black shadow about his jaw, his boyish smirk, his swaggering, aggressive, domineering manner—he could charm and allure, and provoke a little nervous flutter at the same time. But he was a little troubled by his weight. When he went to bed with a new girl friend he preferred to have the light off before he undressed, for fear of being considered a trifle too fat. If the girls wished to reward him with expensive gifts—some of that consumer shit which he couldn't afford and which he despised anyway—he would not refuse it. If they were willing to let him drive their cars, preferably big, fast, and expensive cars, he would do so, without fussing about a driving license. He found he could get a thrill out of driving. It was a taste of dangerous living. Between 1964 and 1967 he was convicted for incorrect behavior in traffic, four times driving without a license, offenses against the car insurance law, misuse of car registrations, driving license forgery.

In 1967 Andreas met the white-faced, intense, shrill-voiced Gudrun Ensslin. She fell in love with him. He went to bed with her, and she found the experience rewarding. Early in 1968 she moved into Elly Michel's apartment with him. But this was too much for the artist, and her displeasure was felt at last by Andreas and Gudrun. The two decided that if they weren't wanted there they had better go. So off they went, leaving their respective children, Suse and Felix, behind them. They had a remnant of Gudrun's scholarship money between them.

Both Andreas and Gudrun were to say that theirs was a "good marriage," sexually; and not only sexually. But what good could come of it was a different question, for it was the marriage of fanaticism and unscrupulousness.

They went south together, to Frankfurt, where Gudrun took Andreas to meet the SDS. They were not a wishy-washy lot, the Frankfurt University leftists. They had been known to beat up fellow students who did not agree with them. They would raid and wreck the offices and studies of professors. They often pelted the facade of their America House with batteries of eggs. There was among them a Marxist-Leninist group whose "praxis" had consisted of wrecking the car of one of their own members because she had only taken off her expensive fur coat before going on a demonstration. They tolerated views only as far right as Rudi Dutschke. They would not shirk disrupting a discussion on Vietnam to prevent the Americans from telling the lies they anticipated. But Gudrun, who would sweep aside their own views as abruptly as she would deliberately sweep a table clean of bottles, glasses, plates, full or empty, with one swing of her arm, wanted action, action, and they began to resent her "hysterical nagging."

Andreas, as the man Gudrun had brought with her, liked being associated with her political theory and the respect with which, at first, they listened to her. He concealed his ignorance by saying little himself, except "shit," so that he too could be taken for the intellectual that she was glad he was not. Yet just by being at her side he was transformed into that difficult intellectual thing, an idealist; and, even grander, that ideological thing, a revolutionary.

6

A Little Night Arson

About the middle of March 1968, Gudrun, Andreas, and Thorwald Proll were visiting Andreas' home ground, the Schwabing district of Munich. They dropped in frequently at the action theater of Horst Söhnlein, where they met an openhanded young man who did not at all mind lending them his sister's Volkswagen, which he had undertaken to sell for her. They borrowed it several times, and when he found it gone on April 1, he assumed that it was someone in the theater who had borrowed it without asking him, probably Söhnlein, with or without his three friends. Everyone at the theater knew that Söhnlein disappeared from time to time but could be relied upon to come back again.

At least that was the story the young man was to tell the court in Frankfurt, possibly to avoid any suspicion of his own complicity. But in any case the chances are that the would-be arsonists, for all their amateurish bungling, would not have told acquaintances what their real intentions were. Certainly their plot was hatched in Munich. The bombs were built there, assemblies of clocks, wires, and plastic bottles stowed in paper shopping bags; and with these under the hood of the gray Volkswagen, some hashish and a notebook in Proll's pocket, and various incriminating bits and pieces in suitcases and other pockets, the four comrades set out for Frankfurt am Main, by way of Stuttgart. There they interrupted their journey to visit Gudrun's family, now atoning in the parsonage in Bad Cannstatt.

At half past five on the morning of Tuesday, April 2, Thorwald Proll rang the bell of an apartment in a block on the Beethovenstrasse, which belonged to a young woman named Cornelia Vogel. Proll had met her at an anti-Vietnam War congress, and they had exchanged addresses. She was not at all delighted to see the four comrades at the crack of dawn, nor was she eager to put them up for an indefinite stay. She had a child and only two rooms, and would prefer it if they could find some other place.

So at six o'clock Proll knocked on the door of an old school friend named Jochen Drews. But Drews said it was quite impossible for them to stay with him.

Back they went to Frau Vogel and persuaded her to let them camp in her living room. They were there smoking a joint when Drews arrived at about eight o'clock to visit them. The four from Munich said that they wanted to borrow a movie camera to make a film. Drews promised to take Proll to look for one later in the day. Frau Vogel, who worked as a cutter for Hessian radio, had to be at work by nine, and Drews drove her there. Then he came back for his old classmate, and the two of them drove to some likely places to inquire about movie cameras, but had no luck. They stopped at a barber's, and Proll had his hair cut. The two high-spirited young men found the barber a "rather stupid person." They set about baiting and teasing the fellow, turning the event, as they put it, into "an art happening." Part of the game was to speak to the barber only in English, which he did not understand. They found it good fun, and at two o'clock Drews dropped Proll back at the Beethovenstrasse, both of them in a state of some excitement, compounded of an infectious exhilaration which Proll had brought with him from Munich and the sadistic glee they had worked up together at the barber's.

At four o'clock the four visitors were walking near the center of the city minding humanity's business, when they saw Drews—who seems to have been very much at a loose end—sitting in a café. They joined him at his table, and there they stayed for a little under half an hour. Then they went on to the Zeil, Frankfurt's main shopping street, where the big department stores and chain-store branches are crowded along both sides: on the corner a Kaufhof and then the Schneider with the post office between them, then a Woolworth, and a Hertie before the Café Becker; on the other side a Neckermann, and so on, a veritable Babylon of consumption terror, degeneration, and overrefinement.

The party broke up into two pairs. Proll and Söhnlein went into the Kaufhof, a huge chain store on the corner, Baader and Ensslin into the Schneider department store.

The Schneider is not one of the grand stores of the Western world, not the most impressive citadel of the consumer-goods imperialists. It is much less streamlined and very much smaller than the Kaufhof on the corner. It was not and is not designed to draw in the hip young. Its patrons are mostly middle-class and middle-aged. Untrendy as stores go nowadays with its yellowy wood veneers, or plastic made to look like wood—which was in fashion in the late forties and early fifties—and its too-crowded wares, it may seem to warn that its goods will be guaranteed reliable and depressingly dull. But in fact the Schneider stocks all the up-to-date paraphernalia, including gadgets which are very much in demand in a prosperous and highly inventive society.

Andreas and Gudrun made no attempt to appear inconspicuous. Dressed in their jeans and sweaters—clothes which at that time and place made a protest against bourgeois conventions all on their own—they entered the store, took the escalator, got off it when they found themselves in the furniture department, and plunged among the garden chairs. With gasps of simulated amazement and delight, and fits of smothered sniggers, they examined an automatic reclining deck chair. "Ah, wonderful! Incredible!" they exclaimed sarcastically, as the head part went up and the foot part went down. This was just the sort of junk that people thought they needed and did not.

The young untidy couple, who didn't look as if they could afford to buy the article they had been admiring so much, went away without even inquiring its price. They went to other floors, looked at a few other things, and then they left.

At half past six, just before the store was due to close for the night, the couple returned, this time each with a shopping bag distinctly full and probably quite heavy. Their afternoon shopping done then, perhaps they had come back to have another look at the garden furniture they seemed to have set their hearts on.

They rushed into the almost empty store. The escalator had been stopped, but Gudrun and Andreas ran up it, hand in hand, laughing all the way. They placed one of their fire bombs in the women's fashion department on the first upper floor, on top of a long wardrobe which formed a partition wall between the main sales area and the fitting rooms. Then they ran on the switched-off escalator to the third floor, the furniture department, and hid the other bomb in a pseudo "Old German" wardrobe.

The sales clerks, no longer busy, waiting for the last few minutes of the working day to pass so that they could go home, watched them as they came into sight and disappeared up the stopped escalator to the floors above, again as they ran down and out. They were glad to see them go, glad to have the doors shut on the last customers. None of them noticed that the young couple had left their shopping bags behind. They all went home. The night watchmen arrived, and a team of painters who were to work through the night on the fifth and sixth floors.

Gudrun Ensslin spent that evening at the Club Voltaire, a step away from the Opera House. The Opera House is an imposing building, as such old opera houses are, only it is quite hollow, a grand ruin. Its solid stone walls enclose nothing except, at night, the darkness. A sculptured figure or two rises at the corner of the great pediment against a sky burnished by city lights. An impressive, thorough, professional job, by Allied bombers in the Second World War.

The street where the Club Voltaire stands is a narrow, poky, bending street, lined with humble buildings. The low doorway of the club is surrounded on the street side with posters, mostly homemade, which advertise forthcoming meetings, demonstrations, congresses, and other opportunities for the public airing of indignations. Basques want a demonstration against the death sentence in Spain. The Young Socialists want one over university reform. Inside is a small lobby, and a door on the left leads into the bar. Above the bottles on the back wall, newspapers are for sale: *Arbeiter Stimme* (Voice of the Worker), *Arbeiterkampf* (Worker's Struggle), *Kommunistische Volkszeitung* (Communist People's Paper). Down a step to the right is a dining area, with molded plastic chairs and Formica-topped tables. The walls are hung with posters: posters tragic, the victims of wars, oppressions, famines, and art; posters satirical, like the one with a house in the shape of a huge cash register (*Kasse*) and a wicked landlord hovering over it spiderlike, his fingers extended toward the keys, with the slogan "Your Home is My *Kasse*."

Basques, Northern Irish Catholics, Algerians, Palestinians, Bengalis, Africans, American Blacks, students from everywhere come in to talk, drink, eat, or just sit and brood. In 1968 Angela Davis (reputed to be Marcuse's favorite American protégée) could be seen at times sitting around in there. And later in the same year one could meet Daniel Cohn-Bendit—called "Danny the Red"—at the bar or at a Formica-topped table. Short, stout, red-haired Cohn-Bendit was an aggressive arguer, but nobody in the Club Voltaire felt inclined to fight back. Some said it was because he was a Jew. Others said that he was, after all, the most daring leader of the French student movement. And in those years, while it is true that the student movements of France and Germany had much in common—both fairly wanting university reform, both claiming Vietnam as their main cause, both vainly hoping to lead the workers in revolutionary uprising—it wasn't so much ideas that flowed between them as Daniel Cohn-Bendit himself. In 1968 he could not get back into France from his native Germany. The French government wanted to be rid of him. He got back illegally, however. And later he returned to Frankfurt, where he could be seen at work in one of those small crowded leftist bookshops which usually have pictures of Adorno on the wall and flattering posters of Rosa Luxemburg captioned: "The SPD does not want socialism!"

But on the night of April 2, when Gudrun Ensslin was there with Cornelia Vogel, "Danny the Red" was making nugatory preparations for revolution in Paris. Angela Davis was perhaps doing the same elsewhere. But Herr Drews looked in for a while. If he had been asked to look in and find Gudrun Ensslin there, to witness her alibi, she either did not know that that was the motive, or he was not going to say so in court. He did say that Ensslin told him that the three others were at the Café am Opernplatz near the Zeil, and he went and found them there, sitting together at a corner table. Proll was writing something in a green notebook. When Drews asked them what they were doing, Proll told him to mind his own business, and Baader told him to "fuck off." He resented Proll being so "peculiar" in his manner toward him, so he went back to the Club Voltaire.

Shortly before midnight a man working late in a taxi company's office opposite the Schneider saw its third story burning and telephoned for the fire brigade. While the engines were on their way, another fire broke out on the first floor. Soon after midnight the fourth floor of the Kaufhof was in flames, two fires having started, one in the bedding department and one in the toy department.

At about the same time a woman telephoned the German Press Agency offices and said only, "Soon there'll be flames in the Schneider and the Kaufhof. It is a political act of revenge."

Baader, Proll, Söhnlein, and Gudrun too, by that time, were near enough to hear the engines arriving and to hurry around to see the spectacle of the buildings blazing in the night. All the bombs, it seemed, had worked. Thus far, it was a triumph, a brilliant success.

On Thursday the fourth, papers carried the news of the fire, the strong suspicion of arson, and the facts that the fires had been quickly put out and that one bomb had been found in the Kaufhof, unexploded and intact.

At one o'clock Drews, either having a forgiving nature or putting commercial interests above hurt feelings, kept an appointment with Proll to see a cheap secondhand car which Proll wanted to sell him. But the transaction was hard to negotiate, perhaps because the car the four were willing to sell to Drews was not their own property. They asked him to lend them money, upon which Drews retreated. But he saw them all again later at the Club Voltaire. Cornelia Vogel arrived with her child, and the suddenly good-natured four offered to drive the child home, while she stayed on with a man at the club. At one o'clock she took him home with her to the Beethovenstrasse. The visitors were asleep in the living room, two on the sofa and two on a mattress on the floor. Cornelia and her friend got into the bed with the child, but he was not happy with this arrangement and complained of the presence of the four in the other room. He wished them gone, and so did she, but they seemed in no hurry to go. Frau Vogel had no doubt what their real business in Frankfurt had been, and after some whispering in the dark, neither had her friend.

In the morning they left with the child before the visitors were awake. When Frau Vogel came home after work they were gone, and she hoped they had pushed off for good. But no such luck; they were back again at seven. And they were still sitting in the apartment at ten o'clock when the police arrived to arrest them "on the basis of a concrete denunciation."

Their persons, the car, and the apartment were searched. In one of Gudrun's pockets a screw was found identical with others found on the site of the arson, and also a piece of paper on which there was a clear prescription:

	MAY APOTHECARY
Red phosphorus	20 grams
Sulfur	250 grams

Potassium chlorate
   for disinfecting skin
Bender and Hohbein
between Sendlingertorplatz
   and Goetheplatz left side
technically uncleaned charcoal
   for stomach troubles
	250 grams
	
	500 grams

Technically clean 4 batteries	

In a bag in the Volkswagen were clock components, the glowing head of a gas lighter, brass screws and nuts, and remainders of adhesive-tape rolls.

On Söhnlein there was found a loan slip from the Munich Chamber Theater made out to the action theater which he ran. It had his name and signature on it. On the back of it was a list: 500 grams of charcoal, batteries, sulfur, four plastic bottles, confectioners' sugar. And as the bombs had been made of an explosive mixture of chlorates with phosphorus, sulfur, and sugar; the glowing components of gas lighters, flashlight batteries, and alarm clocks with the minute hand removed; plastic bottles filled with gasoline; and the parts bound together with adhesive tape—all this was evidence against them. (But when they came to trial the judge expressed doubts that they themselves could have assembled the bombs as they were all "artistically inclined.")

The employees of the Schneider picked Gudrun out of a lineup of seven young women. Her defending counsel was later to complain that as she was the only one wearing trousers, the identification was not properly conducted. But the Schneider ladies insisted that they remembered her by more than her clothes, which were only part of a whole waiflike appearance, and chiefly by her hair in "rat's tails," her deep-sunken eyes, her flat chest. (Prison was to improve her health. By the time she came to trial, she looked better fed, better rested, better cared for, as one of the Schneider ladies was to comment spontaneously in court.)

Baader, Proll, and Söhnlein were lined up with two other young men. The defense was to object that it was only too easy to pick out one of the accused by luck when there were three of them among five, but their objection was to be overruled on the grounds that the Schneider employees were only looking for Baader, whom they picked out without hesitation, and the other two were therefore "test persons" as validly as the two who had nothing to do with the crime.

Baader, Proll, and Söhnlein were moved from lockup to lockup but ended up at the Hammelsgasse jail. They claimed later that they had made three attempts to escape and after each attempt had been "terribly beaten up" by the guards.

For the first time in his life Baader now began to read. Or at least he copied out passages recommended to him by those who supplied his ideological motive—Gudrun and his lawyer, Horst Mahler. Impressive support for doing what he denied having done was discovered in the works of American Black leaders and Herbert Marcuse.

Gudrun spent her remand imprisonment reading, listening to classical music on a record player, and knitting a sweater for Maria Pia Heinitz, the wife of her state-paid defense lawyer, that same professor of law, Dr. Ernst Heinitz, who had found so much to admire in her at the Free University of Berlin. Though nearly seven months went by before Gudrun was brought to trial, the sweater never got finished. But it was the thought rather than the practical success that counted with her admirers, Heinitz and the lady governor of the prison.

Gudrun, the governor said, would always go to great lengths, "to the limit of what was bearable," she stressed, "to support her fellow prisoners." But it was not to be understood that Gudrun's powers of endurance were being put to the test. The governor was expressing a feeling she had about Gudrun's strength and courage. "She would be willing to have herself strapped to the wheel. She had no feeling of guilt." And certainly there was no sign of self-pity in the prisoner. When Heinitz brought her cigarettes and candy, she scorned them as "gifts from the Raspberry Reich," her phrase for the consumer society.

On October 13, 1968, the four were brought to trial. The event drew a lot of attention from the press and the public. One journalist who attended the trial found Gudrun Ensslin strangely impressive in contrast to the rather foolish young men she had taken on as accomplices:

> Next to her sat the three men as if they were incidental figures—her friend Baader, a sonny-boy who had come to read Marcuse by accident; Proll, playing the bourgeois scare in a pair of steel-rimmed spectacles; and finally Söhnlein, the supposed actor, acting being bored through the trial.

Horst Mahler was one of a bank of nine defense lawyers, which also included Professor Heinitz and a young man named Otto Schily, who refused at first to wear the conventional black robe or to stand up when addressing the court, but complied eventually. The presiding judge wisely decided against laying too much stress on formalities and did not insist on a witness standing to take the oath.

When the judge called upon Baader, Proll stood up. As none of the defendants were known to him, the judge proceeded.

"You were born in 1943?"

"No, I was born in 1789."

The judge took it coolly. "You do start off with a lot of nonsense," he said.

Then the state prosecutor pointed out to the court that Proll was pretending to be Baader. The judge asked Proll to explain himself.

"It makes no difference, after all, who is here," Proll said.

The judge ordered that he and Baader should be removed.

Söhnlein shoved the policeman beside him out of the way and shouted, "In solidarity with my comrades I'm also leaving." The policeman grabbed him, and Söhnlein hit out all about him.

The judge raised his voice to sentence all three to three days' imprisonment for this behavior in court.

Proll yelled, "I raise you to four!"

The moment came at last when the one addressed was the one who answered. Did Ensslin have anything to say on the matter?

"For you the roles here have already been totally predetermined. So that this may stay as it is, I would like not to say anything."

"Baader?"

"I will not say anything. I consider this justice a justice of the ruling class, and confronted with such justice, which deals in injustice, I do not want to defend myself."

"Proll?"

"No."

"Söhnlein?"

"Neither on my person nor on the matter."

More clamor and disruption, and Söhnlein was again removed from court, shouting, *"Heil Ordnung!"* (Hail, order!)

Some days later, after a break in the proceedings, Ensslin made a kind of confession. "In agreement with Baader I declare: he and I did it in the Schneider. None of the others were in it, neither there nor in the Kaufhof." With some hesitation she explained, "We did it out of protest against the indifference toward the war in Vietnam" and also against the capitalist structure of society. She shrugged her shoulders, jerked back her long blond hair. "It was a mistake and an error. But I do not wish to discuss that with you. I will have to talk to others about that. You may make a note that at the root of this deed is powerlessness. But frequently justice is on the side of powerlessness."

Baader: "I admit that on April 2, shortly before closing time, I put a paper bag which contained a mechanism into an Old German wardrobe. It was intended to destroy the wardrobe, not more. We had no intention of endangering people or even causing a real fire. . . . Only monopoly capitalism and the insurances, which are suffocating in profits, were to be hit at."

When asked for details after the confession, Baader and Ensslin refused.

Asked how they had obtained the materials for the fire bombs, Ensslin said, "As long as we are not concerned with the true core of the matter I do not wish to comment."

Baader to the same question: "On this I do not wish to comment, as I could be involving others."

The next day Bernward Vesper came to give evidence for Gudrun. Dressed in an expensive maroon short leather jacket, cord trousers, and high-heeled boots, and with his hair fashionably wild, he bounced up to the defendants and handed each of them a single red rose. He was followed by a red-haired woman in crimson slacks and a fur coat who tripped up to Baader and embraced him passionately with one arm. Under the other she was carrying three paintings which she wanted to show the court as evidence of something. She had to be gently but firmly restrained.

Bernward Vesper talked at length, to persuade the judges of Gudrun's nobility; to make them see that she desired only what was good for people; and that if anything had gone wrong in her life, the fault lay not in her but in society, it being full of "inner contradictions."

Faithful Bernward Vesper's own story was nearly at an end. He was yet to commit one act of petty, stupid, pointless destruction of somebody else's property, and on May 14, 1971, to destroy himself, still grieving for Gudrun, with an overdose of sleeping pills. He was well off and left all he had to his son. So little Felix, the "wish-child," was abandoned by both his parents, who had dedicated themselves to nonviolence, before they could teach him their humanitarian values or lead him on the paths of peace.

The trial went on. Vogel and Drews were called as witnesses for the prosecution. With a wary eye on the four defendants, they accused the police of undue pressure to extract statements from them.

Ensslin and Baader changed their confession. They had not known, they said, what was in the two shopping bags. They had placed them under orders from others, they said.

A Dr. Wolfgang Huber had made himself available to the defense to give an opinion for the sanity of the defendants and possibly against the sanity of almost everyone else, as a qualified if not entirely unbiased expert. But the psychiatrist appointed by the court, Dr. Reinhard Redhardt, confirmed that all four were sane, though Proll, Baader, and Söhnlein had refused to be examined. Proll, as Fritz Teufel had done at one of his trials, suggested the judges should be examined.

The prosecution asked for a sentence of six years' imprisonment.

Heinitz and Schily pleaded for Ensslin, and Mahler for Baader.

Ensslin for herself said, "I don't want to give you the opportunity of pretending to listen to me, so I'll say nothing at all."

Proll cursed justice in a long prepared statement, repeating many times that they could or would not defend themselves against a justice which was an instrument of the capitalist order, which since the era of the Weimar Republic had been harder on the Left than the Right (for example, Rosa Luxemburg and Karl Liebknecht, who had been murdered by army officers, and Adolf Hitler, who had not); which convicted "little Jew-murderers" and let "big Jew-murderers" go; which criminalized Kommune I, and so on. Authority was fascist, capitalism was fascist, the court was fascist, and the four accused were heroes of the resistance. He ended, "Workers of the world, unite!" and "¡Venceremos!"

On October 31, when the judge started his final address, the defendants stood up and tried to leave the court. Ensslin shouted, "We are no longer interested in this." More shouts came from the public gallery, where one of the shouters was easily identified as Daniel Cohn-Bendit.

"The defendants should be tried in a student court," he shouted.

The presiding judge directed that "the rabble-rouser Cohn-Bendit be removed from the courtroom."

Baader and Söhnlein dived over the barrier, and part of the public applauded. The judge ordered the court to be cleared, and a strong contingent of police had to be brought in to do it. The court was filled with old people, but also the defendants' own supporters. They were all moved out. In the crush on the stairs a young woman fainted.

Policemen chased Baader and Söhnlein all over the courtroom, with the two laughing uproariously. Baader was tackled and brought down, but went on laughing.

It took a quarter of an hour to clear the court, and after one hour the public were readmitted. Daniel Cohn-Bendit and two others were sentenced to three days' imprisonment. But "Danny the Red" was now subdued. Only a short while before he had been given an eight-month suspended sentence for violent behavior in a demonstration.

Then the judgment was read.

The four accused were found guilty of arson endangering human life, and sentenced to three years' imprisonment.

7

Fugitives

Fritz Teufel observed, "Well, it's better to burn a store than to run one."

But the SDS, which had invited his opinion, was on the whole against the arson. Others were enthusiastically for it: students, communards, youthful individuals, and factions of the APO. Many were stirred by the daring of the deed. To some it was not merely a dangerous act performed to express personal feelings, with a spurious motive tacked on, but "praxis"; and as "praxis" is attached inseparably to theory or "concept," the act inevitably possessed intellectual, political, and, even more loftily, historical significance.

Baader could hardly have hoped that any of his crooked doings would ever have been so complimented. Just doing what he wanted to because he shouldn't, and because Gudrun could supply a great reason for it, had earned him undreamed-of success. But imprisonment for him was very hard.

During a walk in the prison yard, a fellow convict asked Baader what he had done. Baader bragged that he had set fire to a department store in order to protest against the war in Vietnam and to rouse the masses to overthrow capitalism. The other convict was amazed. "How can anyone do anything so nonsensical?" he said.

Baader knew the answer to such a criticism. "Anything," he parroted, "that contributes to the political unrest of the country serves our interests"—which did not make the other prisoner any more appreciative.

Baader suspected that something was put into his food which made him feel woozy and reduced his potency. Still, he had other aids to his *machismo* now. There were his followers and admirers in the world outside. In a letter to Kommune I he wrote, "One further request: When Bonn has fallen, leave NATO to us."

His mother, Anneliese Baader, believed that his conviction was a great miscarriage of justice. She wrote to the state prosecutor to protest. She would not, she said, accept the destruction of the life of her child without complaint. She based her plea on a common maternal illusion: "I know my son." His attitude and beliefs were known to her, she said. His deed was the desperate expression of his thinking. It was a prophecy and a warning, a complaint and accusation.

Golden opinions were earned by the firebrands from quite conservative citizens. Professor Dr. Ernst Heinitz did not lose a jot of his esteem for Gudrun. For him she remained "a highly talented, remarkable person, openhearted and kind." He wanted to arrange for her to get a job in a publishing house after her release or to start on a university career. But when he told Gudrun, she rejected his plans fiercely. "Don't worry about me," she said. "A bourgeois existence is the last thing I'm looking for!" Dr. Heinitz excused her ungrateful and incomprehensible outburst by diagnosing an emotional dependence on Baader, "greater than her intellect would admit," so that he had led her astray.

A quite contary opinion was formed by the court psychiatrist, Dr. Reinhard Redhardt, who turned a colder eye upon her. She was "capable of hating in a very elementary fashion," and it was she, he thought, who was the backbone of the group. She was arrogant, ruthless, and coercive. "She would sell her own brother," he said, and had a driving determination to "involve herself with her neighbors against their will, and so put into practice those ideas which she had learned, in the last analysis, at home in her parsonage." (Or, in an even more ultimate analysis, any ideas which were grandiose and demanding enough and had been given to her early enough. Hers was the kind of fervor which old religious wars, crusades, and persecutions had been fired with; or, in the years of her infancy and long before she put fire bombs into wardrobes, the Nazi movement.)

Gudrun was to be examined by Dr. Redhardt because she had a schizophrenic sibling. He had four or five "examination sessions" with her, which took the form of discussions.

"We do not want to be merely a page in cultural history," Gudrun told him.

What arrogant conceit! Dr. Redhardt thought. He told her that her opinions were generally "inhuman." But their discussions went "round and round," and neither convinced the other of anything, though Dr. Redhardt believed that it was good for him to have to think about the views she had, however opposed to his own.

He asked her about Felix Robert. (Bernward Vesper wanted her consent for him to assume legal custody of the boy, but she would not give it.)

'That's none of your business,' she said, truculently.

She poured scorn on "the trinity of television, judges, and the police."

She said, "Talking without action equals silence."

"Why?" he asked.

She refused the challenge. "I'm not going to discuss it with you," she said.

On the one occasion when he visited Baader, he was accosted by the question, "What are you doing to change society?"

When Dr. Redhardt failed to give an answer which satisified his inquisitor, nothing more could be said at all.

Gudrun's mother spoke more bitterly than Frau Baader. "It would be better," she said, "for Gudrun to be shot before she shot someone else. For one way or another she'll be torn to pieces by the press or in prison. In any case, her life is destroyed." But she retained a fierce loyalty to her daughter, and some years later she was to say that Gudrun and Andreas were "very young" when they committed their crimes, and that should have been considered a reason for leniency. (Gudrun was 27–32, Andreas 24–29.) She would not condemn Gudrun's actions, but said that she herself "would not put bombs about the place" and that she hated terrorism. "The government should be of such a kind that no terrorism could develop at all," she said, but what kind that was she did not stipulate.

One of those who found merit in the arson, though with certain reservations, and caution, and discursive explanations, was Ulrike Meinhof. She did not send in an account of an interview with them which *Konkret* was expecting because, she explained, if she had published what they told her "they would never have got out of prison"—a hint that Baader and Ensslin admitted to her that they had not intended to avoid damage to persons. To others they boasted that they had lit their torch "to celebrate our marriage"; and Gudrun also said that it was an act on her part to "set myself free" (an auto-da-fé this time in lieu of the Alhambra?); but they trusted Ulrike Meinhof with some secret that could not be publicly divulged concerning the arson, although their confidante was a professional journalist and what they confided was of public importance. The journalist wrote, "The progressive significance of department-store arson does not lie in the destruction of the goods, it lies in the criminality of the action, in lawbreaking"—which was a venerable anarchist view.

But she went on, clearly under the influence of Marcuse, and aware of the risks of apparent incitement:

> What can people do with a case of department-store arson? They can plunder the department store. . . . The goods, however, which Frankfurters can take from Frankfurt stores are hardly those which they truly need. . . . In a department-store plundering in this country only the stock of things which in any case serve as satisfaction substitutes, would be increased in some households. . . .
>
> So arson cannot be recommended. But there remains what Fritz Teufel said at the delegate conference of the SDS: "Still, it is better to burn a department store than to run one." Fritz Teufel can formulate things really well at times.

The four arsonists were let out of jail on June 13, 1969, to await the outcome of an appeal which was to be heard in November. They had served fourteen months of their sentence. The authorities believed they could be reasonably trusted not to flee.

They emerged into the sunlight of fame and admiration, heroes to the radical Left; to the chic Left—or Schili—glamorous fun.

Gudrun, Baader, and Proll then joined in a student enterprise which nicely combined Gudrun's missionary urge with Baader's—and Proll's—relish of defiance.

It had begun when students, mostly of social science and education, and some of them members of the SDS (which gave support to the scheme), had distributed pamphlets among the inmates of two Frankfurt boys' homes, one run by the Youth Office and one by the Catholic Church. The intention was to get the boys agitating against malpractices and for reforms—participation in decision-making, more self-administration, and the easing of restrictions. The children in these homes, as in all such institutions, were illegitimate boys, abandoned boys, boys who had been neglected and maltreated, who had come before the courts, boys lonely and deprived, the unhappy, damaged, and often broken-spirited results of parental failure, institutionalization, and inclement fosterings. Suffering had rendered most of them quarrelsome, contrary, dependent, demanding, provoking, ungrateful, uncooperative, and altogether difficult. Some would run away, and of those most would return, having nowhere to go and being unable to find their way in the outside world.

But now they felt that the students—hitherto a remote, mysterious, superior class of persons—were interested in them and concerned for them, so they ran away to them. They were put up in one of the student hostels and in some private homes. A professor of education at Frankfurt

University took in a couple, but very quickly—as one of the social workers who finally had to deal with the situation created by the students put it—"withdrew from immediate consulting activity as he could not meet the concrete demands of assistance in emergency situations." (For heaven's sake get them out of here!) To study them was one thing, to endure them another. The professor approached the Youth Office; and its human, liberal, experienced director, Herbert Faller, met the students and the runaways at the AStA offices of the university, where the police were not allowed, and the boys did not have to fear arrest. He talked to the fugitives and their student advisers-inciters-protectors, and agreed to take up the matter of legalizing their position with the Hessian State Welfare Association. Meanwhile, they were to get help from two organizations—the "Work and Educational Help" charitable club founded by the Youth Office itself and the "Diaconic Work" of the Protestant Church—in getting accommodation and work, usually apprenticeships. They were to continue as the students had started them, in "collectives," but before long student advisers, who after a while found their demands and their behavior intolerable, were replaced by trained social workers who lived with the boys (aged between fifteen and twenty) as "house fathers."

The students and Baader, Ensslin, and Proll when they joined them, tried to politicize the boys, who at first, to please their new masters, put up posters of Mao and Stalin on their walls. (Later, when their position was legalized and they got jobs and started looking for girl friends, they stuck female pinups over the males. Herbert Faller would sometimes see "Mao peeking through" between the bare legs of a model.) They had to stay indoors during the day, for fear of being picked up by the police, and went out at night. Although they were generally called "apprentices," few found work, partly because of their illegal status, and partly because they imitated the students' life-style, which was leisurely.

The number of fugitives soon doubled. Under Baader's leadership, the boys, usually a group of about twenty of them, and about a dozen students, would drive out to state institutions in the country and persuade boys to run away to the big city of Frankfurt and be rehabilitated there. From the first home they visited, about thirty boys ran away. Money and lodgings were found for them. But of course the more the number increased, the more difficult became the practical problems which their benefactors had to solve.

Pastor Hans Brehm of the Diaconic Work did not find the experiment very "meaningful." He said, "They slept by day, jumped about at night, and most of them didn't work at all."

The group was visited by Ulrike Meinhof, who was investigating and writing about state institutions for girls at the time. She asked the boys, who were not practiced in "getting up an action," to get up a few for her, including visiting two homes for girls and persuading the girls to protest against their conditions. She told them exactly what demands should be made. She herself had been barred from one of them by the principal. The boys went, spoke to the girls, and encouraged them to make demands for improved conditions. One of the homes was closed down soon afterward.

Some of the apprentices, in particular one named Peter Brosch, blamed Baader for giving them the wrong kind of guidance and turning the reform school escapees into a riotous band. Baader organized sports activities for them—wild car races around the inner circle roads of Frankfurt and "go-ins" into "bourgeois" cafés, where waiters were jostled, the contents of ashtrays tipped into cups, and suchlike good clean fun. Baader's explanation was that "the apprentices" (as well as Baader himself) "needed first of all some relaxation after the stress of being confined."

At night there were "teach-ins." Baader's instruction took the form of incitement to empty all the homes in the Federal Republic and set free "an army" of the hundreds and thousands of inmates. He was lenient with his boys about going to work and would make excuses for them if they didn't want to get up in the morning. Generally he taught them how to be unruly, defiant, and destructive.

So Baader and Gudrun, who each had abandoned an illegitimate child, enthusiastically took up the cause of damaged boys whose troubles had started with their illegitimacy and abandonment, to champion them against society, whose fault it was.

Financing the good work soon became a chief problem, as the SDS support was insufficient. Gudrun found that she could get donations from the rich who had social consciences or found revolutionary arsonists glamorous. When funds sank she would say, "Well, we've got to resort to writing begging letters to the liberal shits again." The money came.

No one associated with the apprentice experiment ever knew exactly where Gudrun and Baader got the big lump sums of cash which they did get. On weekends the two would drive off to plunder cities in all directions, Berlin, Hamburg—and Munich, where, according to a rumor among the apprentices, "someone was being blackmailed." But they probably did not need recourse to specific blackmail. There was a general blackmail of individual consciences in the very attitudes which created the Schili and made it hard for any of its members to resist an appeal.

The wife of a rich Frankfurt boutique owner presented Gudrun and Baader with an almost new Mercedes car. It was a gift from the Raspberry Reich which Baader did not scorn. But the apprentices eyed it with resentful envy, and they felt mutiny rise in them. Why should they be expected to work, when Baader and Gudrun lived on gifts? Their jealousy and spite needed spontaneous expression, so they climbed on the car and jumped on it until its top and hood were deeply dented and its nice sleek appearance quite spoiled.

Gudrun and Baader did not live in a collective. They were given an apartment by the Diaconic Work which happened to be vacant just then. Pastor Brehm didn't know why his superior did it. "We don't usually give apartments to criminals."

Gudrun's mother, who praised Gudrun for the way she always cleaned and tidied up the family apartment when she came home, would perhaps have been surprised or even incredulous if she had been told that her daughter left the Diaconic Work's apartment "in a filthy state." "I still have a poor opinion of them for that," Brehm said six year later.

But at the time he had been quite impressed with Gudrun. She came to see him about three days before her appeal was to be heard, and he offered to see that she got a job as a social worker, but on condition that she serve out her sentence.

Herbert Faller too retained a high opinion of Gudrun's capability and potential as a social worker—even though she concentrated on her antiauthoritarian mission and once led a sit-in at Faller's office. "Baader, Ensslin, and Proll," Herr Faller considered, "did not give support to the youths in a way that was necessary to them, in starting work, but rather in general antiauthoritarian behavior, and to see themselves as a movement, which kept the boys from developing confidence in us."

Nevertheless he thought Proll was a nice fellow. And the three did, after all, see to it that each apprentice received five marks a day as pocket money. But Baader "made an unpleasant impression" on him. Faller related how once Baader stood on a chair with a wad of ten-mark notes in his hand, bent between finger and thumb, and let them fly, and roared with delight when the boys scrambled and fought for them.

He remembered Ulrike Meinhof too. "She arrived and lay about in the group on the couch. I still have the picture clearly in my mind." She wanted the boys to go with her to Kassel to demonstrate at a trial. She had a bus to drive them there, and she wanted to take pictures of them to accompany an article she would write on the boys' action. Faller advised them strongly not to go. He pointed out that if, as a result, they should be kicked out of the collective they would have nowhere else to go. "In my view she used these youths, without considering their personal future, and exploited them to undertake such actions. But these youths were already damaged, and in their position that sort of thing was dangerous to their lives."

About three months after the start of the experiment, the collectives were granted official recognition. Before that time came, many of the fugitives had done their thing again and run away. About a third of their number absconded between August and November. Many of the rest sank into lethargy, doing little but daydreaming and masturbating (so not, at least, departing from Proll's romantic ideal of "doing something with their hands"), assisted by hashish and LSD. And a few earned money for themselves by prostitution.

Some of them were later to accuse "the Baader group" of "preventing us from distinguishing between the right and wrong kinds of protest and criticism." And though they might too readily shift blame for what they did, there was some justice in their claim. Their "reeducation" in a freer environment under Baader and Gudrun Ensslin was not really helpful to them.

In November the supreme court rejected the appeal against the arson judgment. The four were ordered to hand themselves over for reincarceration. Only one of them, Horst Söhnlein, obeyed the order (but three months later, on February 25, after an appeal for mercy had failed). The other three fled.

Baader left a message for his playmates: "We are physically and psychologically finished. We do not wish the apprentices to attach themselves to us. We just want to relax." (As opposed to what, one wonders.) "And then we'll see how we can carry on."

On the afternoon of the day when the appeal was rejected, Thorwald Proll gave away books and records to the boys in the collective to which he was "adviser" and drove off with his sister Astrid, a masculine girl with a strangely concave face. Then he left the country with the other two.

The flight of Baader, Proll, and Gudrun Ensslin was not a wild dash into the night. It was well prepared. Gudrun was, after all, an organizer; Astrid Proll too. So a comrade was waiting with a tanked-up car in the underground parking garage of a Frankfurt department store, just down the road from the Schneider. The comrade drove them a few miles eastward from Frankfurt to Hanau. There they changed cars and drivers and started westward toward France.

Now the Schili made itself useful again, with its cars and its driving licenses, its international contacts and its high-quality spare housing. The fugitives changed cars several times. Crossing the border between European Common Market countries presented no difficulties. There was no alert out for them, and besides, a German passport held out of the window usually meant one was waved through by both German and French border guards. So they were driven on the autobahn as far as Forbach, where they were put up in a Schili home of good taste, and from Forbach they were driven on to Paris.

In Paris they were provided with a tastefully furnished apartment, nice and central, on the Ile de la Cité, hard by the police headquarters, the Palais de Justice, and the cathedral of Notre Dame. It belonged to Régis Debray, the famous journalist, who was away at the time, in jail in Bolivia. As his father was a well-known lawyer, his mother a city councilor, and he a well-established journalist and theoretician of revolution, his apartment was considered safe from the police. (After his sojourn with Ernesto "Che" Guevara Lynch—that most successful and most thoroughly put down of middle-class revolutionary adventurers—Régis Debray was arrested in 1967 and sentenced to thirty years' imprisonment. But he was released in 1970.)

Someone was paying for the telephone, so it was in working order. The three fugitives spoke to comrades, like Ulrike Meinhof and Astrid Proll. Baader had a special request to make of Astrid: that she bring him his Mercedes, which had been restored to its loveliness, and which he missed painfully. She was also asked to bring them certain books and papers, and money.

When she arrived, Baader drove them at a great rate all over Paris. They ate huge meals, and in two days, according to Thorwald Proll, they "managed to get through some DM 2,000" (about $700).

Then quarreling broke óut among them. Astrid Proll was a fan of Al Fatah and wanted them all to take a trip to the Middle East. Gudrun, still academically minded, wanted to stay awhile in one place and write a book about the "Frankfurt apprentice action." Thorwald, once the spending spree was over, found life underground boring and was more and more inclined to go back to the Federal Republic and give himself up. When he dared to say so, Baader bawled at him, "Shut up, man, we're going to see it through."

In the end they agreed to go to Switzerland.

But Baader, Gudrun, and Astrid began to consider that Thorwald was a danger to them. Baader said that he'd lost his nerve. So they managed to lose him in Strasbourg. Proll waited for about three hours at a fountain where they had arranged to meet, then understood that he had been discarded, went to London and eventually back to Germany, and gave himself up on November 19, 1970.

Back in Frankfurt, those very few of the apprentices who could hold a job were surviving well enough without their advisers. Peter Brosch had a proper apprenticeship. He was responsible enough to be trusted with a commission for Gudrun. She wrote to him and asked him to bring certain papers, which she needed for her book on the apprentice action, to the Zurich address of a writer who had published a book on the Chinese cultural revolution. Brosch took the papers, but when he got there on December 22 he was told that "the people" had moved on.

He returned to Frankfurt. Early in February 1970, Gudrun telephoned him from Naples. The news was that some sick, selfish, greedy, cheap, squalid, twisted shit had stolen their car. Also that they had hardly any money left. And they had heard on the radio something about an application for mercy made on their behalf—was it true? Brosch said yes, it was true. (Many people had written in to support the appeal, including Herbert Faller of the Frankfurt Youth Office, who praised the "good work" they had done for the "apprentices.") But the Minister of Justice for the State of Hesse had refused an application for mercy on February 4. Gudrun said, "O.K., we'll just have to carry on, then."

So they did. And Baader deftly stole an Alfa Romeo. Then he and Gudrun and Astrid went looking for a source of money—liberal shits, or rich chic Leftists. They found a German woman writer who not only gave them all the help she could but succumbed to Gudrun's charm, and later wrote to Pastor Ensslin that Gudrun had found in her "a friend for life."

They drove back to Germany, where their pictures on "Wanted" posters were on public display. Late one evening they called at the Ensslin parsonage in Stuttgart. Gudrun's father implored her to serve the rest of her sentence, but she refused. They would stay underground and "see what would happen," she said.

They had a meal with the family, and drove off later that same night. Baader left a book behind, marked and annotated: *Anarchism: Concept and Praxis,* by Daniel Guérin.

They did not leave Stuttgart at once. It was carnival time, and the city was lighthearted, the streets full and busy. Gudrun wore a wig as a disguise but did not keep out of public places, and those who knew her well could recognize her. Once she walked past her grandfather on the station square. Perhaps she took his stare for uncertainty of recognition.

She didn't stop to talk to him, just passed him by, but she looked back three times, "quite plainly laughing at me," the old man said.

Then after a while the outlaws returned to Berlin.

There Horst Mahler, the legal champion of the Left, had gathered about him a group of political desperadoes, mostly of the professional class, and had changed in appearance, having grown a beard and abandoned conventional dress in favor of a bohemian style. As yet the little band had not done much. Mahler and some colleagues had formed themselves into the "Socialist Lawyers' Collective." And a comrade from Kommune I, Manfred Grashof, was learning the art of forging documents, such as identity cards, driving licenses, and car logbooks. His fellow communard Dieter Kunzelmann was said at that time to be laying property-damaging bombs about the place. But the "resistant" violence of the Mahler group had not yet been translated from concept to praxis.

Gudrun and Baader and Astrid Proll were welcomed and sheltered by Mahler and Ulrike Meinhof and the others: Peter Homann, Renate Wolff, Peter Urbach, and Mahler's assistant, Monika Berberich.

Astrid Proll had a Mercedes of her own and lent it to Baader, who drove it in his usual reckless fashion. He had never been good at keeping himself inconspicuous. A traffic policeman stopped him, warned him, took down the Frankfurt registration number, and let him go. But the cop thought the driver looked familiar and went at once to the state criminal court, where he found out who the driver was and whose car it was. That day, April 2, Schupo, Bepo, Kripo, and Popo started looking for Baader in Berlin. The "Police Defending the Constitution"—Verfassungsschutz—didn't need to look. At least one of their number knew where he was, but was leaving him his freedom for reasons of his own.

The friend and ally on whom Mahler leaned most for help, advice, plans, and moral support was a factory worker named Peter Urbach. On the evening of April 2, Mahler telephoned Urbach and asked him rather urgently to come and see him at his office. Other comrades were there too, including Baader. They discussed the pressing need for weapons. If only they could arm themselves, they could carry out a plan they had made to attack a supermarket and take the money out of the cash registers. Baader complained that he felt insecure in the office and suggested that they move to a safer place, a flat in the Kufsteinerstrasse which was owned by Ulrike Meinhof. She was there, and took part in the continued discussion of how to get hold of arms. Urbach was pretty sure that there were some guns buried in a cemetery in the outer suburb of Rudow very near the Wall. They would go and look for them. That very night they would set out on their Tom Sawyer–type adventure. The hour—after midnight—and the place of meeting were named: not a quiet and secretive place, but right in the heart of the best end of the Ku-Damm. Till later, then, they said, and parted, some to get shovels, and Urbach to an appointment at the Republican Club. He had somewhere to go first, which he hadn't mentioned to the comrades, but he did arrive at the Republican Club, in the Wielandstrasse just off the Ku-Damm, a while before he met the others.

In two cars the party drove to the cemetery. Mahler and Renate Wolff sat near the gate, pretending to be a courting couple and keeping watch. The others dug for the guns without success and then postponed the search to the following night, when they arranged to meet again at the witching hour.

When Urbach arrived with his Volkswagen, the others were already there waiting for him. Mahler was wearing rather surprising dark glasses and a striking cap with its brim pulled well down, like a stage conspirator's. This time, Urbach was sure, they'd find the cache of arms. They set out, Baader driving Astrid's Mercedes, with Peter Homann beside him and Renate Wolff in the back. Mahler rode in the Volkswagen beside his valued friend Urbach, and they followed the Mercedes.

After a short drive, Baader pulled up, Urbach stopped too, and Baader and Mahler got out and went on to a building site where they stole some iron bars which were somehow to help in the search for the buried weapons—as probes, perhaps.

A few minutes later, as they were driving through the suburb of Neuköln, a radio car of the Criminal Police came up beside the VW and traveled along with it for some distance. Mahler became very nervous. "It's the Kripo," he said. Urbach thought it best just to keep on driving steadily as any innocent driver might do. Soon another police car, the kind with an hysterical alarm, swung up beside the Mercedes and stopped it. The officers got out, went to the driver, and asked for his papers. Baader handed over his identity card and driver's license, which should prove that he was Peter Chotjewitz, who had been born on April 16, 1934. He had some children, whose names and dates of birth were entered on the identity card. The police asked Herr Chotjewitz—a writer whose name was well known in Berlin—if he would please tell them his children's names and ages. But Herr Chotjewitz for the life of him couldn't remember. The police then looked inside the Mercedes and found the driving licenses of Mahler and Mahler's wife, and a certain kind of green linen paper out of which car logbooks were made. They arrested Baader, Homann, and Renate Wolff. Mahler and Urbach had driven on past them and gone home.

Strangely enough, no one at the Kripo office the next morning knew who it was they had arrested. An order had been given to find the Mercedes, with no name attached, and the obviously false papers had provided an excuse for arresting the people in the car when it was found. But for a man who had been a pinup for some months in police stations and post offices, a man who was by no means nondescript in appearance, and who had been recognized and identified by a traffic policeman a few days before, Baader was getting very lucky, and might have begun to think that he was going to get away again. But the police had enough on him to hold him for a while, at any rate for long enough to find out his real identity. Sooner or later information from another department would have got through to this department. But they were saved the trouble, because at a quarter to ten Horst Mahler telephoned, as the lawyer of an arrested client, and demanded to be told where they had taken Andreas Baader.

So they found him in their own offices, the wanted arsonist and fugitive from justice. They put him into the Tegel prison, and once again he was very unhappy and wanted to get out.

He was not neglected by the Mahler group. He was visited several times by Mahler, twice by Monika Berberich, and twice by Ulrike Meinhof in the month of April. On the twenty-second one Dr. Gretel Weitermeier was given permission to speak to him. This mysterious visitor was well enough known to Baader. It was Gudrun Ensslin, who wanted him back with her as much as he wanted to get out of prison. Five times in May, Ulrike Meinhof came again, having much to talk to him about.

The prison administration was requested by Monika Berberich to consider giving Baader permission to write a book on the "organization of young people on the fringes of society," for the house of Klaus Wagenbach. They gave their permission. But Baader needed to research the book, and the best place for getting at the information he needed was apparently the German Institute for Social Questions in the quiet suburb of Dahlem. Its library was one of two houses owned by the institute which backed on each other, one facing Miquelstrasse and the other Bernadottestrasse, with no fence between them. The main reading room of the library had three tall windows, from knee height almost to the ceiling, overlooking the garden between the two houses. Ulrike Meinhof had worked in there on social-problem television stories often enough to be known to the director and the employees. But when the director was telephoned from the prison and asked if she would have Baader there to research his book, nobody knew or somebody forgot to say that Ulrike Meinhof would be working on it too. The director of the Institute consulted with her staff and they agreed that as they so often talked about rehabilitation of young criminals, they should take the chance to help implement their own ideas. So it was arranged that Baader would start his researches at the Dahlem library on Thursday, May 14.

Now the Mahler group found the need for arms even more pressing. They had no more time to dig for them in cemeteries (though funnily enough they would have found some if they had tried again, because they had been put there for them to find; but then also, funnily enough, they would have been guns that didn't work). There were two kinds of guns that could be bought legally over the counter: gas pistols and a small-bore submachine gun, the Landmann-Preetz. But something more reliably lethal was needed if one was going to take on armed policemen. The best thing to do was to consult somebody who had contacts in the criminal underground.

One Hans-Jürgen Bäcker was such a man, known to the communes and drug users. Yes, he could find out who would sell them a gun. But when he did, and told them, it wasn't the sort of supplier they'd expected at all; no ordinary criminal gang, but a secret cadre of the NPD, the neo-Nazi party. After some consideration of whether there was any ideological reason why they should not buy a gun from the Nazis, the Mahler group decided there was none. So Astrid Proll, and a girl named Irene Goergens, an escapee from a state home, bastard daughter of an American soldier, protégée of Ulrike Meinhof, set out to make clandestine contact with the Nazis in a Charlottenburg bar called the Wolfsschanze ("Wolf's Lair"). At the door they asked for "Horst," as they'd been told, which produced somebody called "Teddy," whose real name was Gunter Voigt. He asked them what they wanted. "Weapons," they said. "Teddy" sold them a Beretta and 250 rounds of ammunition for a thousand Deutschmarks.

It was not long after eight o'clock on the Thursday morning that Ulrike Meinhof opened the gate in the wooden fence of the Institute, walked up the short path to the locked door under its small wooden portico, and rang the bell. Frau Gertrud Lorenz let her in, but told her that the main reading room was closed to the public that morning. Ulrike Meinhof said yes of course it was, because it was the morning Andreas Baader was to come and work there, and that she had come to work on the book with him. The librarians took the word of the well-known journalist that this was the plan officially approved, and she was let in to the long reading room at the back of the house with its three tall windows. Frau Lorenz expected that they would sit at one of the tables at the end of the room, but Ulrike Meinhof wanted a table at the side. She shifted and arranged the furniture, setting two chairs with their backs to the window. She told Frau Lorenz what books they would need to start with, and she settled down to work. Beside her was a bag with papers, books, and a gun in it.

There were two doors to the reading room. One, in the middle of the long wall opposite the windows, opened directly onto the hall. It was normally kept shut. The other opened into a smaller room, in which Frau Lorenz worked at her desk. This room too had a door, which often stood open, giving direct access to the hall. In the front office Georg Linke, an elderly librarian, and two secretaries were at work. Their hall door was shut. When the bell rang a little after half past nine, they knew who it was. A prison car had drawn up at the curb on the Miquelstrasse, as they could see through their front window.

The prisoner was handcuffed to two policemen. Frau Lorenz led them through her room and into the long reading room. The three stood looking at the empty chair beside Ulrike Meinhof, and it was clear that there was a problem as to how exactly Baader was going to be arranged to do his work at the table while handcuffed to his guards.

It was Frau Lorenz who, out of a sense of the practical as well as a kind nature and a civilized habit of trust, suggested that the handcuffs should be removed. After some hesitation the two officers agreed. They made sure that all the windows were shut and fastened; then each one posted himself on a chair beside one of the doors. Baader sat down beside Ulrike Meinhof, and they started to work. Frau Lorenz and her assistants were kept busy fetching the books which Ulrike Meinhof said they needed. The two researchers talked quietly. The policemen looked on.

There was another ring at the door. A couple of young women were admitted who needed, they said, to look up some facts for a piece of research on therapy for juvenile criminals. They were told they could not go into the main reading room, but were allowed to sit down at a small table in the hall against the side of the staircase. One of them was Irene Goergens, the other Ingrid Schubert. They were both wearing wigs and carrying briefcases with arms in them. They sat whispering and pretending to work, until yet again the doorbell rang. This time it was they who went to answer it. The man they let in was masked by a totally concealing balaclava helmet with an eye slit. He hurried into the hall, holding the Beretta at the ready. Georg Linke, in his front office, had heard the doorbell, the quick opening of the front door, the hurried footsteps and voices, and he opened the door of his office to look out into the hall. The masked man, hardly pausing in his rush toward Frau Lorenz's room, shot at him. Linke slammed the door, ordered the two secretaries out of the window as quickly as possible, and followed them with a bullet in his liver.

The masked man erupted into the other room and pushed his gun at Frau Lorenz.

"Stay where you are," he shouted at her, "or you'll be shot!" The two girls rushed in behind him, guns in hand. One of them opened the door into the reading room, and as the startled policemen rose, Ulrike Meinhof opened the long window and jumped out of it, closely followed by Baader. The other three were shooting, both gas and bullets, but aiming low. Frau Lorenz remained firmly on her chair, with her feet tucked well up under the seat as she watched the bullets scudding all over the floor. The guards beat the Beretta pistol out of the hand of the man in the balaclava, and pulled the wig off Ingrid Schubert's head. The masked man fired a gas pistol. He and the two girls rushed for the open window, and they too jumped out, ran across the garden, around the side of the other house, and out into Bernadottestrasse, where a stolen silver Alfa Romeo was waiting for them with Astrid Proll at the wheel.

There were two mysterious aspects of the affair. One was why the police guards had not used their guns. But every Berlin policeman knew the answer to that in two words: Benno Ohnesorg.

The other was, Who was the man in the woolen mask? For a long time it was believed to have been Peter Homann. But Peter Homann was a man of genuine compassion, which may have led him ingenuously into the group, but which also led him wisely out of it. The man who shot Linke had to be someone more used to handling a gun, and who would do so without compunction.

The escape car was found later by the Kripo. Under the front passenger seat they found a tear-gas pistol, a torch, and a book, *Introduction to Das Kapital* by Karl Marx.

Georg Linke was badly wounded, but he survived.

Nearly three weeks after Baader had been sprung, on the significant date of June 2, a letter was received by the German Press Agency—for maximum publicity—which gloated, or brazened out:

> Did the pigs really believe that we would let Comrade Baader sit in jail for two or three years? Did any pig really believe we would talk about the development of class struggle, the reorganiza-

tion of the proletariat, without arming ourselves at the same time? Did the pigs who shot first believe that we would allow ourselves without violence to be shot off like slaughter-cattle? Whoever does not defend himself will die. Start the armed resistance! Build up the Red Army!

The Red Army Faction—RAF—had come into being. The name was thought up after, not before, the rescue of Baader. And it was not by that name that it became known to the general public, but as the "Baader-Meinhof group" ("group" or "gang" was much debated) or urban guerrilla terrorists. For although Horst Mahler was its chief organizer, theorist, and tactician at first, this was not known to the public for some time; so inevitably the press called it by the name of the "anarchist" who had been freed and the well-known pacifist journalist who had daringly freed him. And from the time she performed that deed, Ulrike Meinhof acquired, in the imagination of many who condemned and eventually feared her, many who were not even leftist or chic, a new glamour as a bandit queen.

PART THREE
THE PEACEMONGERS

8

A Game of Sorrow
and Despair

In the town of Halle in Saxony, not far from the great city of Leipzig, there lived a deacon whose wife Mathilde bore him ten children and died. The youngest was a son named Werner, born in 1901. The deacon married again, a handsome young woman, not much older than her husband's eldest daughter. When Werner reached his later teens he did not get along with his father and stepmother, and in the anxious semifinal year of school he ran away to Hamburg, where he worked as an apprentice in woodworking and metalworking shops. But after seventeen months his father, Johannes Meinhof, hauled him back home again. Without taking his *Abitur* he attended a teacher's training college at Osterburg, where he passed his primary qualifying exams at Easter 1924 and was granted a certificate exempting him from the *Abitur*. He then continued his pedagogic studies at a college in Halle.

By this time he had quite overcome his earlier preference for manual labor and wanted to go on with his studies and achieve higher academic qualifications. He was studying under a Jewish professor, one Dr. Paul Fankl, who thought so highly of him, or took such a personal liking to him, that he "arranged" for young Werner to receive a stipend so that he could go on to take his doctorate. It seems most likely that this "arrangement" was made by the good doctor with himself, and the "private grant" which Werner Meinhof received came simply and directly out of Paul Frankl's own pocket. Werner Meinhof clearly had the capacity to attract friendship and affection.

He put his stipend and his knowledge of woodworking to use on research for a dissertation on Pre-Fifteenth-Century Eastphalian Altarpieces. He traveled about Eastphalia—an old name for an area lying roughly between Göttingen on the west, Halle on the east, and the Elbe on the north—taking photographs and making notes in old churches.

In Osterburg he made the acquaintance of a school inspector named Johannes Guthardt, who was a member of the Socialist Party (SPD). Guthardt had an only child (born 1909) named Ingeborg, who was still at school and fell romantically in love with Werner.

The dissertation on Eastphalian Altarpieces was duly finished in 1927, some 18,000 words only of description, comparison, and dates. But Professor Paul Frankl and others were satisfied with it, and Werner Meinhof was awarded his doctorate. He took a job as a teacher of art history at the Gymnasium St. Johann in Danzig for about one year. In 1928 he and Ingeborg Guthardt were married, and Werner secured an appointment as assistant to the director of the state museum in Oldenburg, Lower Saxony, in northwestern Germany. Because of his special interest in the painter Tischbein (whose most famous painting is the one of "Goethe in the Campagna") he was given a grant to go to Florence for a year's study, and Ingeborg went with him.

In 1931 their first child was born, in Oldenburg: a daughter they named Wienke. Their second child, Ulrike Marie, was born on October 7, 1934—the year after Hitler came to power.

On the Meinhof side, Ulrike Marie was descended from an old bourgeois family of Württemberg, from generations of theologians who had studied, taught, preached, and superintended in the environs of Stuttgart, and a few civic dignitaries, one of whom was rumored to have attained prominence as a burgomaster of Ulm. Among the more distant constellations of the system, the brightest star they claimed was the Romantic poet Friedrich Hölderlin.

The Guthardts were more recently risen. Ingeborg's grandfather had been a shoemaker in Hesse whose wife was left to a long widowhood. The socialist views of Ingeborg's father, Johannes, brought him into trouble with the Nazis; under them he lost his job as a school inspector, and during the Second World War he worked as an insurance salesman.

Ingeborg had not had a religious upbringing. But Werner Meinhof had, of course, and he did not abandon the church but was highly critical of it. He left the Oldenburg State Church and attached himself to a small and ardent group known as the "Hessische Renitenz" (the "Hessian Dissent"), which had been formed in 1874, some three years after the inception of the German state under Bismarck, and ever since then had stood against the state control of church affairs. Now that the churches had come so thoroughly under Nazi domination, this firm independence of the Renitente Kirche (Dissenting Church) was its main attraction for Werner Meinhof: an obstinate independence which was both older and stronger than that of the Confessing Church. And while the Confessing Church was against racial discrimination in the church itself, the Renitente Kirche was against it as a general principle. Ingeborg joined it in sympathy with her husband. So both of them can be said to have belonged to that exiguous class of persons (to which, however, millions have subsequently claimed retrospective membership) who expressly opposed Nazism right from the beginning of Hitler's accession to power.

In 1936 Dr. Meinhof was appointed director of the museum of the town of Jena, not far to the south of Halle. So back to Saxony he went. And in addition to his museum job, he became a lecturer at the College of Art in nearby Weimar.

The family lived in half of a solid, ivy-covered two-family house in a street of solid houses toward the edge of the town. It had a pleasant garden with trees such as children like to climb. Ulrike played in it and climbed the trees and scooted along the paths with the children of the neighborhood, whose householders were mostly middle-class professional and included at least one secret Nazi bigwig. There was a little boy, Reinhard, nicknamed "Bubi," toward whom Ulrike felt particularly protective.

In 1939, about the time of the outbreak of the war, Dr. Meinhof became seriously ill. For some months his illness was not diagnosed and he was treated for diseases he did not have. Early in 1940 he died, and it was then discovered that he had been suffering from cancer of the pancreas. Ulrike received the news of her father's death with the indifference of a young child to an event that means nothing to her.

Dr. Meinhof had been an employee of the city and not of the state, so when he died there was no state pension for his widow. However, the municipal authorities offered to pay for her to study and qualify for a profession so that she could support herself and the children. She had passed her *Abitur* before her marriage but had not started formally on any higher education. Now she chose the subject she knew something about, art history.

Ingeborg found it hard to look after home and children and to study at the same time, and to keep the three of them on the grant from the city of Jena. She talked of taking in a lodger.

In seminars at the university she became acquainted with a clever, good-looking, strong-minded, crop-haired, friendly, and generous young woman by the name of Renate Riemeck, who was studying history and Germanistics as well as art history. The nineteen-year-old Renate was already a polymath by taste and aptitude. One day when the two women were still only colleagues rather than friends, Ingeborg sent Ulrike to Renate, who later recalled that meeting:

"I was a student in my first semester; her mother had just lost her husband and had also just begun to study. It was Ulrike who established my connection with her mother the day she brought me a scientific book which her mother and I had to work through jointly. The heart of the child Ulrike flew to me. I devised games for her to play, and the child organized everything further. She said, 'Mother has to let a room, so you come to us.'"

She was a chatty, perky, happy child with bright brown eyes under straight eyebrows, her fair but darkening hair tied in two bunches behind her ears. Quick, appealing, affectionate, she had a winning way about her.

The next day Ulrike came to Renate again, with her mother. "I want to play with you," she said. "I want to show you how I can walk down the mountain two steps at a time." She had a small rucksack on her shoulders, and they all went for their walk up and down the mountain, Ulrike holding Renate's hand. Renate went with them to Ingeborg's apartment, and the children went to the nursery to play. After a while Ulrike and Wienke came to Renate with a broken toy. "Can you fix it for me?" Ulrike asked, and Renate did. Ulrike said, "Renate can fix my toys, Mother, so if she comes to live with us you won't have to marry again." When Renate left the two little girls asked her to come again. They also took to calling so regularly on Renate, who was lodging with a family not far away, that Ingeborg felt she had to apologize to her for their interruptions of her work. Ulrike repeated her invitation to Renate to come and live with them, but Renate knew that Ingeborg could get a better rent than she could afford to pay.

One day when Renate was walking with Ingeborg on the road to the university, Ingeborg asked, "Do you think that we shall win the war?"

Renate replied, "No, I do not think so," which was a dangerous declaration to make in Nazi Germany.

"But I believe it," Ingeborg said.

Renate turned away. "Good-bye," was all she said. But she suspected that Ingeborg did not believe it and did not trust her enough to say so; because the children had told her that their grandfather had been a school inspector and was now selling insurance, so she guessed what the background of the family was. The next day the young but strong-minded student decided to take a risk in order to make her own views clear to Ingeborg Meinhof.

She went to her house just before two o'clock in the afternoon, the time the BBC broadcast war news to Germany. It was a punishable crime to listen.

"Do you have a radio?" Renate asked.

Ingeborg did, and showed it to Renate, who switched it on and turned it to the BBC news. After a little while she switched it off again and then said, "I don't believe you when you say that you believe Germany will win the war. But if you like you can now go to the Gestapo and tell them that I listen to the BBC."

Ingeborg did not go to the Gestapo. Instead, the two women became friends. Neither of them told anyone, not even the children, of the "political incident" which established confidence between them and began their relationship. Renate became Ingeborg's lodger, the rent having been adjusted satisfactorily to both, and thereafter was on the spot to mend Ulrike's toys, "until the 'toys' were not toys any more, but life situations which had gone wrong."

Ingeborg was lively, gay, and amusing; also practical, conscientious, and kind; properly cultured, with approved, international, yet decided tastes in art and literature (Tolstoy, but *not* Dostoyevsky) and seasoned by a relish of humor (Boccaccio, Goldoni, Cervantes, Gogol). She suffered from asthma.

Both Renate and Ingeborg took their doctorates in 1943. Ingeborg's thesis was on the subject of "Ornament in Medieval Art." Renate, who had studied German and history as well as art history, wrote about "Medieval Heretical Movements in Middle Germany." As soon as she got her doctorate she became a junior lecturer at Jena University. The state exams they both passed a year later qualified them to become primary school teachers. But very soon the war came to an end, the Meinhofs and their neighbors were surprised to learn that Bubi's father had been a member of the Gestapo, and everyone or nearly everyone wanted to move west.

At the time of Germany's capitulation, Jena was in the hands of the Americans, but by an agreement concluded between the Allies in 1944 and ratified at Yalta in February 1945, Saxony was to fall into the Russian zone. The hand-over was scheduled for July 1, 1945, so the two women had only a few weeks to find a place of refuge.

An acquaintance of theirs who had been imprisoned by the Nazis was now in an official position, a sort of "head of the district" of the town of Berneck in Upper Franconia, in the American-held territory of Bavaria. He was able to offer them both jobs as primary school teachers—

the only sort of school that was open at the time—so they moved the short distance to Berneck. But they could not take their second qualifying exams there in order to get promotion and higher-paid jobs, and in the spring of 1946 they moved to Oldenburg, where Ingeborg Meinhof had many friends. It was in the British zone, but it was not difficult to get there. The women hired a truck with a trailer to transport them and all their belongings, and in one day the move from Berneck to Oldenburg was accomplished.

It took them only a fortnight with the help of friends to find an apartment in a large straight-fronted three-storied house, number 4 on the Ackerstrasse. It had a fair-sized garden, not too formal a place, just right for children to play in. The house was not far from the center of the town, in one of the older but still solidly respectable suburbs, where many of the streets were still cobbled, and though in those hard and hungry years many of the houses were in a state of disrepair—not because of bombs, for the town was one of the few that had not been destroyed in the last phase of the war—most were as well kept as the times allowed, with polished brass plates beside the front doors announcing names and degrees and professions.

Oldenburg is a conservative town, largely Protestant. It had become staunchly National Socialist in 1932. It is chiefly remarkable for the bicycle paths which run along the edge of most of its sidewalks. With such a facility, and a general flatness of the land, tinkling flocks of cyclists become an irresistible force bearing down upon pedestrians everywhere. Once there was a horse market in the middle of the town, and a *Platz* still goes by that name, though only automobiles line up there now. The population of the town swelled from 80,000 in 1939 to over 120,000 in 1945 as refugees poured into it from the east.

So the schools were understandably full. The state high school, the Cäcilienschule, could accept Wienke but not Ulrike. Ingeborg managed to get Ulrike into the Liebfrauenschule, a half hour's walk or ten-minute bus ride from the Ackerstrasse: a school founded and run by Catholic nuns, but welcoming pupils of all denominations. A pretty building, stone and creeper, four stories high with a gable and dormers, it stands in a suburb of large bourgeois houses and quiet wide streets and big trees, a monument to the middle-class respectability of Oldenburg.

Ingeborg and Renate took their further exams and went to work at the Cäcilienschule—Renate until April 1948, when she moved to the Oldenburg Teacher's Training College as a lecturer, and Ingeborg until 1949.

They had both joined the Socialist Party (SPD) in 1945. They were against Stalinism but were "not blind anticommunists." "We thought, like Thomas Mann, that 'anticommunism is the fundamental foolishness of the twentieth century.'"

Toward the end of 1948 Ingeborg was found to have cancer. She had an operation, which was considered successful, and she was quite soon fit and eager to go back to work. But in that time of want, many adults went short of food and warm clothing to give more to their children, and it may have been a general debility and lack of resistance caused by not taking sufficient care of herself which made Frau Meinhof too susceptible to illness; and when, in late February 1949, she caught flu, she did not have the strength to recover, and she died on March 2.

For three or four days she had lain in bed, nursed by Renate Riemeck and attended by a careful and sympathetic woman doctor. Then an attack of asthma came on in the night. Reante heard the agonizing sound of her friend gasping for breath, sent for the doctor, and stayed helplessly watching beside her bed. "I saw that she was in agony," Renate recalled later. For two or three hours she struggled, and died suddenly of a heart attack, before the doctor arrived.

"The children were restless. They had heard the ringing of the bell, the doors opening and shutting, the voices. I went to them and told them that their mother was dead. At first neither of them cried. Then Ulrike asked me to read to them from the New Testament. So I opened it, and my eye fell on John 3:16, and I read: 'For God so loved the world, that he gave his only begotten Son, that whosoever believeth in him should not perish, but have everlasting life.'

"Ulrike said, 'That's Mother's verse for the burial ceremony.' And then she cried. But not much.

"I took them at once to the deathbed. Ingeborg looked more beautiful than in life. Both the children said she looked 'wonderful.' They were comforted by seeing her, the beauty of this face. None of the agony of the death showed in it—that had quite vanished. But of course the death was a shock. Ulrike was very brave. She didn't cry at the burial. 'Now we've only got you,' she said to me. She had said it too—'Now we've only got you'—on the night of her mother's death. I thought of how I had tried to save them from air raids, and a lot of other things, and it seemed to me now that I had no choice."

There were no relatives who could take the children. Ingeborg Meinhof had a married cousin, but the couple were refugees and in no position to help others. Of Werner Meinhof's large family two were doctors of medicine and several sisters were married to parsons, but either they lived in the Russian-occupied zone, in very reduced circumstances, or if in the Western zones their houses had been destroyed. "None were well off, and they had children of their own—of course they would have had to take Ulrike and Wienke if I had not." As it was they were happy to let Renate become the girls' foster mother and reserved to themselves only the right of criticism, implicit when not explicit. (Once, for instance, several years later, when Ulrike was about eighteen and wanted to go on a hitchhiking trip with Thomas Lenk, son of an artist friend of her parents and now a highly successful sculptor himself, Renate could not permit it "because of what the relatives would say.")

It was Grandfather Guthardt who had to make the decision. He had lost his wife in an epidemic during the war and was delighted that Renate was willing to take the children, for the children's own sakes. "He was a very good man, he did all he could." He sent DM 50 a month for the children. And in addition the foster mother received DM 18 from the state for each of the girls, the statutory orphan's allowance.

But Renate Riemeck, who was as warmhearted and kind as she was brilliant, did not find them a burden. "I am very grateful to the children, because they compelled me to earn money—so I began to write books to supplement my salary, and the books helped me to get a professorship."

Yet there might have been a reason, which she never told, for not being grateful to the children at all. About the time of Ingeborg's death, she and a certain young academic, who had been a friend of hers and Ingeborg's for some time, had been thinking that they might marry. But when she undertook responsibility for the children, their marriage was put out of question. The young man was sympathetically understanding of Renate's decision, but he had a mother to support, times were hard, and by the time general economic recovery brought circumstances which might have been more favorable for their marriage, he was killed in an accident.

So Ulrike chose Renate, and Renate chose Ulrike. The foster mother was only eleven years older than Wienke, fourteen years older than Ulrike, and she became, or rather continued to be, a loving and responsible second mother to them both. "Ulrike was upset by her mother's death, but she was not inconsolable," she found. And yet, beyond the brief tears, the religious consolation, and the appeal to the heart, there was the insecurity and abnormality of being left an orphan. And Ulrike needed, and was to seek in the years to come, "family" groups to which she could belong and be central.

The child Ulrike made an impression on adults in a way that Wienke did not. Ulrike enjoyed and courted the approval and delighted praise of adults. She liked to be the center of interest. Wienke was more retiring. And Wienke seems to have lived her childhood in the shadow of her younger sister. Wienke suffered at times at the hands of the littler girl who only meant fun, didn't really mean to hurt at all, was only teasing, was so kind and bighearted really, but just had a little mischief in her—which nevertheless to its victim must have felt less charming. Ulrike knew that Wienke was afraid of mice. So when she found a dead mouse she put it in Wienke's bed, and Wienke shrieked. "I thought it was stupid. Ulrike was a little beast to Wienke. But she had a good heart," Renate believed. She would tell Wienke to defend herself, but Wienke was not able to. And it was Ulrike all the same who attracted notice, who unfairly mattered, and whose childish clever sayings were remembered, and her charm responded to; and whose fourteen-year-old needs came first even with the woman, however just she wished to be, who felt that Ulrike's "heart had flown" to her.

"I loved this child Ulrike. She reminded me so much of my own childhood. I too liked climbing trees. And I had not known many children. Ulrike was always full of ideas. She invented games, and liked to take on the leadership. She could tell stories—remembered fairy tales well as a little girl and could retell them well. When I was a student and went for a walk with Ulrike, my mind would be on other things as she talked. But she'd know I wasn't paying attention to her, and she'd tug my hand. 'Did you hear me—are you listening to me?' she'd say."

And yet Ulrike did not have the self-confidence that her youthful ability to impress others would seem to imply. By temperament and circumstance she needed to please: to win approval, to be accepted, to belong. She was not, and never became, a daring loner. Her later oppositionism, like her even later "radicalism," resulted from an urge to be part of a dedicated elite rather than from critical independent thinking. In adolescence she acquired a soulfulness. Like most children she was quickly moved to pity, and in her teens to strong feelings for this and against that—the puerile sense of right and wrong. But again like most children she adopted the views of the adults on whom she emotionally depended. She adopted them with more than usual intensity, however. And on the whole they were not the views which were generally held in the environment in which she was growing up. Oldenburg was far from being the mental home of Renate Riemeck, a scholar who arrived at convictions which were often avant-garde. Ulrike might have learned method from her foster mother by which to reach conclusions of her own; but lacking Renate's gifts, and out of emotional need, what she learned were Renate's conclusions.

Renate Riemeck was a gifted teacher, and had a great deal to teach. She was born in Breslau on October 4, 1920, the daughter of a businessman. He was liberal in politics; yet in 1932, along with a third of the whole voting population, he and his wife voted for the Nazis, and their daughter Renate was entered into the ranks of the Bund Deutsche Mädchen. This meant that when Hitler became Chancellor in 1933, she was awarded the Golden Hitler Youth Badge, the reward for those who had committed themselves to the Party before obedience to it began to be compulsory. Later her parents regretted their rashness. Her mother found that the anti-Semitic action which the Nazis had always threatened had been meant in deadly earnest, and for that in particular she turned her opinions against them. Renate passed her *Abitur* and then studied at both Munich and Jena universities, and formed her own views.

To look ahead from the point where she undertook the care of the Meinhof girls: She became a lecturer at the Oldenburg Academy of Education in 1951, and in the same year professor of education at Brunswick, and continued as professor for another nine years, first at the Institute of Education in Weilburg and then the Academy of Education in Wuppertal. She published her first book, a study of Friedrich Schlegel, in 1945. Between that year and 1975 she wrote or edited some fifteen others, including collections of poetry, a history in four volumes for schoolchildren, and two atlases; for one of which, published in 1949, she was severely criticized because she called the German Democratic Republic the German Democratic Republic several years before it was accorded recognition as an "independent" state—but the edition of 136,000 copies was by that time already distributed. In 1964 she published a two-volume work, *Moscow and the Vatican*, and this was followed by several books on religious teachers, including one on Jan Hus, the Czech religious reformer. She got into trouble with her state employers of North Rhine–Westphalia for opposition to the remilitarization of West Germany in the late 1950s, and in 1960 became one of the first directors of the German Peace Union (Deutsche Friedens Union, DFU). In 1967 she was awarded the Carl von Ossietzky medal of the DDR "for her efforts to promote peace." ("I believe that Germany treated the Poles, Czechs, and other Slavs so badly that we owe them recompense," she has explained.) In 1971 she was awarded an honorary doctorate by the Lutheran Theological Academy of Budapest.

The fourteen-year-old Ulrike, under Renate Riemeck's guidance but free to follow her own tastes, read nineteenth-century German literature, the mainline Romantic novelists, looked at reproductions of great pictures, learned to play the recorder and the violin, and continued her religious observances. She was confirmed. The text on her certificate of confirmation was again a passage from John—this time, Chapter 16, verse 33: "In the world ye shall have tribulation: but be of good cheer; I have overcome the world."

Her teachers and other adults who observed Ulrike during her school years saw her as a well-cared-for child, intelligent, generous-hearted, and without superficial vanity, since her clothes, though serviceable, did not look fashionable or even new, but like hand-me-downs from relatives who had a proper sense of both charity and economy and the enterprise to seize an opportunity to combine the two; and her lack of stylish clothes did not seem to trouble the teen-age girl at all. Her exercise books were neat, her homework regularly and conscientiously done. "Good" was a frequent comment in her school reports at this time, and someone wrote "Has intellectual ambition," and someone else wrote, "Likes to dream." The views she liked to repeat were of a high moral tone, and she added an insistence all her own. She consciously emulated Renate in many ways. Renate wore slacks and sensible rather than glamorous clothes, so Ulrike was content to do the same. Renate had her hair cut short, so Ulrike had hers similarly cropped and swept back from her rectangular forehead. Ulrike even tried to imitate Renate's handwriting, small but clear, and managed to do it very well.

Renate Riemeck, though she would be firm in her decisions even if they were not pleasing to her foster daughters, was neither disciplinarian nor conventional. When in 1950 she was invited to England to lecture at a teacher's training college in Hertfordshire, she took Ulrike to relatives in Wuppertal, a parson and his family, and arranged for her to attend a Rudolf Steiner school in the neighborhood. But on returning to Germany in the first vacation to see how Ulrike was getting on, she found that the aunt and uncle objected to the teaching at the school of Renate's choice, and Ulrike did not want to go to the conventional school they preferred. So Renate took her back to England with her, where she lodged with a married couple, friends of Renate's, improved her English, and enjoyed outings with Renate to look at old churches and cathedrals. "She loved art and architecture, just like me."

They returned to Oldenburg. But the Liebfrauenschule did not take its pupils as far as the *Abitur*, so to study for her exams Ulrike moved to the Cäcilienschule, which by then had room for her. Wienke—and Renate—had both left it by then.

Ulrike's childhood was not an unhappy one. Yet she was fatally attracted to unhappiness. When the day's lessons were over, she would often go home with other girls. In the privacy of someone's own room, with the door closed on adult interference, their cigarettes lit, she would expound to others her views on art, morals, politics, history, religion, literature—by that time mostly Hermann Hesse, whose romanticism particularly appealed to them, warming their feelings, who were already emotionally in heat. He wrote about individuals who were different from (better than) most people. Knulp the vagabond. Steppenwolf, who is a "genius of suffering," and who despises those who do not suffer, who are bourgeois—which is to say smug, vulgar, little, brash, insensitive, American, ordinary, dull, lukewarm, or engaged in the bakery business. He exhibits the snobbery of the romantic egotist:

> If the world is right, if this music of the cafés, these mass enjoyments and these Americanized men who are pleased with so little are right, then I am wrong, I am crazy.

And he blames "society" for his own boredom:

> But the worst of it is that it is just this contentment that I cannot endure. . . . A wild longing for strong emotions and sensations seethes in me, a rage against this toneless, flat, normal, and sterile life. I have a mad impulse to smash something, a warehouse perhaps, or a cathedral, or myself, to commit outrages, to pull off the wigs of a few revered idols, to provide a few rebellious schoolboys with the longed-for ticket to Hamburg, to seduce a little girl, or to stand one or two representatives of the established order on their heads. For what I always hated and detested and cursed above all things was this contentment, this healthiness and comfort, this carefully preserved optimism of the middle classes, this fat and prosperous brood of mediocrity.

In this small private society, this cabal of the afternoon, where the eternal verities were chewed like gum, other girls felt privileged to be chosen by Ulrike. She was the oracle, the guru, the leader of some undefined, incipient mental crusade. Years later one of them remembered, "She conveyed a sense of daring, of rebellion, of risk; of being for things that our parents and most of the world were probably against." She even turned her utility clothes to advantage, as the others (who had families like fortresses into which they could retreat) began imitating her carelessness of appearance as being somehow an indication of intellectual and moral and spiritual superiority, or at least freedom from the dictates of convention. It made them feel special and significant. Altogether it was an atmosphere that adolescents can revel in. The intimacy of those long afternoons, and the pride of leadership, the sense of personal importance, the warmth of belonging—though perhaps always just a little insecurely—formed for Ulrike a pattern of adolescent need and satisfaction which, though the emotions of puberty may be glandularly caused, was not forgotten. (That thick schoolgirl atmosphere, with its hints of lesbianism, romantic sadomasochism, and full-blown hero worship persisted into Ulrike's later life and emanates from her play *Bambule*, which she wrote in her mid-thirties.)

One of her school friends recalled those days like this:

"We belonged to the 'trouser-wearing' girls who smoked and read books which one should not yet have read. Ulrike had a nice generous and casual way which at the same time was provocative. There was something distinctly antiauthoritarian about her, although that word wasn't used at the time. I felt definitely distinguished by her liking me. She had a conspiratorial air against everything that was considered normal. We enjoyed this kind of elite feeling without defining it more precisely. My mother instinctively feared this company for me, although she couldn't say anything about it but that 'the curtains would turn yellow with all our smoking.' No doubt she felt the uncompromising quality of this girl whose sympathies could be neither broadened nor deflected.

"At the time we talked primarily about literature—all the things that were now being published after the Nazi time—Jünger, Hesse, Sartre. That was also the subject of our correspondence when I moved away and she went to Weilburg in Hesse with her foster mother, who had become a professor at the Weilburg Institute of Education. At that time we lived in a deliberate austerity, 'consumption abstinence'—that is, despising all externals, refraining from all concern with appearances—so that at the time I was counted among the most slovenly girls in my circle, and I am sure that that was attributable to her influence. But I know that the connection, on my part at least, was a source of pride and gave me an aura of 'sorrow and despair' which I enjoyed very much. There was something forceful, vital; it had a touch of the forbidden, but also a touch of the 'profoundly genuine' in the meaningfulness of which we believed ourselves to be thinking and acting. As we did not encounter each other again, our correspondence also finally dwindled away. We sent each other quotations from books which we were reading. I remember one of them, at least the sense of it—at the time I wrote it in my diary. I believe it was by Jünger. 'What does the frog in the well know of the ocean?' In any case, everything was still fermenting and very adolescent.

"Important in all this, too, is her foster mother, Professor Renate Riemeck, whom we all admired passionately while she was a teacher at our school. She was a boyish woman with a man's haircut and a deep forehead, who sang naughty songs at school celebrations, and in whose classes one was allowed to sit on the tables and smoke. She was certainly a great influence on Ulrike."

Ulrike was just eighteen in October 1952, when she moved south with Renate, now a professor of education, to the old town of Weilburg in the state of Hesse, to finish her last two and a half years of schooling. So the game of "sorrow and despair" broke up, and the young players moved on.

9

Becoming Engaged

Weilburg in Hesse, in a curl of the River Lahn, is an old town with a few remaining steep-roofed timbered houses, and a fairy-tale *Schloss* on the top of the hill. The road that dips out of the town through the old gate arch rises again, and toward the top of the next rise stand the big buildings of what used to be the Institute of Education. There Professor Riemeck had an apartment to go with her new job, and Ulrike had a nearby but separate room in the same building. Wienke was away, training to be a children's nurse, but she came often to visit them.

Ulrike now attended the venerable Gymnasium Philippinum. With two of her teachers she got along well. One of them, the English teacher, a kindly, generous, and broad-minded man, remembered her later as "a very intelligent young lady" who was not like the other girls of her age, concerned with looking fashionable—"her stockings were twisted"—but who made friends and liked dancing. Again, as in her friendships in Oldenburg, it was she who exerted the stronger influence even when the other girl was older than herself.

But her closest friend now was the son of a pastor of a neighboring village, Werner Link, who came to study at the school at the same time as she did in 1952. He was a gentle, highly intelligent young man with warm brown eyes and leftist sympathies. He would often walk home with Ulrike in the afternoons, down the road through the old gate and up the steep hill to the college near the top. They would do homework together, smoke, and talk—until the last bus of the evening took Werner home—about art and politics and religion and books: Kafka, Thomas Mann, but mostly the novels of Hermann Hesse and the poetry of Friedrich Hölderlin. These were interests which the two shared almost exclusively with each other and Renate, and made them feel rather apart from the other members of the class. Sometimes, after Renate had gone into her own room to write, taking several packs of cigarettes with her, and Werner had gone home, Ulrike would go on reading into the small hours. In the morning she would creep into Renate's room to see if there were any cigarettes left, but they would all have been smoked. Such was the atmosphere then, intimate with starry ideas, smoky and nocturnal.

Sometimes Professor Riemeck gave a talk at the school. There too, as in Oldenburg, she was quickly and ardently admired, and was applauded long and loudly. "There was a very intellectual atmosphere about her," as Werner Link recalled. "And at eighteen Ulrike was different from the other girls in the class. In her there was a special combination of intellectual interests and a very charming feminine way about her. Not like a teen-ager. She was not interested in clothes like other teen-agers. She liked to argue very seriously—intensely, but not aggressively. She was unwilling ever to make compromises, a characteristic which seems to have remained constant (though I never saw her again after 1965)—that absoluteness!"

Ulrike practiced her violin conscientiously, but—considerately—not at night. If she was alone in the evenings she would read for long hours. Sometimes when she couldn't get up in the mornings she would say that it was because she had been absorbed in art books. No one could have emulated a parent or teacher, or pursued recommended goals, with more conscientiousness.

Ulrike, Werner, and two or three other girls and boys founded and edited the school magazine. It was Ulrike's first venture into journalism.

Under the burden of the approaching *Abitur* a certain anxiety began to oppress Ulrike. Perhaps a less than absolute confidence in her own abilities was troubling her. She confided to Werner that she dreamed of some way out from the burden of study, the strain of competing in exams, the pressure to achieve academic success and then—it seems an endless vista, a surely exhausting and futile pursuit—professional status. How much more real and meaningful was a life in which bread was earned by the work of the hands, skill, craft, sweat of the brow: the simple life— how attractive in romantic fiction. There was Goldmund in Hermann Hesse's *Narziss und Goldmund*, who wandered about and found a master to teach him woodcarving. And hadn't Ulrike's father done the same? She often spoke of her father in this connection to Werner in those days. How he had left school without taking his *Abitur*, and learned the craft of woodcarving, and then when he felt ready he had taken his doctorate of philosophy and become an art historian and a director of a museum. So one needn't give up the ambition to become a university professor, one could just defer it for a while. And in any case, what were all these intel-lectual things *ultimately* all about? Would it not be better to be appren-ticed and become familiar with material things?

Werner, less doubtful of the uses of learning, could nevertheless sympathize with her view:

"She did find that what we were learning then would have no rele-vance to our further lives. She went on with it, but there was this proto-type of someone who had taken this step, who had left home and still made it in life."

After talking it over with Werner, Ulrike concluded that it must be possible to achieve a balance of intellectual and practical activity.

In 1955 they took their *Abitur* exams. In the German paper there was a choice between a political and a literary question. Ulrike chose the literary one. The written papers were followed by oral tests. In English Ulrike had to read and answer questions on a poem by Carl Sandburg called *Chicago* ("Hog butcher to the world . . ."). She did well with it, and when the oral exams were over and the *Abitur* candidates gathered to hear their results, she found she had achieved a first class in English, though only average grades in most subjects. Her weakest had always been mathematics and science. Werner achieved a first in math, Ger-man, and Latin, and a second in English. It was a good class; the general standard of achievement was high. One of the boys got firsts in all eight of his subjects—and went on to become a priest.

Both Ulrike and Werner then set about working for scholarship grants. Both tried for one offered by the Protestant Church, and Ulrike also applied for the scholarship of the Study Foundation of the German People, which was not only the most generous but also carried the most prestige. Both were awarded the church scholarship. But Werner felt he could not fulfill the religious obligations which the award imposed, al-though the study foundation assured him that they would take a most lib-eral view of them. He won grants of other kinds. And Ulrike turned down the church scholarship because she won the coveted Study Foundation of the German People. It was usually awarded only for very high academic achievement, but in her case it was given not because of good grades but because of her situation as an impecunious orphan whose father and mother had both been doctors, and helped by letters from Renate Rie-meck and several professors, one of whom had been a friend of her fa-ther. It was an honor that gave her complete financial independence.

So later in the same year, 1955, Ulrike went to Marburg, a univer-sity which is still a stronghold of the right-wing student *Korps*, in a beautiful old city, farther up the Lahn, built on a steep hill crowned with rock and a grand *Schloss*. On some of the old cobbled streets stand the timbered houses, gabled and painted with flowers and mottoes, but also the large buildings, old and new, of the university institutes. The country round about is fat and fair. Ulrike lived in a furnished room, smoked a pipe, studied educational science and psychology, and attended occasional lectures in other subjects such as art history. She never entertained the idea of studying politics. That was Werner Link's subject. He too had gone up to Marburg, but the two drifted apart and seldom saw each other.

The professor under whom Link studied was Wolfgang Abendroth, a Marxist who had been ill-used by the Nazis, taken prisoner of war by the British, returned after the war to the Russian zone, and, being ill-used again by his communist comrades, had fled to the West in 1948. During the fifties, as professor of politics at Marburg, his reputation grew, and he became one of the heroes of the New Left in the late sixties when West Germany had recovered economically and was thriving and prosperous under a Social-Democrat government. Despite all of these circumstances he yet maintained that the worst socialist state was preferable to the best capitalist state. Presumably he meant for theoretical consideration only, and not for living in. He wanted to support youth movements and student insurrection even when they were antidemocratic, so that socialism—as he conceived it, which was quite differently from the SPD government—could be established. But for all his personal charisma and great powers of persuasion and Werner Link's initial bias in his favor, he did not make a permanent convert of Link, who was to become a professor of politics himself, a liberal and a rationalist.

Ulrike's interest in politics still amounted, it seemed, to little more than a general acceptance of vague leftist sympathies, tinged with a sentimental preference for Eastern Europe with its austerity, idealism, and suffering, and a particular opposition to the atom bomb. Religion was still her favorite mystique, particularly the forms favored by the "Berneuchener Kreis," the Brotherhood of St. Michael founded in Berneuchen. Neither a sect nor an order, the Brotherhood revived the liturgy of Luther and practiced various spiritual exercises. The Bishop of Oldenburg, Professor Dr. Wilhelm Stählin, had been the head of the brotherhood at the time Ulrike lived there. Renate Riemeck had been critical of them, although she "appreciated many of their intentions." She found Stählin "too authoritarian" and recognized that one of the sources of his wisdom was Rudolf Steiner's anthroposophy, but Stählin not only would not admit being stimulated by Steiner's teaching, he denigrated it. Ingeborg Meinhof had been less critical of them, but disliked their exclusiveness.

Their Luther liturgy was used, however, in Sunday services in Oldenburg, and Ulrike became familiar with it. When she went to Marburg, she found a very active "Berneuchener" pastor, and she joined his group. It was her Christianity, fortified with pacifism, that brought her into close sympathy with a Marburg student of nuclear physics named Lothar Wallek, a scholarly, rather shy, shambling bear of a man, with dark curly hair, who was quietly against the atom bomb. Wallek was able to tell Ulrike more about it technically than she had known, thereby raising the temperature of her own opposition to it, while not becoming fervent in the cause himself. Yet it was Ulrike's opinions, and above all her religiousness, that engaged his affection. So closely did their common piety bind them that they talked of marrying, and for a while regarded themselves as engaged. But then certain differences within the context of their general agreement arose and proved insuperable. It was not so much that he, whose knowledge of atomic physics fed the flames of her antinuclear fervor, was not prepared to become as involved in antibomb protest as she; more irreconcilable were his Catholicism and her Protestantism. In which church would they raise their children? Her convictions would not permit her to become a Catholic; and though he would have been willing on his own account to change over to being a Protestant, he knew that his parents would be strongly against it. She hoped to get him interested in Protestantism through the "Berneuchener" group. But he remained Catholic, the problem could not be overcome, and the engagement lapsed. While it lasted it was, by his account, a chaste affair, though they slept under the same roof for a couple of months, when Ulrike had to stay in Marburg during a vacation to finish some work, and his landlady rented her a room.

While she was at Marburg, Ulrike befriended a fellow woman student by the name of Eva-Marie Titze, who was also an orphan and had some similar views and beliefs and interests. Ulrike liked to discover as many similarities as possible, as though she needed to confirm not only her opinions but, more deeply, her personal validity.

Ulrike continued for some time after leaving school to call the place where Renate lived, wherever it was—Wuppertal after Weilburg—home. In matters of personal tradition she showed a conservatism which those who had known her longest did not expect. Once when she had come "home" from Marburg at Christmas and found that the usual decorations had not been put up—in deference, her foster mother believed, to her own views—she was very disappointed. But then, it was a time of her life when she went in for contrariness. Renate Riemeck remembered: "When she would come to Wuppertal from Marburg she was very talkative. We had debates. She always took the opposite point of view, like a game, and we never came to any agreement, but we enjoyed it. She defended a point of view, that was all—it didn't have to be any matter that concerned her personally. That was the time of my strongest contact with her. She was never angry—just liked to put up a proposition and a counterproposition. She was never aggressive. The sin I accused her of was her old failing of lack of modesty."

Ulrike was trying out other opinions, but still Renate's were highly important to her.

Renate Riemeck had left the SPD in 1955, when it gave up the struggle against remilitarization of Germany and voted for the law introducing universal conscription. She was never "an absolute pacifist," but she thought that West German rearmament was a disastrous step in the escalation of the cold war. In the next five years, she became well known (or "notorious," as she herself put it) as an opponent of Adenauer's atomic rearmament plans and an advocate of reconciliation with Poland by recognizing the Oder-Neisse border, and of coming to terms with East European states in general—for which she came under attack from the Christian Democrats (CDU), who were then in power. (But ten years later, under Willy Brandt's government, the recognition was made and a kind of reconciliation achieved.)

Ulrike left Marburg at the end of the 1957 academic year and moved north to the University of Münster, a predominantly Catholic city in Westphalia, to continue her studies under Professor Heinrich Döpp-Vorwald; and although she sometimes over the next year or so visited Lothar when she went to Marburg, the affair of the heart—or more accurately the alliance of moral accord—was virtually over.

At the University of Münster, Ulrike and a student of politics, Jürgen Seifert, busied themselves with campaigning against the atom bomb and rearmament. In answer to a call from several professors and scientists in 1957, committees against the bomb had begun to be formed all over West Germany (the Berlin Working Committee Against the Atom Death, for instance, which included, in April 1958, Heinrich Albertz, later Mayor of Berlin and later still convert to the antiauthoritarian viewpoint; and Willy Brandt, the even more famous future Mayor of

Berlin and later still Chancellor of the Federal Republic). Having made herself heard on the subject at student protest meetings, Ulrike was sent to represent the students of Münster at an antibomb press conference in Bonn. She found herself among famous socialist politicians, academics, and journalists. And most importantly for Ulrike, as it turned out, there was the editor of the student paper *Konkret* (or *konkret* as it decapitalized itself on its own cover), Klaus Rainer Röhl.

Of that meeting in Bonn, Röhl later wrote in his book *Fünf Finger sind keine Faust* ("Five Fingers Are Not a Fist," an autobiography centered on the history of *Konkret*):

> It was dislike at first sight. For both parties. For me she was the type—quite uninteresting—which I simply could not bear: bluntly direct, with a deep, earnest look, anything but superficial, chock-full of intellectual sincerity.

Ulrike, he says, saw in him a "show-off" with a crooked face, an impenetrable, arrogant type, in whom one would surely find no integrity, "so alien" was what Röhl pleases to call his "ironic manner" to "this Christian pacifist." He asks, "How did this 'dreadful type' turn into the man to whom she directed the greatest affection of her life, her only great private love?—of whom she would later say, if someone did not take to him, did not consider him 'the best man in the work,' with a finality that was unanswerable, 'Only quality can recognize quality,' pronouncing at the same time an irrevocable judgment on whomever she was talking to."

Although "the meeting was not a success," he recorded that they worked together at the conference, and, despite sincere Ulrike's dislike of supercilious Röhl, and ironic Röhl's dislike of earnest Ulrike, they "already recognized each other as useful."

Ulrike herself was editing a paper. With a student of theology named Peter Meier and, for the third issue and those that followed, with Jürgen Seifert, she brought out a small pamphlet-paper *Das Argument*. It was irregular, issued seven times between June 21 and July 15, 1958. It propounded the antibomb–antirearmament creed. In the first issue there was an article on the Democratic Cultural Association of Germany. Democratic? Cultural? Used together, those two words could produce a redolence of East European propaganda, but only in the nostrils of the disingenuous. What was it? "An association of culturally creative people . . . for the security of peace as the first cultural task of our time, . . . against the Third World War and the philosophic belief in its inevitability, . . . for unity of the fatherland, . . . for freedom of scientific and

0

cultural creation, . . . against misuse of art and science in preparation for war." So it was for peace and the reunification of Germany, terms unstipulated.

The third issue joined battle with seven Catholic theologians who had proclaimed that defense is legitimate, even by means of atomic weapons. Ulrike Meinhof and Jürgen Seifert replied, "Have the bishops, confronted with the threat of freedom-robbing communism, . . . become so blind that they dare to destroy the highest good of a Christian— the irremovable freedom of conscience?"

Editors who could speak of "freedom-robbing communism" were no conscious propagandists for the East. Ulrike was still a Christian and not yet a Communist. "From the very beginning," Ulrike Meinhof and Jürgen Seifert wrote in the seventh issue of their paper, "our circle has held to the principle not to enter into any common action with those who are working for the East."

Renate Riemeck did not give Ulrike any direct help with *Das Argument*. But it was no doubt important to Ulrike that Renate believed in the cause. "Ulrike was involved in the antibomb struggle, and it was a political struggle, but for her it was more a moral than a political question. She said to me at that time in relation to the antibomb issue, 'Don't let yourself be eaten up by the politicians.' " Ulrike was excitedly involved in it. The involvement was at least as important to her as the ideal. Monika Mitscherlich, a daughter of the psychologist Alexander Mitscherlich, met her about that time and observed that "Ulrike forgot herself in politics. There was no distance between her and her politics." Organizing, arguing, talking absorbed her, but not, Monika maintains, learning or reading about politics, or considering what others had written on the subject. "She was not really a Socialist. Perhaps in her own mind she was. But she did not understand Marxism. I am sure she never read Marx"—not even later, her friend believes, who continued to be her friend well beyond the time when she and Jürgen Seifert (who became Monika's husband) and three others, constituting the SDS committee, expelled Ulrike and Röhl from the SDS in 1960 "for wanting to make the SDS serve the purposes of the Communist Party through the Peace Campaign."

Ulrike and Röhl and the Communist Party. Her interest in politics really began, Röhl claims, with her interest in him; "her love affair with communism" and her love affair with him were "the same thing." Communist literature came her way after her association with Röhl began, and she may have read some of it. She did read a lot of books about "the anti-Nazi resistance" in her late teens and early twenties—but not, unfortunately, books by Nazis, which might have helped her identify and resist certain ideas which were yet to entrance her.

In his book Röhl tells how he came to see a possibly fruitful partnership between her "intellectual sincerity" and his "intellectual finesse." He went to see her again, about a month after the Bonn meeting, with the prime object apparently of pandering for the Berlin editor of *Konkret*, one Reinhard Opitz, who had recently met and fallen in love with Ulrike. The meeting took place in Marburg, and in his book Röhl describes it like this:

> Marburg is surrounded by wooded hills, and somewhere at some spot with a beautiful view is an excursion restaurant. There Reinhard Opitz and I met Ulrike to win her for the cause of peace and progress. She was still undecided. I came as matchmaker for Reini and the Party. It was June, after all. A high pressure area. Forest and a warm evening. All the preconditions for peace. I talked at Ulrike like a book, I was not all twisted, nor arrogant, had my great evening. I praised my friend Reini and socialism in the highest terms, I looked deep into her eyes: Opitz, the marvelous fellow. Her childhood friend, whom she had always protected at Jena, was also called Reinhard. Opitz, the selfless comrade. I described socialism to her as the only possibility of realizing what true Christians (I already knew my partner) had really always wanted. What the greatest thinkers of antiquity had wanted—the greatest dreamers of humanity. Foremost the mighty dream—justice— would be realized solely through communism. And reconciliation and kindness, the opposite of hate.
>
> It did not turn cold on that summer night, Brecht and Busch and Lenin and Christ and Mao and Plato spoke, and in the background someone played the same song again and again on the music box, a pop song, it made us mild and wild and sensitive and dreamy, we shall never forget it, that song. It was not "The International" . . . and not "The East is Turning Red," but it was the south wind: "Do you hear the south wind?"
>
> This we want to hold on to. Praise of communism and insight into necessity and into solidarity did not stand at the beginning, but something entirely private, something apolitical . . . and in this particular case the American hit tune "Tammy." . . .
>
> Maybe I overdid my matchmaking efforts. That happened which is called "transference" in psychoanalysis. Ulrike found more pleasure in the matchmaker than in the bridegroom. We did not know that she decided then, simply, in the first instance, for

us, for progress. A few months later we dragged her off to East Berlin, like some precious loot. The Party was wildly enthusiastic, felt itself confirmed in its assessment. She has, Manfred Kapluk [one of the apparatchiks] said admiringly, a great political career ahead of her. A really great career.

So the Party felt confirmed in its assessment of Ulrike Meinhof. Ulrike might have "held to the principle not to enter into any common action with those who are working for the East," but those who were working for the East adopted no reciprocal antipathy. In *Die Genossin* (The [Female] Comrade), a fictionalized account of Ulrike's life in politics, Röhl describes meetings in East Berlin with Party men, where contacts had to be made in public places on the hour precisely, or else one moved on and returned on the next hour, and did not return at all if a third attempt failed; and dodgings about on the S-bahn—the East-West train system—so as to shake off pursuers. But in a novel facts have to be improved to match the realities which spy-story readers have come to expect.

Klaus Rainer Röhl—born in Danzig, 1928—was the son of a teacher who blossomed under the Nazis into a writer of radio plays, the "*Blubo*" (Blood and Soil) type of poetry, and literary criticism for local East Prussian papers. The family moved to the West in 1945. Klaus took his *Abitur*, went to the University of Hamburg to read philosophy, was keen on acting, and developed a lasting admiration for Bertolt Brecht. He married and had a daughter, Anja, in 1955. Early in that same year he started a news sheet, *Das Plädoyer* (The Plea), with two friends, Eckart Heimendahl and the poet Peter Rühmkorf. The paper was financed at first by Klaus Hübotter, law student and member of the East German organization the Freie Deutsche Jugend—illegal in the West. "Money is no problem," Herr Hübotter said. He could "organize" it. The first issue cost DM 800. After a few issues the name of the paper was changed to *Studentenkurier* (Student Courier).

Röhl himself was still a student, preparing for his state teacher's exams.

Then, late in 1955, Hübotter was arrested. This did not cut off the money flow, however. A representative of the original donors appeared, to escort Röhl to meet them—in East Berlin. Satisfactory arrangements were made.

A few months later, in the summer of 1956, Röhl took a trip to Moscow with his wife, Bruni, and a pair of married friends. Röhl and the other man's wife became involved with each other, Bruni and the husband returned to Hamburg, and Röhl and the wife together went on to the "Fourth International Student Congress" in Prague. There they met Peter Rühmkorf, who was a delegate of the West German student press. In one of his own books Rühmkorf recounts how some virus caused an epidemic among the delegates, and he found himself in a crowded ward with Algerians, Cubans, Venezuelans, and others of the Third World, all with inflamed throats and fever. In the next bed was an Arab whom the ward called "Mr. Palestine." He moaned expressively, wailed colorfully, at first on his own behalf, but as he recovered continued to do so on behalf of the "bitter fate of a whole people." As throats became able to manage discussions of refugee policies and problems, "Mr. Palestine" became more and more excited and began to drive the Jews into an imaginary sea on the other side of Rühmkorf's bed, and to turn his blanket into a map to show how the campaign was to be conducted. The attack became so violent that Rühmkorf had to defend himself by gripping the Arab's wrists and finally pinning him to the floor, until he was released, not by sympathizers of the Third World, but by hospital staff. Mr. Palestine's real name was Yasser Arafat.

That was in August 1956. On the seventeenth of that month, the Communist Party (KPD) was banned in West Germany. But Röhl continued to be a Communist, now secretly, and the money for his paper continued to come from the East. Yet the paper carried articles which criticized the DDR on cultural and political issues—overfulfillment of plans, army recruitment, and so on. He liked to write these articles himself. And the paper was not overtly pro-Communist. It was more for supporting such policies as those of Dr. Gustav Heinemann's party, the short-lived All-Germany People's Party, which was against rearmament, for reunification, and against "bourgeois tendencies" in the Federal Republic.

On November 4, 1956, Russia invaded Hungary. There were some pacifists who raised their voices in protest along with others in the West. But the *Studentenkurier* and a majority of those who were concerned with the Peace Campaign and sat on the committees against the bomb did not swell the sound of that protest. There were students who protested against the aggression of both the Russians in Hungary and the English and French in Egypt. The VDS (Union of Student Associations) put out a pamphlet specifically protesting against the Russian aggression, but at a meeting on November 17, delegates were angry that it had not also protested against the Suez invasion, and the VDS president had to resign.

In October 1957 the *Studentenkurier* was renamed *Konkret* and was soon being printed in local editions in Berlin, Munich, Frankfurt, and Cologne as well as Hamburg. Its circulation was then nearly 20,000.

In 1958 Röhl, much concerned with the Peace Campaign and the committees (augmented by the SPD campaign started in March of that year called the Struggle Against the Atom Death), went to Munich in pursuit of his mission and had a brief affair with one Erika Runge, a dedicated antibomb committee member. It was to be a year of romantic involvements for him. In the summer he entranced Ulrike Meinhof by pleading for Reini Opitz. In the autumn he took her to visit East Berlin but started an affair with another young woman; or, as he put it in typically self-mocking and yet simultaneously conceited style, "I now became seriously involved with the working classes by having an affair with a shop-girl." But he did not gratify their aspirations. When his wife, Bruni, divorced him in November, he did not marry the girl and so she broke off the affair with him.

At the same time he had trouble over the paper. The contact man with the fund source was a man known as "Ralf," who, Röhl suspected, kept back a little of the money which was passed through him. Röhl accused him of doing so, and "Ralf" retaliated by reporting to the East Germans that the Konkret staff did not want Röhl to stay as its editor in chief. Röhl himself says that what with his affair and his divorce he was rather neglecting the paper, letting Reini Opitz and others put it together and only coming in himself to add the gloss. Before the lords of the purse, Reini Opitz stood up for Röhl, but maybe he overdid his advocacy. Or perhaps "that happened which is called 'transference' in psychoanalysis." The bosses found more pleasure in the advocate than in the defendant. They appointed Opitz editor and instructed Röhl to become an occasional contributor and gradually ease out.

But Röhl was not an easer-out or a giver-up. He returned to Hamburg and whipped up support from the correspondents and the "atom" committee. Among those who supported him were Erika Runge, Ulrike Meinhof, and Reini Opitz. Röhl won and was reinstated.

Years later it transpired (so Röhl relates) that "Ralf" had not only misappropriated funds but as a secret capitalist had set himself up in a little business with his ill-gotten gains. Confessing this to Ulrike Meinhof, the enterprising fellow apparently wept; tears of laughter and triumph, dare one hope, rather than remorse?

In January 1959 Röhl and Ulrike came together again at a student congress against the atom bomb at the Free University in Berlin. Professor-and-Pastor Gollwitzer gave the opening address on behalf of the twenty-five members of the presidential committee to 318 delegates of the twenty West German and West Berlin antibomb committees. Among the student representatives were Eva-Marie Titze, Peter Meier, and Ulrike Meinhof.

The central question which the congress had to decide was whether it was an essential part of the antibomb movement to demand recognition of East Germany and negotiations with it.

The Münster student delegation—led by Peter Meier—put their angle. How can the antibomb movement in West Germany get ahead— what hinders it? First of all, we have to clear away blind anticommunism.

Erich Kuby was there, and said that "we have to learn to think properly," and demonstrated the need for rethinking by hypothesizing a situation in which three quarters of the city of Cologne in West Germany was in Communist hands and year after year leading West German politicians were defamed in its broadcasts, spies maintained, and so on, on the pattern of West Berlin.

But many voices were raised against the timeliness of urging negotiations. One of the strongest was that of Oberleutnant H. Schmidt of the Reserve, an SPD man from Hamburg, who said that while he conceded that negotiations with East Germany would have to take place some day, it was too early now to put forward a resolution to that effect. He went on to say that such a resolution must have been inspired by a meeting at Humboldt University in East Berlin.

Shouts of "Pfui!" and loud heckling made Schmidt leave the hall in disgust. He was heard of again, however. In 1974 he became Chancellor of the Federal Republic of West Germany.

The victory—then—went to the "no anticommunist statement" faction. Röhl claims that Ulrike took a leading part in the "debate with Schmidt"; that she pursued the "no anticommunism" line with such zeal and tireless energy that she did not sleep for forty-eight hours. And perhaps it felt to her almost like a personal victory. Certainly those who won had fought fervently, and Ulrike was among them. The atmosphere of crusade was no doubt very exciting, and the issue would tend to swell in importance as the knights and the Joans of Arc remained sleepless in the fever of the battle.

In June 1959 both the SDS and the SPD declared that membership in their respective organizations was not compatible with working for *Konkret*. But in September Ulrike Meinhof began to work for it. Her first article was on the meeting of Khrushchev and Eisenhower at Camp

David. It was full of rhetoric and gush, but in it she dealt with what were to be her main themes as a columnist for years to come: peace and East-West détente in Europe, which she was for, and atomic rearmament, which she was against.

Two events of the month of September have put the population of our planet into breathtaking excitement, have opened up perspectives in the field of scientific and political efforts, one of which has appeared so far only in the dreams of humanity and the other hitherto only as an illusion in the clothes of hopelessness. A thing made by human hands has successfully been shot to the moon, and the starting signal has successfully been fired [at Camp David] for a new concept of international negotiations on questions of détente, peace, and coexistence on the broadest front. . . .

Khrushchev traveled to America. The Prime Minister and first secretary of the Communist Party of the Soviet Union was a guest in the high citadel of the capitalist West, the originating country of McCarthyism. . . .

It is necessary to bring up for debate once more the atomic rearmament of the federal army, to bring the SPD plan for Germany emphatically into play once again as an alternative to the policy of the Federal Government [Christian Democrat], to demand without compromise a decision for a policy of détente in Central Europe.

That autumn, Ulrike Meinhof became the paper's "foreign editor." *Konkret* was soon to provide her with "that longed-for ticket to Hamburg" (to use Hermann Hesse's words). Meanwhile, she had fallen in love with Röhl.

This became clear to her friend Eva-Marie Titze—who was an archivist for the paper—at a *Konkret* conference which was held in a hotel in a wood near Göttingen. Erika Runge was there; she was a little older than Eva and Ulrike and had been greatly admired and envied by both of them for her "sophistication" in their Marburg days ("She even wore earrings!"). Erika unpacked a bottle of perfume and put it on the dressing table of the room which the three women were sharing, and it was the very same perfume that Röhl had recently given Ulrike. She concluded that Erika's too had come from him, and that, Erika being so much more sophisticated—even wearing earrings—he must prefer Erika.

Overwhelmed with unhappiness, she went off alone into the wood. Eva noticed she was gone and went to look for her. She knew that Ulrike was given to moods of melancholy. She found her sitting under a tree and weeping. With tears Ulrike told her how she loved Röhl, but he could not be in love with her, for he had given the same perfume to Erika. "Her last, me now, you next," she cried to Eva, who tried but failed to console her. They returned to the hotel together, and Eva was so worried that Ulrike might try to kill herself that she arranged with Erika that they would take turns sitting up that night to watch her. The two solicitous young women had a rough night, but Ulrike slept peacefully till morning.

Röhl's awareness of a rivalry, or at least of Ulrike's fit of jealousy, prompted him to observe, "Erika and Ulrike were in keen competition for the palm of the most beautiful and politically interesting *Konkret* woman."

So "sophistication" was an exotic quality to the intense, puritan, and provincial Ulrike, a quality that both fascinated and intimidated her. Röhl was sophisticated too, and hedonistic, sardonic, and rather exhibitionist, but with the right and good antibomb opinions. But Röhl, for all his need to seduce, for all his sentimental description of the leafy warm night and the dreamy music which made them mild and wild, probably did only believe, as elsewhere he more frankly states, that she could be "useful" to him. He was not, except briefly and perhaps out of a male urge to win the female another buck is courting, eager to win Ulrike. He was loved by her more than he was loving. Later, in retrospect, he was to find that he had loved her—but by then she had become part of his life.

It is interesting that she was not able to tell Renate how strongly she felt about Röhl—perhaps because the qualities in him which most fascinated her were not the ones which stood highest on the scale of values to which she had been raised. Renate believed that Ulrike was always "very objective" about Röhl. Ulrike did tell her that she loved him, but as though excusing the fact: "He is not the right man for me, but I love him," she said, and most probably with genuine recognition.

Happily involved in the paper, she soon became powerful, took a leading role, and exerted a certain authority over others, though not, according to Röhl, over him. He and she, he relates, tried to get away from each other.

So that winter Ulrike went to Jena, the town of her early childhood, in East Germany, to examine original material for the doctoral thesis she was working on. She had decided to write about an obscure seventeenth-century pedagogue and scholar by the name of Weigel, a friend of Leibnitz, who had been unearthed by Ulrike's father; and it was Renate who suggested that she go and find the original documents at Jena. She stayed there for a few weeks, living with friends, but did not finish her thesis.

Meanwhile Röhl sought further experience of the working classes in the form of a hairdresser from Hesse, as he puts it himself.

In 1960 Ulrike gave up the autopsy on Weigel and went to live in Hamburg. She wrote for *Konkret* and renewed the relationship made up of love on her part and friendly affection on Röhl's. At first they lived separately, but then, as Röhl puts it, "Ulrike vanquished me, with a vast quantity of fine vegetables, fine peas, carrots, asparagus, chanterelles and kohlrabi, 'Rikibaby's kohlrabikins' as we called them because Rikibaby knew how to cook them so inimitably, but also of course the steaks which went with them."

So she, he would have it understood, was wooing him with all a woman's wiles—or wilikins. And to kohlrabi, and also of course to steaks, if not to his own feelings, Röhl yielded, and on September 13, 1960, they became officially engaged with a celebration in the Kröger Bierstube.

In *Die Genossin*, the character Michael, an actor who is not unlike Röhl, sees his engagement to Katharina—Ulrike—as some kind of joke which Michael hopes that Katharina will not take seriously, but she does. Perhaps it was so with the real engagement. Renate Riemeck knew that "Ulrike did not want to marry him at first. She was in love with him but did not want to marry him. Then she said she would marry him. 'I think it is more sensible to marry because we are both involved in the political struggle, and we can't live together with every magazine saying so. But perhaps we shall be divorced.' "

So the commitment seems to have been without confidence on either side.

10

A Lefter Shade of Chic

Ulrike Meinhof and Klaus Rainer Röhl were not married until the very end of 1961. For Ulrike it was a busy and exciting year. Röhl was busy working as propagandist for the German Peace Union (DFU)—founded by Carl, Count of Westphalia, and directed by a triumvirate, including the Count and Renate Riemeck—with its preparations for the Bundestag elections which took place in September of that year. The Count and his group had founded the party because they felt let down by the SPD. They had invited Renate Riemeck to help them. The Count himself, a Catholic, had been a founder member of the CDU, but left the party because of strong disagreement with Adenauer's rearmament policies. Those who gathered about him were described by Renate Riemeck as "prominent bourgeois and aristocratic anti-Nazis—professors, literary people, anti-Nazi officers from resistance circles"—which demonstrates that some leftist opposition circles were resolved that Nazism itself was still a threat, and resistance to it a live issue. Ulrike Meinhof adopted this resolution, as did protesting students and the APO generally.

Ulrike took over as editor in chief of *Konkret*. After only two months in the job, she made herself noticed by the government, or at least by one member of it, when she published her leading article, "Hitler in You." It was a tirade against Franz Josef Strauss, then Minister of Defense, who was *for* German rearmament.

A brief and, in the light of subsequent events, interesting extract:

"A revision of anti-Semitism cannot exhaust itself in study trips to Israel, for pro-Semitism is only half an answer, as what is required is the refutation of any kind of political terrorism."

The article ended:

"As we ask our parents about Hitler, someday our children will ask us about Herr Strauss."

Herr Strauss sued. The case was to drag on for some time, but Ulrike and *Konkret* finally won, in 1962, thanks to their able defense by no less a person than Dr. Gustav Heinemann, who was to be President of the Federal Republic before the decade was out.

Meanwhile, in her private life, Röhl alleged, Ulrike saw herself in the role of "Hanna Cash," heroine of a Brecht ballad which asserts:

> Whether he limps, or whether he's nuts,
> Or whether he beats her up,
> The question for Hanna Cash, my child,
> Is only whether she loves him.

Their social life was full and pleasant. Peter Rühmkorf records of that time, in his book *The Years That You Knew* (*Die jahre die Ihr kennt*):

> We spent many nights with beer and whiskey and sympathy, on which occasions such curious night-wanderer groups formed as the dissimilar pair Ulrike Meinhof—Günter Grass. . . . Elevating hours at the "Lonely Hearts Ball" opposite Mantheys at the corner of Lehmweg . . . where Ulrike and Grass indulged in wild open dancing, so that they were asked over the microphone to stop it.

However much Hanna Cash's uncertainty bothered her at home in the apartment she now shared with Röhl, Ulrike in the office was decisive, energetic, and thorough. *Konkret* was helping history advance toward its Marxist goal. It was on the side of the proletariat. It sent pamphlets down to the Hamburg docks to be distributed, DFU pamphlets entitled "Your Telephone Too Is Being Tapped"—and the editors were a little put out when the reaction they got from the dockers was: "So what? We haven't got a telephone."

In September the DFU failed to get the 5 percent of the total votes cast which was required for Bundestag representation. Its leaders did not get the kind of support they expected from left-wing intellectuals, partly because the "goodwill of the leaders seemed unduly naïve" and partly because "they did not show enough independence vis-à-vis the communist bloc." (Renate Riemeck herself did not help in the election fight, as she fell very ill in the middle of 1961 and was confined to a hospital in Freiburg for nearly a year.)

In that same month in an issue of *Konkret* there were two articles defending the Berlin Wall, which had been thrown up in August. Students, who reacted fiercely to the Wall and became outspokenly anticommunist for a couple of years as a result while devoting much effort to helping escapees get over to the West, were understandably outraged. At the Technical University of Berlin, fifty-nine copies of the paper were burned by a couple of dozen students, and permission for its sale on the campus was withdrawn.

In October Röhl and Ulrike both felt the need of a vacation, so they took a trip to Bulgaria and were "horrified" at the Bulgarian standard of living.

In December they were married. The reason which Röhl gives Michael in *Die Genossin* for marrying Katharina is that he had answered an ad for a house in Lurup with a vegetable garden, four rooms, kitchen, and bathroom for DM 300 (about $70) per month, but the owner would only rent it to a married couple. So perhaps Röhl wanted to explain it away, but marry her he did. Ulrike put on an off-white calf-length raw-silk dress with daisy buttons studded with diamanté, and married Klaus Röhl on the day after Christmas in a magistrate's office with two friends, a married couple, as witnesses. And they celebrated in their home, a small apartment in Lurup, on the street called Sprützmoor. Lurup, a lower-middle-class suburb of Hamburg, had neat new houses and neat new apartment blocks and rather empty gardens, since its saplings had still a long way to go to bosky maturity.

It was not a happy marriage even to start with. And its first year was particularly full of troubles—though success of a competitive, capitalist kind was to come to the unhappily matched pair after a few years more, when the "economic miracle" had lifted the nation into prosperity.

The first trouble of 1962 was over the paper, as the East Germans threatened to withdraw financial support. The business manager was Klaus Steffens, and he began to plan for independence. The format was reduced from a giant to a more conventional magazine size. Its circulation then was about 30,000.

Ulrike was continuing as editor in chief, and also contributed a column to almost every issue. She hailed the arrival of the New Left with less than enthusiasm:

> One cannot love the political atmosphere of this city [Berlin]. Between a shabby East and a glittering West the Wall is drawn, and in addition there are the politically empty phrases in the East, and in the West a terrible irritability in matters political.
>
> Pressure, however, produces counterpressure. The pressure of the East produced the counterpressure of the West, and since in West Berlin so much nonsense is talked officially and publicly, and Willy Brandt is continuously hoarse, and all Leftists have run over

to the Right to boil the common pot and cook in it, there is nothing but one anger, one hatred, one lament . . . and the exclusion, the hereticizing, the bedevilment of what remains has sired a kind of Left.

A "New Left" as it calls itself, so as to doubly signal its appearance.

She continued to urge the cause of peace, to be against the bomb and against rearmament.

"One does not change the world by shooting," she wrote. "One destroys it. One accomplishes more by negotiating, avoiding destruction."

Early in that year, 1962, Ulrike had become pregnant. In the summer she began to suffer severe headaches and to have trouble with her vision. She turned at once to Renate for help and comfort. As Renate had no telephone, she wrote to her address in Freiburg, but Renate was away and no answer came. She sent a telegram, and eventually Renate heard the news.

The eye specialist sent Ulrike to a neurologist. A test of reflexes showed that the source of the trouble was in the brain, perhaps a tumor, perhaps a benign one. But naturally in the light of her family history Ulrike feared cancer. She was put through the unpleasantness of a lumbar puncture and was told that she must choose between having the child and having an operation to remove a suspected tumor. She wanted to save the child. The symptoms grew worse. One of her eyes moved erratically, and one eyelid would suddenly and uncontrollably flop down. She could not open her mouth wide, and she smiled lopsidedly. It became unsafe for her to drive a car. She began to have a continuous headache. Eventually, when she was seven and a half months pregnant, she went into the hospital to have her baby delivered by cesarean section. "The baby" was twin girls, Bettina and Regine, born September 21, 1962. When they were strong enough to be taken out of the incubator, they were taken to Freiburg, where they were cared for by Renate—recently recovered from her own illness—while their mother had a brain operation.

The question of whether they should be baptized now arose. Ulrike had moved away from the church after her marriage to Röhl, but had exchanged many letters with Renate expressing her doubts: "How do you act if you're a Christian?" And "Why do so many Christians not act in a Christian way?" And "What should I believe?" Now she wrote that it was Röhl who wanted the children baptized. But, she wrote, "I don't want them baptized because that would not be honest in our marriage, which is not genuinely Christian. Klaus is not a Christian. I have doubts about Christianity, but I cannot misuse baptism."

So it was not done.

Ulrike had to wait four weeks in the hospital after the birth before the brain operation could be performed. In the interval she wrote an article on the emergency laws, on a typewriter which Röhl was much reproached by his private chorus of critics for setting upon her knees in the hospital bed.

The operation took about five hours. A third of her hair was shaved off at the back of the head. A small hole was drilled through her skull, and a triangle cut out of it. Then the "tumor" turned out to be nothing serious after all, but only a swollen blood vessel, probably worsened by pregnancy, at the bottom of the brain on a level with the eyes. The patient endured great pain after she woke up, and it was only on the second day that pain killers could be brought to her aid.

It was nearly three months before she could go home. She had help with the children, but three times in their first year they went to stay with Renate, while Ulrike was recovering and also starting to work again, "much too hard," Renate felt. "She was trying to recover confidence in herself after the operation. She was determined to get back to normal life, but was afraid the trouble might recur. Her self-confidence had never been as great as she made it seem. She had always needed someone stronger than herself to back her up. She was intelligent as a child, and her character was good, but she always reflected her environment. In a way that was her strength. She wanted to explore her limits, to go as far as she could. Sometimes I'd say, 'All right, do it—you are right to do it.' Then if it was the wrong thing, she would find out it was wrong. That's how she needed to work things out. Very much as a woman. She never had a cold hard intellect."

At Easter 1963 Ulrike wrote an article on the annual antibomb march, but did not get back to normal work until the end of the year. When Kennedy was shot, she wrote a lament—although it was Kennedy who had first involved the United States in Vietnam, and explicitly promised protection to West Berlin. It seems she chose to notice neither fact.

Grief ebbs away, emptiness remains. The man who the peoples of the world believed would make peace is dead. The man on whom even those who were living in conflict with their own governments had placed their bets exists no longer.

He was a discomfort to the conservatives and would not let the Left have its way. But the mighty had to come to terms with him and the faint put their hopes in him.

Emptiness remained. Ulrike herself went two or three times a year to visit Renate. She told her that she had thought of divorcing Röhl, but that she wanted her children to experience a normal home with both parents, not just a mother.

In the spring of 1964 the crisis came to *Konkret* which had long been expected. The East Germans finally withdrew their financial support altogether. The paper's debts amounted to about DM 40,000 at the time. But Röhl was determined to find a way to save it.

They had to drop the July issue, but were able to put out several excuses without, of course, giving the real reason. A change of layout was mentioned, and that an employers' association had included *Konkret* on a list of "dubious publications" and a suit for libel was being brought against them by a general: for all of which they appealed to readers for support, and got it. On top of that, the senior shareholder of the *Stern* publishing company came to their aid. In fact, with the next issue the circulation of *Konkret* shot up to 50,000. A report in *Der Spiegel* on their miraculous survival helped them further. The "economic miracle" was reaching their offices in the Alte Steingasse, and was soon to translate them to better premises in the Gänsemarkt.

In that year, 1964, Peter Rühmkorf married Ulrike's old friend Eva-Marie Titze, apparently to the surprise of Ulrike, who had thought of a match for Eva, but not this one. The Röhls gave them a party in the Rühmkorfs' prefab home, at which Ulrike, raising her voice above the noisy rock music, said, "I'll never understand you two. You are something quite different." But how very different she and Eva really were Ulrike had yet to discover.

It was Peter Rühmkorf who suggested to Röhl that the addition of sex to *Konkret* might boost its sales. They tried it. Röhl had undertaken the translation of a Swedish novel for a publisher of pornography, and they put some extracts into the paper. It worked. *Konkret* began to acquire its reputation as a porn-with-politics magazine—or an "all-porn rag," as some of its political critics put it—but it was saved, and even began to make the Röhls' fortune. That was also helped along by the fees which Ulrike began to earn in 1964 from broadcasting work. Her first piece for radio on the Hamburg trial of a Nazi mass murderer, *Karl Wolff—SS-man*, was transmitted on September 5, 1964, though the piece, written "on spec," had at first been turned down by Frankfurt Radio.

In November she attacked her old enemy Franz Josef Strauss again in an article called "Row in Bonn," in which she alluded to him as "the most infamous German politician." Strauss sued again—and this time he won. He was awarded damages of DM 600. But *Der Spiegel*, in January 1965, praised Ulrike for her attack, calling her "the courageous columnist of *Konkret*," and printed her picture, which made her face known to the nation, or at least to a fair portion of it. So they were not distressed. "Strauss has the case," Röhl said, "and we have the publicity."

Ulrike was now contributing regularly again to *Konkret*, but left to Röhl the job of editor in chief, which he had resumed when she fell ill. If the editorial policy changed after the connection with East Germany was severed—"after we broke with the Stalinists," as Röhl put it—it was not at once or very obvious.

It was the "sex wave," started in May 1964 with the smaller format and the first nude that made the noticeable difference. Röhl translated another pornographic novel. For the solitude needed for this work, he went for the first time to the fashionable North Sea resort of Kampen, on the island of Sylt, just west of the Denmark border. Ulrike had visited the place, but not Klaus. It was to become a frequent weekend vacation resort for the Röhls, who were soon to be fashionable themselves.

The pornography which boosted the circulation was objected to by some six thousand persons who signed a petition to the Federal Agency for Youth Publications in an attempt to stop the sale of *Konkret* to juveniles. But supported by other influential papers. *Konkret* won against the petitioners in court. And the publicity boosted its sales to 100,000.

In Röhl's view, the four years after the "break with the Stalinists" were not only the best years for *Konkret* but also, or because of that, the best years of the marriage. As always, they had help with the housekeeping, but both of them liked to cook. The twins were being properly brought up, their mother teaching them, in the time she had with them, good manners and correct habits: sit up straight, elbows off the table, don't talk with your mouth full—a little too strictly, some friends considered, but then they were parents themselves, which is always a condition of unique expertise. Renate Riemeck thought she was a lenient mother. "She always regretted that she could not spend more time with the children, but she liked to do her work too."

Ulrike's view of the marriage was not, it seems, as enthusiastic as her husband's. But she still wanted her children to have the experience of growing up in a normal family, with a father, as she had not. She did, however, attain a degree of personal success, fame, and money which could not have disappointed her; by all accounts she seemed to revel in it.

In March 1965 she returned to Weilburg for a reunion of the 1955 *Abitur* class. She wrote up the event for the school magazine. The piece starts with a pleasant description of a bus ride, which gives rise to poli-tico-moral judgments of an oddly conservative if not merely puritan nature:

> The bus still had the same dark red vinyl seats as ten years ago. And it still jangled and rattled and puffed and swayed exactly as before. The two-and-a-half-hour trip from Frankfurt to Weilburg had not grown any shorter in the meantime. And when it grew dark, again a light was turned on so that one could not make out the landscape outside, any more than the newspaper, nor could one write because of the swaying and the bulb giving out such a dim light. The railway bus from Frankfurt to Weilburg has squeezed past the economic miracle. A homely, comforting fact, at any rate if one makes no usé of it. But I believe I was the only one who made use of this method of transport. When we finally said good-bye to each other on the night of Saturday–Sunday on that 13–14th of March, 1965, at about 1 A.M. at the Weilburger Hof— "Nice that you came"—"Everything of the best, then, especially for the children"—" 'Bye"—"Until 1967, then"—there were stately and gleaming cars of the sixties, whose motors purred and no gears crashed—practiced drivers, therefore, the fathers and mothers and the childless of the *Abitur* year of 1955.

After giving personal news about everyone, she ends:

> That's it. The first ten years that is: training, the professional start, marriage, small children, trouble with housing. Less es-tablishment and consolidation than I had expected. And all of us still totally and utterly civilized. Our class was neither part of the Hitler Youth of the past nor yet in the Federal Army. Perhaps that is why no one has totally changed. Because one could not lump our years into some cliché.

Ulrike continued to send her changes of address to the old school magazine right up to the next-to-last address she had in Berlin before she went underground.

In May, at the Hamburg artists' club, Die Insel, *Konkret* celebrated its tenth anniversary. New offices were acquired in the Gänsemarkt—the

Goose Market—a *Platz* with a statue of Theodor Lessing seated thoughtfully on his bronze chair. On the wall they put the *de rigueur* portrait of Che Guevara, not tacked up poster-style as he was in the rooms of students, but in a conventional and rather ornate frame. Also in this year Stefan Aust joined the paper, coming from the editorship of a high-school paper which he had shared with Röhl's younger brother, Wolfgang.

And it was the year in which Vietnam became the big protest issue for the Left, for pacifists, for the increasingly politically active students. Ulrike wrote, in a tone characteristically intense, but pedantically, not fiercely:

> It looks as if in Vietnam the era of Kennedy is being borne to its grave while the era of John Foster Dulles is being exhumed. Militarily: the threat of the Bomb is the threat of massive retaliation; that was John Foster Dulles' all-or-nothing strategy; that is the policy at the edge of the abyss of the great war. Politically: Johnson's offer to negotiate without preconditions is an offer to negotiate under the threat of heavy and heaviest weapons; this is the policy of strength for which Dulles and Adenauer have stood, not John Fitzgerald Kennedy. In terms of alliance policy: the news that European partners in conversations with American diplomats have it pointed out to them continually that the attitude of Western allies to the war in Vietnam is a kind of litmus-paper test of their faithfulness, lets one recognize the friend-foe thinking which tolerates no neutrality.

By the end of 1965 the Röhls owned "a smart six-cylinder Opel Rekord, red," as Röhl describes it.

As it was Klaus and not Ulrike who now ruled the roost, she was not involved in the manipulations which kept the paper richly supported. Its managers were becoming more enterprising and adventurous. Their capitalist ventures did more than keep the paper afloat, it was making them personally rich. When a *Panorama* (television news show) journalist was dismissed for political reasons, Ulrike wrote an article about his dismissal, but it was Klaus Röhl and his fellow managers who had to face the problem of direct competition when the same journalist started a paper called *Panorama*, financed by the Metalworkers' Union. They came up with a clever solution. They offered to distribute the competition through their own established chain of wholesalers. The arrangement was to last for over a year, and when *Panorama* wanted to get out of the contract it had to pay a dissolution sum with which Röhl was to buy his first Mercedes, white.

In the autumn of 1965 the Röhls went on another excursion into the lands of disillusionment. This time it was Yugoslavia. Again the misery in a communist country disappointed Ulrike.

She wrote busily, not only for *Konkret*. For the *Frankfurter Rundschau* she reviewed a book on American foreign policy. She wrote for radio. She was doing more television stories: on topics like the boredom of stopwatch production-line labor; on the *Gastarbeiter*—foreign "guest" workers—and their difficulties and disabilities in their host country; on the job and pay inequalities of women.

The year 1966 marked the Röhls' entrance into fashionable society. Ulrike began to appear on television talk shows, which spread her reputation as a political polemicist and champion of the social underdog. It was becoming necessary to have a token woman, preferably one engaged in public life, adding her views to the predominantly male panels, and when a woman journalist was needed there was no great choice. Ulrike Meinhof was almost the only one. Which is not to say that she was anything less than competent, or that she did not thoroughly earn her increasing financial rewards with hard work and good ideas.

To make her films and radio features on subjects like *Gastarbeiter*, women in industry, the poor, the underprivileged, she would descend briefly into a world of poverty and struggle and return thereafter to the sunny heights where the greater amount of her time was spent, where her life was lived, her comfort secured; and the sunny heights became very sunny indeed. Socially, she herself was a grand success. She was taken to the heart of Hamburg society, of the "beautiful people" whose faces were shown to the rest on the society pages of the newspapers and glossy fashion magazines: captains of industry and their wives; international playboys; powers of the press and television; film makers, writers, artists, advertising executives, gallery owners, photographers, kings of commerce and their wives.

In Kampen she lay in the sun with an empress of soap powder, perhaps, or a queen consort of typewriters. Perhaps with Inge Feltrinelli, wife of Giangiacomo Feltrinelli, first publisher of Solzhenitsyn in the West, yet despite that belonging very devotedly to the Schili, admiring Castro (whom he visited), marching with the APO and students in Berlin demonstrations, and finally dying in a mysterious incident involving the blowing up of a pylon in northern Italy in 1972. The crowd was generally known in Hamburg as the *"erotische Schickeria,"* and it overlapped but was not exactly the same as the Hamburg section of the Schili. In other words, all were chic, some were Left. And most were naked on the beaches of Sylt in the summer. In the nightclubs they twisted to the new English pop music, the Beatles and the Rolling Stones. (Hectic, frantic, corybantic, the tempo of the time—why not, some felt, of student politics too?)

Ulrike enjoyed dancing as much as ever. She dressed fashionably now, the old carelessness of appearance quite gone. She had her hair styled. It was, after all, professionally necessary for her appearances on television. The rich socialites adopted her as their *Revolutionskasperle*, as she put it herself ("little revolutionary punchikins"), a role which inevitably aroused ambivalent emotions in her, for had she not always been anti-Establishment, and against money privilege? And for all her enjoyment of dancing and company, she had never been lighthearted. She was inclined to melancholy still, especially when she was not busy in a group, and was unhappy still—or more so—in her marriage to a man who was unfaithful to her ("the sort of man who has two affairs a week," his friends would say more with admiration than with envy or censoriousness). He was also given to outbreaks of violent temper. She needed all the friendship and appreciation she could get. She also needed, as from her early youth, to dedicate herself to great causes. And for the idling in the sun, the omnitanned twisters, the private-jet set, the chairman of the bored, it was her very radicalism, her criticism of the whole structure that sustained their way of life, which made her attractive to them. She did not want to antagonize them, and had never in her crusading fervor been aggressive, but only bent on proselytizing with intense argument. And she did not merely put up with this society; she enjoyed being favored by it and enjoyed luxury. What she could not enjoy was her own enjoyment—perhaps because she was, by temperament and training, puritan, or because she felt she was betraying some old principles of youth, when she had intended to devote herself to something quite different, when Hesse-like ideals had seized her imagination—self-sacrifice, perhaps. Or possibly she was beset by guilt, or insecurity, or *Leidensneid*, that strange envy of suffering which was to become so general in the prosperous sixties in the West. Some of those who knew her well believed her to be more than a little masochistic, "in a clinical sense."

And her circle chose to regard her radical ardor as amusing. She was a subversive in their midst—well dressed and not actually guilty of any crime—and so could provide a slight thrill of danger, like the possession of a firearm.

A new small-bore gun did in fact become available, license-free, for anyone to buy and play with at that time: the Landmann-Preetz, made to look like a submachine gun. (Röhl got one, and amused a contingent of *Konkret* correspondents from Berlin, including Rudi Dutschke, with target shooting in his cellar very late one night, until the neighbors threatened to call the police. The correspondents had come to discuss the turning of the Berlin office into a "collective," and were not very affable at the beginning of the evening. Old wine and the fun with the gun sent them happily to bed at dawn. But that was in 1968, after Ulrike had gone.)

Ulrike professed a hatred of guns. One day she was walking with her young brother-in-law Wolfgang in a wood when he was carrying a shotgun. He fired suddenly, and she burst into hysterical weeping—"almost had a small nervous breakdown." Perhaps she was oversensitive to noise since her operation, but later, when her name was linked with many incidents of violence, one of her fellow bandits was to say, "Ulrike was always pleased when we could do without shooting." (She was, however, reported by a French woman journalist to have replied to a question about the morality of shooting people—policemen particularly—"Of course one can shoot." But the report, though incorporating material from taped underground conversations, was repudiated by Ulrike Meinhof, who claimed she was misled as to her interviewer's intentions and accused her of distortion.)

In her days as a socialite Ulrike was a plump, matronly woman, in stylish clothes, her hair wound up modishly. And Röhl too was fashion-conscious, a snappy dresser without the least of puritan reservations. Their twins, blond and brown-eyed, were thriving.

One day Röhl found a few pages of diary notes "accidentally" left lying on his desk at home where he could not fail to find them. They tell how Ulrike herself saw this life:

> The relationship with Klaus, the entry into the Establishment, the work with the students, these are three aspects which appear uncombinable in one life, drag at me, tear at me.
> The house, the parties, Kampen, all that is only partially fun; it provides me with a basis, among other things to be a subversive element, to have television appearances, contacts, to be taken notice of; belongs to my job as a journalist and Socialist; provides me with a platform via radio and television beyond *Konkret*. It is even pleasing personally, but does not fill my need for warmth, solidarity, for belonging to a group. The role that gave me an entrée here corresponds to my nature or needs in only a very minor way, because it involves my attitude as a "punchikin"—it forces me to

respond with a smile to things which to me, to us all, are deadly serious: therefore grinning, therefore masklike.

The "work with the students" was for radio. For her this was a way of becoming accepted by them, though she was so much older than they. To them she was useful for the sort of publicity which they sought.

Throughout 1966 *Konkret* continued to flourish. The people who worked on it were particularly taken at the time with the views of Herbert Marcuse and Wilhelm Reich, and published articles on subjects like "sexuality and the class struggle." It was selling 150,000 copies. Vietnam was thriving as the major protest topic of the Left. In June Fritz Teufel and his friends gathered at the Kochelsee, and in July Mao went swimming in the Yangtze River and Ulrike Meinhof in the North Sea at Kampen. She and Inge Feltrinelli and their trendy circle played day and night one particular pop song more than any other—"A Whiter Shade of Pale." And the circulation of *Konkret* soared to 200,000 at the end of the year.

Ulrike Meinhof wrote on the Grand Coalition in a tone of resignation, and clearly under the influence of Marcuse:

> The step was due. One can be angry about it, one need not be amazed at it. . . . It has been prepared systematically since Godesberg. . . . The SPD . . . wanted to prostitute itself, what matter if it now does it? . . .
>
> The precondition for the change of the SPD into a people's party was an economic miracle which sucked in all strata of the population so that the conflicts of the state and society could be veiled over. . . .
>
> The chance for everyone to improve his standard of living gave rise to a feeling of satisfaction which was not suited to a concern about the limits of one's freedom; it made one happy in having confidence in the rulers and little inclined to criticize.

Ulrike, whose own rise of living standard did not lessen her inclination to criticize, found a house she wanted to buy in Blankenese, the most expensive suburb of Hamburg: a large pre–First World War house, old for Hamburg, so much of which had been smashed to rubble in the Second World War; and therefore a house with cachet. At the end of 1966 Röhl acquired a mortgage loan which let them buy the house. It cost DM 150,000 (about $50,000): thick hedge, big shady trees, tiled roof with dormers, ivy under the eaves, large rooms, cellars, and french windows onto a long shaggy lawn. The street on which it stands, Ferdinands Höh, among the hills above the Elbe, is one of those quiet shady streets of big houses, some, like the Röhls', old and ivy-covered, some new and architecturally proud, in long gardens with plenty of sunshine and plenty of shade in the summer, and pervaded with the scent of lilac and the buzzing of bees on summer afternoons—the peaceful scents and sounds and quietly shifting shadows of a world where security and domestic order and bourgeois solidity seem to be accepted as the invariable norm of civilized life.

The Röhls moved into it in 1967. Klaus wanted one room furnished with Old German furniture (chairs, wardrobe, of the sort Gudrun Ensslin and Andreas Baader were to plant a bomb in a year later); and an ambience, or ambivalence, was created, of hesitation between grandeur (curtains restrained by chains, branched candelabra), and coziness (the Old German leather-and-wood chairs, paneled wardrobe, grandfather clock, capacious desk).

The demonstrations in Berlin (Easter March, antibomb, anti–Vietnam War marches, Ho-ho-ho past America House and the eggs and the paint), and the outbreak of mass apoplexy over the Shah, were musts for the Schili of Hamburg and anywhere else within tolerable traveling distance. The Röhls, Feltrinelli, Stefan Aust—who, since he had joined *Konkret* in 1965, had become its editor, production manager, crisis solver, and almost everything else—would join Günter Grass, Horst Mahler, and all in Berlin for the placard-carrying giant processions which chanted their way through that city. In May 1967 Ulrike wrote her "Open Letter to Farah Diba," adding her voice to others who "taught-in" the students, who in turn protested their moral outrage at the Opera House on June 2. But if the shooting of Benno Ohnesorg affected Ulrike emotionally, if savage indignation was lacerating her breast, or if she thought much about it, she certainly gave no sign of it. She was busy that summer and autumn hunting through the Hamburg antique shops, for— according to Röhl—"art noveau bric-a-brac," and generally feathering her new nest. She had also begun in 1966 to explore the theme of authoritarianism and misery in state homes for girls. She continued with her work of exposing social injustices, but went with her rich friends to smart shops to find a Tiffany-type lamp, to buy handmade jewelry, to lie in the sun and listen to "A Whiter Shade of Pale."

Of this time Peter Rühmkorf, the poet friend and sometime *Konkret* associate of the Röhls, recalls:

It is, however, important to learn that these contradictions, between her day-to-day contacts with social misery on the one hand

and turning them into effect-sure features, or between her sharp-
ened consciousness of social injustice and her beautifully socially
insured private existence, were quite readily accommodated by her
then. If one of the two Röhls was heading for society in a determined and contact-seeking manner, then it was first of all Ulrike;
Röhl rather had the gift or the compulsive need to annoy, to make
enemies for himself, to step on some people's toes, to break off con-
versation brusquely, to bring discussions to shrill heights or provoc-
atively hold himself aloof. While he was the one whom people put
up with, she was lovingly clasped to their breast and used as a deco-
ration; and she decorated herself for society and liked to wear
Gloria model clothes and with them handbeaten Skoluda gewgaws.

She did write that Benno Ohnesorg was a "victim of SS mentality
and practice," in the context of a piece on Israel after the Six-Day War,
which had been pending at the time of the operatic events in Berlin. The
article asserts a "solidarity" of the Left and the young with the Jews, while
denying absolutely that victory in the 1967 war was essential to the survival of Israel.

The Röhls' move into their Blankenese house in 1967 did not produce domestic happiness. Klaus' infidelities had been, by his own admis-
sion, numerous. They were not expected to count. And a sexual adventure mattered hardly at all to Röhl or to anybody else—unless perhaps to
the Adventure herself. But that year, at a demonstration, something new
happened to Klaus Röhl. He met someone with whom he fell in love.
The woman who conquered his heart at last was a Greek. "She came
from a country which had a real political problem," he saw apprecia-
tively. It was a serious affair. It was to last seven years, the same length of
time as his marriage, but there was no question of a second marriage for
him with this lady. She was a married woman, who wanted to remain in
the security not only of her existing marriage but above all of her social
class. And Röhl saw no reason why his own family life should be
disrupted in any way simply because he was having a love affair. Life for
him at the time was sweet. For Ulrike too. And becoming sweeter.

That summer they journeyed south to visit the Feltrinellis at Villa-
deati. They were impressed. "In the hill landscape of Piedmont—a mil-
lionare's castle with cooks and chauffeurs and 'faithful servants,' " Röhl
records. And from this Socialist's home they went on to visit one of
Konkret's oldest contributors in St. Moritz, and flew back to Hamburg in
the private jet of one of the owners of *Stern*.

In October the Röhls gave a housewarming party—though they had been living in their house for some months—which was also to celebrate Ulrike's thirty-third birthday. The lady with the beautiful political problem was there, and emotions ran high. In *Die Genossin* a similar event takes place:

> It was Katharina's birthday party and "everyone" was there, or nearly everyone. And all became witnesses to how the party turned from a birthday party for Katharina into a wedding party for Michael and Ines Cabral; toward midnight [Michael] Luft simply walked out of the house arm in arm with the Portuguese lady, a bridal couple, which let its guests carry on the celebration. Everyone was to know it and everyone was against Luft and felt sorry for Katharina and admired her at the same time, but this time pity had the upper hand. . . . .
>
> The next morning Katharina moved out. She took the children.

So Ulrike made the decision at last to leave Röhl. But to do something so decisive all on her own was not easy. Other marriages in the circle were breaking up, but it wasn't a Movement. Someone—one other at least—should go with her.

She went to see Eva Rühmkorf. She tried to persuade her to leave her husband and come with her to Berlin. She had such convincing arguments against marriage that Eva wrote a letter to Peter, who was away in Italy at the time, handing on the theories against it with such conviction that Peter came home again half expecting his wife to be gone. But Eva did not go. Ulrike might be able to defend a point of view very well, but Eva had her own ideas, and they were all tending in quite a different direction from Ulrike's. In mid-1967, when after returning from a Berlin demonstration Ulrike had written that instead of smashing some of the cars in the streets they should have smashed all of them, Eva had called her a "writing-desk activist," and if this accusation had had any effect at all on Ulrike at the time it was to make her qualify her remark and explain herself as less violent than she sounded, rather than more active than she seemed. She said, "People like you and me may think about throwing stones at other people, but we wouldn't actually do it." Now, at the end of that year, when her marriage broke up, Ulrike was beginning to find violence less and less morally inexcusable.

Immediately after Christmas, Ulrike took her twins to Renate, who was then living near Frankfurt working for a publisher. She asked Renate if she would look after the twins during the divorce proceedings. She said she thought Röhl might try to take them. Renate asked what she should do if he came to her for them, and though Ulrike said she was sure he would not do that, she did not leave them with Renate after all. She drove them to Berlin, and the divorce proceedings started, and Röhl did not try to take them from their mother. But he missed them painfully.

He believed it quite possible that Ulrike wanted him to go after her and ask her to come back. But he did not.

11

Nothing Personal

In November 1967 a solemn procession of doctors in academic gowns and regalia emerged from the University of Hamburg, and as they started down the steps two neatly dressed students carrying a banner stepped in front of them and walked at the head of the procession. On the banner was a verse:

Unter den Talaren   (*Under the academic gowns*
Muff von 1,000 Jahren.   *The mustiness of a thousand years.*)

One of the robed doctors, a professor of Islamic studies and an erstwhile member of Hitler's brownshirted SA, exclaimed, "You all belong in concentration camps!" Others laughed, and the prank was attributed to Fritz Teufel by many who appreciated it. It was certainly in his style, and his spirit may well have inspired it, but Teufel himself was in prison in Berlin at the time, where most of whatever he did was done, and where the question of what exactly he had done was being considered gravely by the law courts.

This was the time when play-the-devil tactics were at their most fashionable, inspired largely by Fritz Teufel. But it was also the time when the first warnings against terror tactics were beginning to be sounded, not just by ex-SA professors who provided the militant Left with more justification than it deserved, but by liberal intellectuals, and even leftists such as Jürgen Habermas, who had denounced the tendency of a "fascism of the Left" in the aftermath of Benno Ohnesorg's death. To some uncommitted observers it seemed clear enough that beside the devil-play an arrogant nastiness was growing up among some increasingly aggressive groups of students, whose personal attacks on individual professors were becoming intolerant to an intolerable degree. Lectures would be interrupted by as many as three hundred students shouting down the lecturer. These tactics, wrote a commentator in the liberal newspaper *Die Zeit,* were very close to terror.

Ulrike Meinhof, in quite a different style from Teufel, protested. Her always rather heated manner, the vehemence that goes with views seized upon rather than reached, clung to rather than defended, intensified further in 1968. Her writing became fulminant, bombastic, grammatically ungainly, at times almost hysterical, as in the February issue of *Konkret,* in which she attacked the article in *Die Zeit* and defended "counterviolence"—her name for the increasingly violent student tactics against university authorities. She gave her own version of what had happened at the ceremony at Hamburg University before the procession:

> When, at the Hamburg immatriculation ceremony . . . last November a few SDS students disturbed the festivities, and these disturbances became gradually more boisterous during the economics lecture of the new Rector and more obtrusive and intolerable for the new Rector's lecture, which justified Schiller's economic policy and put forward anti–trade union theses such as a thesis on the wage-price spiral and talked about development aid, as if there were no exploitation of the Third World, and when that gradually got too much for a majority of students in the Audi Max and they therefore no longer wanted to accept this reactionary lecture without contradiction, did not want simply to remain silent, where the working people were being insulted and German imperialism being justified, there was a point where the mood finally threatened to switch over against the Rector and the professors and the celebration and all this immatriculation to-do, and nobody could hear his own words any more and no microphone could cut above it and the ceremonial threatened to break apart. . . . The students have through bitter experience—as, for instance, through the Hamburg immatriculation celebration—come to understand that they cannot achieve anything quietly and decently, but only with noise and rigorousness.

Yet as it would have been quite impossible to compose the rhyme and make the banner between the end of the Rector's speech and the procession's reaching the steps, it is obvious that protest on that occasion was well prepared in advance, and Ulrike Meinhof's insistence on spontaneous indignation (even if that or anything else would justify under any circumstances the attempt to stop the Rector's saying whatever he wished to say) could simply not be true.

The article demonstrated that although the fervor of her immaturity had not changed except perhaps to grow hotter, the great causes to which she would apply it had changed radically. Not peace, but violence, was now her great good—violence intolerably provoked by the fascist-capitalist-imperialist powers. Because that winter, when satire was making its point quite effectively, and viciousness only too effectively, was also the winter of Ulrike Meinhof's deepest discontent. She was not in a mood to see reason, or to be less than absolute in her judgments of what she was against. She chose her side; she had chosen it long ago, but now she went where she could be in the thickest group of her fellow believers, and where rebellion and militant aggression was—to Berlin, that Western island in an Eastern sea, where political intrigue, unrest and protest, experiments in alternative ways of living, talking, acting, learning, teaching, provoking, and attacking, abounded in the universities, the communes, the SDS, the Republican Club, the Argument Club, apartments and studios, the drinking dives, the streets, and the elegant Dahlem houses of the Schili (who would not choose any alternative to their lives unless it was a material improvement, so that their sons and daughters felt morally superior when they embraced radical politics and went to live in communes). At the Republican Club Ulrike Meinhof took her onion soup or bean soup or lard-on-bread ("simple fare of that sort, and we had a huge bottle on the bar which everyone just tossed coins into, and we couldn't make the catering side pay and we went bankrupt," one of the erstwhile catering committee recalled ruefully) with the others who were burning with a resentment against this-and-that which had a few public names but many private ones.

On the surface of it her divorce was to be "very civilized"; she was to continue writing for *Konkret*, and Röhl could come and see the children, and the divorce settlement was to be negotiated and agreed amicably.

At first she lived in quite a small flat in the Gosslerstrasse, in Dahlem, near the university—a pleasant street with luxurious houses, cared-for gardens with clumps of white-boled birches, and a small park at the other end where the children could be taken by their nurse to play. As always, she had domestic help. The sister of Dr. Bahman Nirumand (the Persian expatriate) helped her for a while. But for all that, friends who visited her from Berlin found that the children "had a neglected look, like children in an institution."

In February 1968 her suit for divorce was heard. Her lawyer was Kurt Groenewold. By agreement Röhl kept the house and the publishing business; Ulrike had the care of the children and was to be compensated with a capital settlement. She was to receive one third of the value of the Blankenese house, DM 50,000. In addition Röhl was to pay DM 1,200 per month as maintenance. This alone would give Ulrike an annual income equivalent to about $5,000, to which she would add her own considerable earnings—DM 1,500 for every article for *Konkret* (monthly, then fortnightly from September 1968), and much more from television and radio work. She was very well off.

But Ulrike was not in a peaceful frame of mind. She told her friends that she was not feeling well. Upheaval from an environment, a home, a society, a way of life, a circle of friends, a sphere of personal importance, could not leave her unaffected; and it might reasonably be supposed that a sense of loss or failure, thoughts of all those years invested in trying to make something work—a marriage, a home life for the children—now wasted and come to nothing, might assail a woman approaching her mid-thirties, especially one who was not and never had been independent of mind. Her old melancholy had not left her, and her actions and words began to express an increasing bitterness and anger—not, she would insist, over hurt pride, remorse, and regret, a sense of having been a victim of unfairness, injustice, of having been exploited and misprised, held too lightly in esteem, humiliated; not over Röhl as faithless husband; but over Röhl as misdirector of *Konkret*, and over the coalition government, the American government, the police, the state and university authorities, the bourgeoisie, the Shah of Iran, Israel, the international companies, capitalism: these were to blame for the injustice, the oppression which the world was feeling through her own nerves, her own emotion. She wrote now about "resistance," "struggle," "counterviolence." And there was the ready-to-hand alliance of a whole rebellious movement, protesting, indignant, self-righteous, passionate, claiming the same noble motives as she, with which to fuse her own cause. Ulrike had always "reflected her environment," as Renate Riemeck later pointed out; now she reflected the New Left, the student protest movement—but not the devil-playing, she was far too serious for that—and though she expressed appreciation of Teufel pranks, her own feelings demanded more forceful, more dramatic, more earnest expression.

Peter Rühmkorf expressed his view of her condition:

> The divorce . . . which Ulrike receipted with a move to Berlin, meant separation from her social life as well, one into which she had been fully integrated. . . .
>
> The role that she had played in this cannot be overestimated: as favorite child, as a spoiled exception, as a lovingly passed-around exotic, as crowning glory of a pluralistic Establishment, relentless in pursuit of her subject matter, but privately very happy to be part

of it. Nothing of this in Berlin. There was an attempt to continue a life with the external attribute of a free and open home, but that experiment failed from lack of substance. Few friends, too few at least, who corresponded to her uncompromising feeling for quality (Ulrike: "Only quality can recognize quality," a maxim in which Röhl liked to see himself reflected). Not even a climate which would appear to make the formation of new interesting groupings possible. On the contrary the so-called new society, the New Left, was in its intensest period of breakup, so she came from the private rain into the public fountain. Her role as teacher and missionary (which one can trace right back to her 1956 student days, when she wanted to put new soul into the liturgy with the "Berneuchener") she now continued, as it were, by correspondence course. Friends from Hamburg flew in, fragments of the great marriage crisis of 1965–67, victims mostly, like her, of divorce and separation, damaged people, problem bunnies, those dropped-off remnants of the merry libertinism; and there she sat in her Dahlem shell like a grand sybil and advised one of a pair this way and the other (separately arrived) that way, but always so as to come out for break-up and emancipation and splitting and division of what was. Above all, she was out for the dismemberment of the idea of marriage as private industry with the husband as industrialist. . . .

So the sentimental identification with victims slowly grew into a naïve ethic of action.

Furthermore Rühmkorf observes that the rich and powerful prodded Ulrike into terror action in order to be proxy-activist for them, to implement the ideals they dared not (or to give them a vicarious thrill).

For her work as an "exposure" journalist, and also because of an "I'll show-'em" sense of mission upon which she now placed even higher priority than formerly, she busied herself with exploiting the "exploited."

In a high-rise district of north Berlin, the Märkische Viertel, built originally for workers but mostly only affordable and afforded by middle-class tenants, she and her colleagues visited teen-agers and the children in the playground, and explained that they should not have to obey the authority of parents and teachers. (Ulrike's own children were entered into an old-fashioned disciplinarian type of school.) This housing development, though it probably had too high a population density, was not at all like a slum. It was new, and immediately beyond it lay open country. But Ulrike Meinhof and her friends believed that here were exploited workers whose eyes, and above all whose children's eyes, needed to be opened for them.

Ulrike found it hard being separated from the *Konkret* comrades. She wanted to form, with Rudi Dutschke, Bahman Nirumand, and others, an authors' "collective" to be called "Konkret Berlin," which would have some nineteen pages of *Konkret* to do with as they would, for a fee, and with an office and telephone paid for by the *Konkret* publishers. The authors, some of them very well known, would not sign their own names as they did in other periodicals, because *Konkret* as a leftist paper should not make money and so did not need sales based on "personality cults." To be part of a collective was necessary to Ulrike, now more than ever, it would seem. "Everyone here is so loving," she wistfully told her friend Eva in a telephone call to Hamburg.

Early in April the Frankfurt arson was committed, and soon after came the shooting of Dutschke, and Ulrike piled up stones which she never actually threw and parked her car ambiguously during the Springer blockade.

If her active participation in the riots which followed the denunciation of Axel Springer as scapegoat was less than effective, she did, however, go back to words to justify and defend the action of the students and the APO in her column.

> The boundary between verbal protest and physical resistance has been transgressed in the protests against the attack on Dutschke these Easter holidays for the first time in a massive way, by many, not just individuals, over days, not just once, at many places, not only in Berlin, in actual fact, not only symbolically. . . . Resistance was practiced. Was that all senseless, unrestrained, terroristic, apolitical, powerless violence?
>
> Let us state: Those who from political power positions here condemn stone throwing and arson, but not the incitement of the House of Springer, not the bombs on Vietnam, not the terror in Iran . . . their commitment to nonviolence is hypocritical. . . . Johnson, who declares Martin Luther King to be a national hero, Kiesinger, who regrets the attempted assassination of Dutschke telegraphically—they are representatives of the power against which King and Dutschke stood, the violence of the system, which brought forth Springer and the Vietnam War. They lack both the political and the moral legitimacy to protest against the students' will to resist.

That Easter, after the mob attacks on Springer, she drove back to Hamburg to fetch the remainder of her possessions from the Blankenese house—or at least those possessions which she regarded as suitable to her new life. She left behind her fur coats (perhaps because she had heard of the fate of the young lady of Frankfurt who took off her furs in the SDS office before going on a protest march) and her wedding dress, and her violin. Some of her loving supporters from Berlin helped her to load her unshameful possessions into a furniture van. Röhl was on holiday in the Canaries with his problematical Greek.

The Berlin *Konkret* collective had a trial run, and it wasn't a success. They presented nine pages only, at a cost to the paper of DM 6,000. Then in the middle of 1968 they objected to the inclusion, in an issue on violence, of a piece called *Love with Violence*. They thought it a profanation of this high, even holy form of political activity to discuss it in connection with sex. Violence was deeply revered by now in the student movement and the APO. Make violence, not love.

In August Röhl offered Ulrike her old job back as editor in chief, but she replied:

> I now have to concentrate seriously and intensively on my television play (*Bambule*) and cannot flit about and allow myself to be diverted, but I am of course basically prepared to assist you in relation to *Konkret*. If only one could talk with you! I believe one really should discuss all these matters thoroughly again. . . . I am not nursing a grudge. I am now recovered and can again do something. But cannot allow myself to be taken over by you. I do not want to find myself compelled to collaborate with you. But of course I am willing to contribute to thoughts and plans.

But she insisted that Röhl did not have the necessary "human qualifications" to deserve her return to Hamburg as editor in chief of the paper.

In September, when *Konkret* began to come out fortnightly, Ulrike wrote two articles on the occupation of Prague by forces of the Warsaw Pact on August 21. She, the practiced protester against militarism and imperialism, the gallant champion of the victimized, did not find it outrageous. This was all she found to regret: "On August 21 the European Left gave up its solidarity, its sympathy, its gratitude toward the Soviet Union as the first Socialist country, as that state which defeated German fascism at Stalingrad."

And in the second article she wrote: "Just this is what must be held against the Soviet Union, and it has absolutely nothing to do with anticommunism, as the intervention powers right up to the German Communist Party would like to interpret it: that its blow against Czechoslovakia has no positional value in an antiimperialist counter-strategy."

So much for pacifism.

At the end of October Ulrike attended the arson trial in Frankfurt of Gudrun Ensslin, Andreas Baader, Thorwald Proll, and Horst Söhnlein. The article she wrote on the arson was almost incoherent in places and altogether more prolix than any she had written before. It candidly praised lawbreaking for the sake of lawbreaking, but ranted puritanically against plentifulness of consumer goods and was grumpy about the spending of money on anything which was not public, healthy, utilitarian, and necessary. Puritan to the point of prudishness, or even priggishness, it prescribed what should and what should not be regarded as necessary. Money should be used "in the educational system, in the health service, for public transport, for peace and clean air and sex education, etc." Not for pleasure, or possibly for pleasure only with a civic sanction—a rather bleak treat, like having a picnic in a bus depot instead of Versailles.

After the trial Ulrike went to see Renate Riemeck. She told her that she did not know what to write about it. "None of the arsonists can be taken seriously politically," she said. "But I've got to write something." Professor Riemeck got the impression that Ulrike really wanted to write an attack on all forms of terrorism. But what she did write was sympathetic to the arsonists. Perhaps Ulrike already knew, when she misled Renate about what she wanted to write, that the choice she was making would lead her to commitments which her friend and foster mother would never approve of.

She defended the arson at a public meeting too. It was a political discussion on "the duty to disobey" at the Hamburg Academy of Arts, which she attended at Peter Rühmkorf's suggestion. Ulrike urged this duty upon her listeners by holding up the example of the Frankfurt arsonists. There was a protest from the audience, but Röhl was there and leaped to her defense, saying that one stone was a "harder-hitting argument" to revive the Vietnam debate than ten marches around America House.

After the meeting Ulrike returned home with the Rühmkorfs to spend the night in their apartment at the top of a house in Övelgönne on the bank of the Elbe. (They had got it by a lucky chance. Peter Rühmkorf had gone to read some of his poems at a gathering where some of the gathered were hostile to the very idea of public readings of poetry. "Why don't you poets stay in your garrets?" someone called out. "I would if I had one to stay in," Peter Rühmkorf called back. Some days later a letter arrived from the landlord of the Övelgönne house, offering him the "garret" which he had said he would stay in if he had one.)

Ulrike went on with the talk of violent resistance. "We must force

exposure of the fascist in the police," she said, "for all to see, and
en the people will turn to us for leadership."

She also waxed hot against the authoritarian harshness in state
homes and reform schools. There too she saw the answer in rebellion,
resistance, overthrow, breakup, violence.

The ways for Ulrike and Eva were becoming widely separated: Eva
was an SPD supporter and believed that there was need for reform and
improvement in many places, but that one could work toward it best
from within the system. (She eventually became the governor of a juvenile prison and fought the difficult day-to-day battles, to help the boys
themselves with their own problems and in relation to the authorities.)

For all her spirited arguing that night after the meeting, Ulrike
seemed very low in spirits herself. Eva felt this, and wanting to comfort
her, to show her some special kindness, to give her a token of her sympathy in a way Ulrike would recognize, she put an apple on her pillow to
find when she went to bed. Ulrike was touched. She sat up in bed eating
the apple and talking. She seemed to Eva to be vulnerable, in need of affection and reassurance. Then Peter came in to say good night, and an
argument developed between him and Ulrike. She adamantly and passionately defended the case of the Palestinian refugees, while he maintained, as he had to Yasser Arafat years before, that Israel too had a case.
She denied that Israel had any case at all and would not concede an iota
of right to the "Israeli imperialists." She was emphatic, intense, and obstinate. This was no pacifist speaking now, nor a passive resister, nor even
an apologist for violence, but an advocate of terrorism.

"Over the breakfast egg," Peter Rühmkorf writes in his book, "Ulrike
exclaimed over 'the peace' of our Övelgönne house. And then she returned to her theme of how it was necessary to 'provoke the latent fascism
in society.' "

He replied, "No, no, no, no. That must mean in practice to help it
unfold, Ulrike!"

When she left her friends they felt "a precognition of disquiet yet to
come."

On September 28, 1968, a new German Communist Party was
formed (DKP) which had nothing in its program about overthrowing the
democratic state—the aim which had outlawed the old Communist
Party. For this very thing Ulrike Meinhof criticized it. It could not be
radical enough for her.

At Christmas Röhl went to Berlin to visit the children.

"With an almost embarrassed smile she puts an article in front of me and says, 'Read that, Klaus, I'm keen to know whether you'll print that.' "

It was an angry article accusing him of being undemocratic in not permitting the Berlin *Konkret* collective to contribute ten pages to the paper after its initial failure. His belief in editorial democracy was therefore, the article maintained, hypocritical. His only real concern was with deadlines and profits, the author or authors alleged.

Röhl's choice was either to print this attack on himself or to reject it and risk losing the paper's columnist. He decided to print it with his own reply beside it, in which he dealt with some of the specific charges, such as the one regarding deadlines, but did not answer the main point about his refusing space to the collective. He ended, "Her [Ulrike Meinhof's] columns will continue to appear in *Konkret*. Where else?"

A few more of her columns did appear in *Konkret*. Their style reflected a confused state of mind, and the logic (something Ulrike Meinhof had never been good at) became increasingly hard to follow.

One of the last columns was a protest against the refusal by the state of a residence permit to Bahman Nirumand, the exiled Iranian writer who, she wrote, "represents as hardly anyone else at present the process of the internationalization of the anti-imperialist movements." But in addition to that recommendation she urged that the refusal should be reconsidered on humanitarian grounds, because "the family will be destroyed, or the German wife and child torn from their normal environment." Enlarging on this to make an obtuse if not entirely unintelligible political point, she did make one clear assertion: that mothers are irreplaceable and indispensable to their children. It was an opinion, however, which she was soon to abandon, or a fact she was able to ignore, a year later.

The desire to make a revolution within the little world of *Konkret* grew stronger in her as it was encouraged by the Berlin comrades. With an eagerness to incite rebellion she went to Hamburg to see Stefan Aust, the friend who had got her off the hook at the time of the Springer riot charges.

He had been quarreling with Röhl, who was seldom in the office but would come around to disagree and change things at the last moment and wanted to have the last word, leading to disputes over trivial matters. Stefan Aust was sharing an apartment with a couple of friends, one of whom was a painter from Berlin named Peter Homann. Ulrike would come often to see them. She asked Stefan Aust why he worked so hard for *Konkret*, why he let Röhl exploit him. Aust had not felt exploited because he—though he almost alone, it seems—had been earning a fairly high salary. But he had had enough of the job and wanted a change, so not much persuasion from Ulrike was necessary. He suggested to Röhl that Peter Hormann could come in to replace him, but as Aust had done the work of several men, several men would be needed in his stead. So Aust suggested that Röhl's younger brother, Wolfgang, be asked to come onto the paper too. Röhl agreed, rather reluctantly, and it was Aust who had to arrange it with Wolfgang, and also to telephone one Uwe Nettelbeck and ask him to do some work for *Konkret*. And Peter Rühmkorf, who had left the paper some three years earlier on discovering that others were being paid for working on it, returned to it on improved terms. Aust went to America.

Peter Rühmkorf's reentry onto the editorial board was disliked by Ulrike's Berlin supporters. They conferred with her on how to provoke rebellion in *Konkret* and overthrow Klaus Rainer Röhl. But Röhl (he reveals in his book *Fünf Finger sind keine Faust*) was informed of the plot by a pair of innocent spies—Bettina and Regine, who told him chattily when he next telephoned, "Mommy wanted to arrange that Uwe Nettelbeck and the others don't listen to you any more."

The new men in the office in Hamburg began to take on employees, some of them so young that they were still at school. Röhl (he relates) asked them what they were doing there.

"Important work," they replied—and added that the office was a lovely place to do it: lots of space, lots of paper, and a photocopier.

Soon they demanded the right to speak at editorial conferences. Röhl suspected that it was all part of the take-over plot hatched in Berlin.

One day he asked a strange young man what he was doing in the office, and got the reply, "I am working for *Konkret*."

Röhl said that was impossible, as he had not employed him.

The young man dismissed this objection. "That," he said, "is a bourgeois view."

"But you don't know how to write," Röhl persisted.

"That's what I'm here to learn," the irrepressible youth returned.

"Well, anyway," Röhl insisted, "there's no place for you here."

"That is a matter we shall have to discuss," came the answer.

On another occasion Röhl found a new photographer who said he had been employed by Ulrike.

"What photographs have you taken?" Röhl enquired.

"None," the "photographer" said, but added that he thought Röhl had "authoritarian ideas about professional training."

Röhl called an editorial conference. Ulrike was there, and an assortment of strangers, packing the meeting.

"Only editors of *Konkret* have a vote here," Röhl said.

Shouts of "Why? Who says? How come? It's not for you to determine that! We want a full discussion of that first, then we'll take a vote on it!"

There was a debate—a furious one—but almost exclusively between Röhl and Ulrike.

At the height of the angry exchange, several more people walked in—a number of women, including Astrid Proll, sister of the poetic diarist Thorwald Proll, who was in prison in Frankfurt for arson at the time. Astrid and the others sat on the desks of the editors, punctuated Röhl's speeches with regular cries of "Shit!" and after a while began to chant, "*Raus, kleiner* Röhl! *Raus, kleiner* Röhl!" ("Get out, little Röhl!")

Finally it was agreed that the office of editor in chief would be divided between Röhl, Rühmkorf, and Uwe Nettelbeck.

In March Ulrike delivered an article written not by her but by her Berlin collective. Röhl said he would publish it but only under her name. She refused and got Nettelbeck to accept it. But Röhl found out and retrieved it just as it was about to be printed in the middle of the night.

Röhl was away from home in April. Some visitors arrived at his house, found it empty, and moved in for a few days. They were youths from the Märkische Viertel in Berlin, who had been paid some weeks earlier to tell *Konkret* what it told them it wanted to be told about life in the Märkische Viertel. They had come, no doubt at the instigation of the "countereditorial office," to demand an "additional fee." At the offices in the Gänsemarkt their demand was turned down—so the youths went looking for Klaus Rainer Röhl at his house in Blankenese, on Ferdinands Höh. When they found that nobody was at home, they broke in and took possession of the place for a few days. They drank everything they could find to drink and were noisy enough to alert the neighbors, who called the police. But by the time the police arrived they were all gone. Only the signs were left that people had eaten, drunk, slept, and played. On the living-room floor lay a broken violin, trampled and jumped on and splintered to pieces. But the youths had not stolen much, only a few clothes.

Worse was to come to the house in Blankenese.

First some warnings were sounded:

On April 26 Ulrike announced in the newspaper *Frankfurter Rundschau*:

> I have terminated my collaboration with the paper *Konkret*
> . . . as the paper is about to turn into an instrument of the coun-

terrevolution, a fact which I do not wish to hush up with my collaboration, and which cannot at the moment be prevented from happening.

It is well known that major rows have taken place in *Konkret*'s editorial offices in the last few months. If Röhl claims that the uprising of the editors never took place then he does so only because he disclaims that those involved held positions as editors, by taking a legalistic view of the situation.

A group of leftist employees of the paper had started to organize themselves with the object of turning *Konkret* into the paper required by the Left. . . . Too late, however, did we come to recognize the solidarity declarations of Uwe Nettelbeck for what they were: attempts to ingratiate himself.

She ended with a reference to "our desperation and horror over the imminently bad use of the instrument we have built up."

Then, early in May, Ulrike's Berlin collective published an article in a Berlin underground paper, *Red Press Correspondence:*

After the attempts of comrades . . . in the spring of 1968 failed to force Röhl to work together with the most prominent names of the movement, now the second attempt—this time by the leftist editors and authors—to force him to cooperate has failed. A third attempt must be made on a different plane, with different means.

On May 3, Röhl and Rühmkorf heard, "as one hears these things"— apparently through a member of the *Konkret* staff—that Ulrike intended to storm the editorial offices on May 7. They discussed whether to inform the police and decided against it. The antiauthoritarian movement had made "the bulls" into the bogeymen of the Left—or revealed them as the tools of authoritarian oppression, depending on how you looked at it. Röhl looked at it both ways and chose the view that might be best for *Konkret* in the long run. He moved into the peaceful Rühmkorf house at Övelgönne. Machines and documents were taken to the homes of the staff. When night came on May 6, Peter and Eva and Klaus Röhl found they could not sleep. They went out at 4 A.M. to get sleeping pills. They did not wake up until noon the next day, when the raid was all over.

Wolfgang Röhl barricaded himself into the old offices at the Alter Steinweg. Klaus Steffens, the business manager and 30 percent shareholder (against Röhl's 70 percent), moved out of his house and stayed with a friend, but his wife was left behind; and although no damage was done, she came under a barrage of hard-sell propaganda by the rebels, who turned up to do their good work on Wednesday, May 7.

On that day, at 1 A.M. a convoy of minibuses and cars left Berlin to drive through the DDR into West Germany. There were about eighty resolute and intrepid invaders making for Hamburg, including Astrid Proll and Bernward Vesper, the erstwhile fiancé of Gudrun Ensslin. There were also two reporters from the Berlin offices of *Der Spiegel*. They arrived early enough in the Gänsemarkt under the bronze eye of Theodor Lessing to park their cars in metered spaces. Then they went into a café for breakfast. The excellent breads of the bakery did not tempt them. Most of them must have been watching their weight because the general order was for black tea and soft-boiled eggs.

At 10 A.M. the troops assembled in the Gänsemarkt. But the police (informed by whom—*Der Spiegel* perhaps?) also arrived. The invaders entered the building, whose door was a few yards down one of the streets radiating from the *Platz*, and stood in the entrance and on the stairs, which *Konkret* did not own. But the police stopped them from going any further. The frustrated invaders nevertheless handed out pamphlets:

> To all employees in the editorial offices and the publisher of *Konkret!* We have today occupied [they had not actually, of course, but that was an unanticipated hitch] the editorial and publishing offices. Why? Of course this occupation is not directed against you. The occupation is only directed against your and our employers, Röhl and Steffens [the business manager].
>
> This paper is just as shabby and authoritarian as the behavior of the authorities Röhl and Steffens toward you and us in the editorial and publishing offices. When you have to arrive punctually in the morning to attend to your work, that is, to Röhl's profits, then Röhl is still lying in bed, but his watchdog Steffens is already keen and sticks his nose into your business.

> Above the desk the Che Guevara,
> Under the desk the MacNamara.
> The streetcar brings you to the job,
> The boss arrives by Porsche.
> Call an end to *Konkret* stench
> And create an APO collective.

At 11 A.M. Ulrike appeared. She had arrived by plane from Berlin and was well rested. She was wearing dark glasses, trousers, and a raincoat, whether against private rain or the public fountain. She found everyone standing about. The Hamburg press had arrived too. The operation could not be allowed to fizzle into bathos. Somebody called out, "Off to Blankenese!" The cars were fetched from the meters. Ulrike Meinhof climbed into one of the proletarian vehicles, and off they went, along the road beside the Elbe, up into the quiet respectable suburb where the house stood which Ulrike had coveted, bought, decorated with devoted care—and still legally owned a third of.

Perhaps the first to get to Ferdinands Höh was gentle Bernward Vesper in his Volvo. (Röhl believed it was he who led the marauders.) Or perhaps someone even more eager beat him to it. But whoever it was had painted a phallus on the front wall of the house by the time the main body of the cultural democrats got there.

They trooped—about thirty of them—belligerently and excitedly into the garden, carrying their placards, "*Konkret* Wage Writers Demand Codetermination" and chanting, "*Raus, kleiner* Röhl! *Raus, kleiner* Röhl!" Ulrike let them in. They tore the telephone wires out of the wall, overturned large pieces of furniture, threw small objects through the closed windows, smashed what was smashable, tore what was tearable, flung pictures from the walls, ran upstairs to Röhl's bedroom and urinated into his bed. It was an orgy of vandalism. Or rather a blow against the iniquitous system of private ownership. And a lesson to the authoritarian Röhl that the Left would not put up with his sleeping late any longer. Praxis.

Satisfied with their day's work for Vietnam, or on behalf of History, or against consumption terror, or whatever it was for, they went on to the Hamburg Republican Club to slake the healthy thirsts they had worked up, regale themselves with fresh discussion, beer, and *Schadenfreude*. There they met some SDS members, and the talk over whether they ought to have done what they had done went on for some hours.

Peter Rühmkorf bravely turned up to hear what they had to say.

"At last someone has done something!" was what Ulrike said. "And some," she predicted, "will say it's 'first class,' and others will say it's 'shit.' "

And by way of justification she said, "Thirty percent of the readers of *Konkret* are active Leftists." (And some had just been more active than others.) "The paper can do without the other seventy percent."

Neither she nor any of the others would have countenanced the suggestion that the action had been taken for any but sound political reasons, not at all for the relief of any personal feelings, neither Ulrike Meinhof's nor anybody else's, such as Bernward Vesper's.

The "protest" pamphlet with the Guevara-MacNamara verse bore the signatures of many well-known persons, but Röhl believed them to be forgeries. And he found he was not without sympathizers from the ranks of the Left. Over the next three months, the offices were "purged" of the infiltrated staff. Röhl had won.

Ulrike wrote no more for it, and expressed disgust at what the paper had become—"that jerking-off aid," she called it—ignoring the fact that it had been a sex mag since 1964 without her having raised any objections. It continued to print nudes, and articles presenting the case against the United States' waging war in Vietnam, and the case against the junta in Greece. And Röhl continued to be a supporter of the anti-Vietnam protest movement, as he had been through the last years, when he had carried his placards through the streets of West Berlin, and past America House, in the company of the other APO demonstrators.

In the Berlin suburb of Dahlem, Peter Homann, who had returned to Berlin, was living with Ulrike Meinhof, cooking for her and Regine and Bettina and driving the twins daily to their expensive, private, old-fashioned disciplinarian school. Ulrike was foolish enough to malign their father to them, or at least within their hearing.

She had finished writing her television play *Bambule*. It was filmed. She had quarrels with the director and complained that she was not happy with the work she was doing, most of all because, she said, her work as a journalist, exposing such things over the years, could not change anything. It was probably quite true that she was sick and tired of being a journalist.

At the Eichenhof home for girls in West Berlin, she had talked to the inmates: orphans and half-orphans with whom she no doubt had sympathy, having been orphaned herself in her childhood; illegitimate girls; girls fathered by American GIs who had long ago returned to America; girls abandoned, or from homes too poor to keep them, or homes from which they had needed to be rescued; girls institution-formed, hurt, bored, rebellious.

The story of her play is set in a welfare home of that kind. Two of the girls, sick of labor at the ironing board, of stupid lessons where they are taught nothing worth learning, of punishment in isolation, restrictions on smoking, hair styles, and makeup, run away. One is caught and put into isolation as punishment. The other eventually gives herself up. Another rebel in the home leads a destructive riot—"*bambule.*"

The parts of the girls were acted for the film by their Eichenhof originals, while actors took the parts of the teachers and other adults. The girls afterward complained that the actors had not done their parts convincingly. Some of them also complained that Ulrike Meinhof had "tried to politicize them."

Ulrike also did factual programs for West German Radio about girls in homes. And she went to Frankfurt, to see how the "apprentice" experiment was going there, the one in which Gudrun Ensslin and Andreas Baader were taking a hand, and persuaded Baader's escapees to incite rebellion and flight in two girls' homes, one of which was closed down soon after the "action" which the boys provoked. Impressed with the "apprentice" experiment in Frankfurt, she wanted to try the same sort of thing in Berlin. There one girl in particular engaged her sympathies, Irene Goergens. Ulrike arranged with the Youth Office that she be allowed to stay out of the home, and the despised authority even provided her with a subsidized apartment.

Ulrike bought for herself a large apartment in the Kufsteinerstrasse, not far from the Ku-Damm, in the fashionable heart of Berlin, and moved into it in October 1969. But from time to time her need for a family group brought her to share living quarters with others. For a while she and Peter Homann and the twins lived in a sort of commune, or at least a "group-living situation," with the brother of her old friend Monika (Mitscherlich) Seifert and his paramour, and one Marianne Herzog and a quiet young man by the name of Jan-Carl Raspe.

Raspe, born July 24, 1944, in Austria, was the son of a chemical factory director who had died of heart disease four months before he was born. Like Baader, he was raised by women—his mother, two aunts, and two sisters. In his teens he attended a *Gymnasium* in the western sector of Berlin, traveling to and from it by S-bahn from his home in the eastern sector. On the night of the August 12, 1961, he was spending the night with an uncle and aunt in the western sector, having been at a concert late that evening. The next day, August 13, the Wall was raised. He stayed in the West, and wrote to his mother, "In any case I cannot see any future in East Berlin." So like other radical Leftists in the story— Abendroth, Dutschke, Mahler, Röhl—he was a refugee from the communist East. (It seems that communism is like suffering: it has a great reputation for being mysteriously good, but no one actually wants to be subjected to it.)

Jan-Carl Raspe was, by reputation, a gentle boy, who was very fond of animals and found it difficult to communicate. "He couldn't stand violence," his uncle avowed of him, and added that it was lucky for him that in West Berlin he did not have to do army training. Most of his pursuits were peaceful. He liked to swim and ski.

But he demonstrated against the atom bomb and the emergency laws. He became increasingly involved emotionally in the student actions of the later sixties. When Benno Ohnesorg was shot "he saw it as plain murder." It was then that he became politically engaged. He joined the SDS.

In 1967 he helped to found Kommune II, that Psychoanalytic-Amateur-Dramatic-Society which put on Mao badges and shoved the Rector of the Free University and distributed the "specialist idiots" pamphlets. Four men and two women moved into a roomy apartment in an old building in the smart and central Charlottenburg district of Berlin, sharing everything, including the two children. They kept a record of what they said and did in the commune, and later published it. The communards felt that although it was a worthwhile record of an experiment, of an alternative way of life within the consumer society, the experiment itself had not, after all, been a success. They were pleased with certain of their achievements, however, such as "an openness about sex."

Raspe found it hard to study in the commune, what with the communal children—to whom he was a benevolent substitute father—being properly noisy and all, but described it as a "life-deciding experience": he could never go back to bourgeois one-family existence. He had entered the university before the commune and had felt strange and angst-ridden. In contrast, the commune was a "tender womb." It took him four months, he said, to loosen up. "I was often speechless when we had to have discussions." In the commune's book he wrote of himself that he had "contact difficulties, angst when faced by authority, with sweating and stomach pains." Later he told one of the gang members, Beate Sturm, that he had joined the commune to overcome his difficulty in making contact with people.

He initiated a scheme that became quite a popular cause with New Leftists called the "child shop" scheme. It did not buy and sell children as an accessory of commune life, but organized children to resist organization, instructed them in how to refuse instruction, and how generally to rebel against authority, whether parental or institutional. The Märkische Viertel was one of the sites for these "shops."

After two years he left the commune and moved into a shared apartment to start a political life with like-minded comrades. The object was to overthrow the system. His preference for living in the West did not involve any anticommunist foolishness.

Ulrike's large and luxurious Berlin apartment in the Kufsteinerstrasse soon became a meeting place for APO supporters, SDS members, communards, girls from the Eichenhof, and a flophouse for drifting idealists of the sort who had found shelter and succor with Baader's friend Ellinor Michel: the Great Refusers who would not be part of the system, who would deny themselves to the wage-slave labor market, and who were all "so loving"; students of philosophy, sociology, psychology, politics, and the arts; radicals who lived on their nerves; members of the legal profession and the leftist press; the ragtag and bobtail of the New Left.

Ulrike was appointed a part-time lecturer by the Free University. She was to give one lecture a month at the Institute of Media Studies on the topic "the Possibility of Agitation and Exposure in Radio Features"— not an illiberal requirement by a university bitterly accused of high-handed authoritarianism.

She had plenty of money, but it ran through her fingers: partly because she "lent" it to borrowers who saw no reason to return it since property is theft, and partly because she did not go in for bourgeois housekeeping—as some critical visitors remarked—which meant that she preferred to replace things that got dirty rather than wash them. There were also rather a large number of people who needed to be fed, and needed light and heat, and whose telephone calls had to be paid for. After a while she decided that austerity was desirable, more for ideological than economic reasons, and discarded the lampshades.

The transmission of *Bambule* was scheduled for Sunday, May 24, 1970, at a peak viewing hour of 8:15 P.M., but it was never shown: before then, Ulrike Meinhof became an outlaw.

Earlier in that spring of 1970 the fugitives Gudrun Ensslin and Andreas Baader had arrived secretly in Berlin. They had to be hidden, sheltered, fed. Others must be moved out of this or that apartment, so that they who had suffered in jail could be made comfortable and not be seen by too many eyes. To Horst Mahler—bearded now, and balder and thinner, with the look of a religious ascetic—planning violence against the state which was "fascist or tending toward fascism," Baader could only be an asset.

Whatever her view of Gudrun and Baader had been a year earlier, Ulrike was now more than ready to share their views. At this time of emotional weakness and need for acceptance and inclusion, for direction and inspired confidence, she reencountered Gudrun Ensslin and her indomitable willfulness. For Ulrike—who had always liked to have her attitudes confirmed, her views shared and bolstered, her actions praised and supported, the details of her personal history matched by another—

Gudrun Ensslin was made to measure. Gudrun too had beer
Protestant, an ardent pacifist, had read the great Romantics,
violin, won the Scholarship of the Study Foundation of the Ge
ple, studied pedagogy, gone in for publishing, had a child, b
pointed by the Grand Coalition, committed herself to the antiauthoritarian movement, become politically active, protested against the bomb
and rearmament, carried banners through the streets of West Berlin,
shouted Ho-ho-ho and sung "The International," hated the CDU and
Franz Josef Strauss, helped to free the victims of illegitimacy and abandonment from the restrictions of welfare homes, possessed the tempera-
mental quality of "absoluteness," and was only ahead of Ulrike Meinhof
in that she had already taken violent action on behalf of Vietnam.
Gudrun, six years younger, was the true crusade leader of Ulrike's aspirations. And Gudrun had attached Baader's daredeviltry to herself when she
attached him to herself. Such an influence on Ulrike at this time, added
to that of the students and communards, the young hotheads of Berlin,
the exaggerators of the APO, was not likely to be ineffectual.

Gudrun and Baader said that one should not talk and write, but do
something. And Ulrike agreed.

Baader was arrested on his way to dig for arms in the cemetery, and
Gudrun Ensslin pined for him. She said she could not live without
"Baby," as she called him. Ulrike and Horst Mahler and the others must
help her get him out of prison. Ulrike was not one to ignore pleading,
and it was Gudrun Ensslin who was wanting something of her. This was
Ulrike's new, best "family." If anything had ever been expected of her by
those whose approval she needed, it was now. She did not clearly visual-
ize what it would mean to go underground, but she did take one precau-
tion. She arranged for the children to be hidden from Röhl.

Peter Homann, who was with Ulrike when the freeing of Baader was
being plotted and went underground with her for a while afterward (and
was the first to leave the group), later asserted positively that there was no
question of political motive, not even discussion of it. Gudrun wanted
Baader out. The idea of the "Red Army Faction" came afterward, when
they found themselves in any case outlaws with Baader and Gudrun
Ensslin, and after the "Minihandbook of the Brazilian Urban Guerrilla"
by Carlos Marighela was published in Berlin at the end of May 1970,
after Baader had been freed.

On May 14, 1970, there was a party in Hamburg to celebrate
the fifteenth anniversary of that triumphantly surviving paper, *Konkret*.
Everybody who had ever had anything to do with the paper was invited.

Ulrike was expected. Peter Rühmkorf, recently returned from a guest lectureship in Texas, was there, and Eva, and Erika Runge, and contributors from everywhere, and employees of the present and past, such as one Jürgen Holtkamp, who had come from nearby Bremen for the party, which started at three o'clock in the afternoon.

Röhl made a short speech. He had only just finished when a secretary told him that there had just been a telephone call, some important news he had better know at once.

It had been announced over the radio on the midday news broadcast that Andreas Baader had been sprung, that Ulrike Meinhof had participated, with several others, in his escape from the Institute of Social Studies in Dahlem, and that the police were now looking for them.

Röhl's first thought was naturally for the children. He telephoned everyone he could think of in Berlin who might know where they were.

Jürgen Holtkamp listened to all this going on, calmly said good-bye, and drove back to his home in Bremen, where Bettina and Regine had been brought a few days before to be looked after and hidden from their father.

For Ulrike Meinhof, her leap with Baader out of the window of the library in Dahlem was an act as irreversible as suicide; and for a while at least it did very well instead. To leap out of an old unsatisfactory life into a new, of excitement and urgent purpose, romantically at pitch and in peril, and with a new name, was virtually—so she must have hoped—to lose the old identity and to leave the old melancholy separateness behind; for the new identity was that of the group. So now too there would be the close companionship she had always craved, this time welded by mutual dependence, shared danger, and common aims to be pursued with total dedication, at extreme personal risk, and without scruple. For once one had broken the law, one was surely freed from all constraint: if there was no going back, there was also no limit ahead, other than the limit of the outlaws' own capabilities. An illusory sense of power and a certainty of victory would make them feel their own capabilities to be great. Each could seek personal relief through acts of violence and blood and terror, and always with a grandiose moral justification. They could call a lust for revenge "a thirst for justice," and terrorism a righteous fury that "society" had called down upon itself. In Ulrike's case "society" was a euphemism (which she could not recognize, her insight into her own motives not having matured with her years) for her own failings, and for Klaus Rainer Röhl. And her committing of herself to a life outside the law was a venture to overcome not governments, not systems, but private despair.

PART FOUR
BANDITS

12

Going Places and Doing Things

On June 8, 1970, Horst Mahler and Hans-Jürgen Bäcker, who were both wanted by the West Berlin police in connection with the freeing of Baader, flew with false passports from East Berlin to Beirut. With them went Mahler's assistant Monika Berberich, a student from the Free University named Brigitte Asdonk, Manfred Grashof, and his nineteen-year-old hairdresser girl friend, Petra Schelm. From Beirut the party traveled to Jordan to a PFLP camp (Popular Front for the Liberation of Palestine, an extreme Marxist group clamoring for world revolution—hence their special attraction for bourgeois rebels of the free and prosperous democracies). They were soon joined by Ulrike Meinhof and Gudrun Ensslin, with her beloved Andreas Baader restored to her by Ulrike and other comrades. These three had taken a more devious route, through Italy, Yugoslavia, Bulgaria, and Turkey, Lebanon, and Syria. Ulrike's passport was in the name of "Sabine Markwort." Later that same month Peter Homann too arrived at the camp, but kept apart from the other Germans. He had parted company with them before the freeing of Baader and had broken off his personal ties with Ulrike Meinhof.

At the camp the comrades were to be trained as urban guerrillas. But the scheme was not a success. The Germans and the Arabs could not get along with each other. Each side accused the other of being cold and arrogant. Baader refused to undergo the commando training offered, through mud and under barbed wire, because he said such skills were unnecessary to an urban guerrilla. None of the men in the German group were able to train with the Arabs because there was too much antagonism between them. But the women did learn something. They were taught to handle pistols, particularly Firebirds, and Ulrike Meinhof declared that learning how to lift weights and fall out of a fast-moving car was much more fun than sitting at a typewriter. The Arab terrorists, who were training many women deliberately in spite of the Mohammedan attitude toward women generally, found the Western women too domineering and less able to stand up to the training exercises than their own, and they liked neither Ulrike Meinhof nor Gudrun Ensslin. In all, there was only one German woman who found the Spartan life in the desert congenial. Her name was Ingrid Siepmann. She had come to the camp a year earlier, with her fellow communard Dieter Kunzelmann and some comrades from Munich, and had stayed on, working in a pharmaceutical center for the Palestinians.

Baader, Meinhof, and their fellow factioneers were eventually asked by their hosts to leave, and they returned to Germany on August 9. Peter Homann returned a day later and went into hiding for a year and a half because he was suspected of being the man in the mask who had taken part in the freeing of Baader. His weeks with the conspirators had infected him with the fear which the wanted criminals among them had, that if they walked into a police station to give themselves up they would be shot dead on the spot. Such a belief, though it might have been conjured up out of a wish to dramatize and exaggerate the dangerousness of the enemy, could only be confirmed and enlarged within a close and secret society. He ventured into public places, but had moments of considerable anxiety. Once, in a public sauna bath, he sat next to five naked policemen who were chatting about their assignments in the Baader-Meinhof hunt. They did not recognize him. "But I was in quite a sweat," he said. At last, on November 17, 1971, he gave himself up to Josef Augstein, a Hanover lawyer and brother of Der Spiegel's publisher. In an interview he gave to Der Spiegel he told how the Palestinians regarded the RAF: " 'It's no revolutionary group, it's a gang' "; and Ulrike Meinhof: " 'Her problem is an immense need to be protected, and at the moment she could only satisfy that in this group' "; and Baader: " 'He is a coward who is performing the whole revolt to cover up his cowardice. We couldn't even take him on a patrol.' "

Revolutionary group or bandit gang, when the comrades were back in Germany they got the People's War under way.

They had fun choosing cover names, dressing up, getting the right equipment—money, cars, electronic devices, weapons. Mahler ordered a consignment of watches and distributed them among the group, for synchronization, as in the movies. ("Baader wanted to be Marlon Brando," some of his Berlin acquaintances guessed. He and his pals were apparently specially devoted to Westerns, but spy stories, cops and robbers, anything action-packed was also to their taste.)

They had to have lots of money, not only because revolutions need capital like everything else, but also because they liked to live well. They got it mostly by robbing banks. Capitalism must finance its own overthrow. Besides, Carlos Marighela's do-it-yourself book instructed students of urban guerrilla warfare that robbing banks was the best first action and the best preparation for further action.

There were new recruits to the People's Army—two of them even from the ranks of "the people." Eric Grusdat was a mechanic and the owner of a motor-repair workshop in a southeast district of West Berlin, near the Wall. He had repaired Hans-Jürgen Bäcker's car. Bäcker brought a new customer, who asked Grusdat and his assistant, sandy-haired Karl-Heinz Ruhland, what they thought of the idea of making a revolution. They both thought it was a great idea. So the customer asked them if they'd like to meet some comrades who thought the same. They said they would. On the day appointed for the meeting, the customer arrived with only one comrade. "My name is Mahler," he then revealed, "but now I am called 'James'." The other was Baader, now called "Hans."

It seemed to Ruhland from the way they tucked into Frau Grusdat's homemade plum cake that they were both very hungry. Mahler asked the two mechanics whether, to assist the upheaval of society and the overturning of the system, they would be prepared to change the appearance of stolen cars, their serial and registration numbers, color, and so on. This was necessary, Mahler explained, as he was building up a group to lead the revolution along the lines laid down by Carlos Marighela.

Ruhland and Grusdat regretted that they hadn't heard of Marighela. But they said they would read about him if Mahler gave them a pamphlet, and, yes, they would doctor stolen cars in return for good payment. Also out of political conviction, Grusdat added. Ruhland needed the money to pay debts.

This form of political participation started very soon. They covered chassis numbers with a special kind of plaster, filed down motor numbers, and substituted new ones as ordered by the Baader-Mahler group. They changed doors and ignition keys, removed extra parts, such as fog lamps, and resprayed the car bodies.

Ruhland had an obvious passion for cars—those supreme instruments of capitalist consumption terror—even greater than Baader's, and of a different kind: Ruhland understood, cared for, and respected the machines; Baader liked to show off in them. However, the respective passions of the two men for social justice may well have been quite evenly matched.

On September 1, 1970, Horst Mahler came to the Grusdat workshop, wearing a full beard and a toupee but dressed "inconspicuously," according to his own rules at that stage. (The middle-class members of the gang had to "try to look bourgeois," and Ruhland and Grusdat could dress as usual.) He asked Grusdat and Ruhland if they were ready to take part in a bank robbery. When both said they were, they were invited to a meeting at the apartment of Hans-Jürgen Bäcker in the (very central) Keithstrasse, number 15. It was a two-and-a-half room apartment with a telephone installed, but not yet working. To Ruhland's eye it was uncomfortably empty: a camp bed, a plank with books, a record player, "a table without a tablecloth and the floor without carpets." The comrades sat on the floor and drank coffee and beer, and some smoked black-tobacco cigarettes of the Gauloise type. Ruhland had a good memory for such details. He was arrested a few months after joining the gang and gave clear descriptions, at his trial and to the newspapers—notably *Die Welt*, which published his life story, from which most of the quotations given here have been taken—of how the gang lived and worked during the first weeks of its activity.

Ruhland said that he found Baader's way of talking "puke-making," but that his "velvet look really had an effect on the girls. Hardly any of them dared to contradict him—only 'Grete' [Gudrun Ensslin]. And Mahler often ticked him off."

Ruhland himself admired and respected Mahler. And at the meeting in Bäcker's apartment it was Mahler who did most of the talking.

Mahler expounded his plan to rob four banks on the same day, in the same hour. The gang was divided into four groups. One of them—Gudrun Ensslin, Ingrid Schubert, Hans-Jürgen Bäcker, Karl-Heinz Ruhland, and a new sixteen-year-old recruit—went several times to case their bank, which was in the Siemenstrasse. They observed that it was on the ground floor; they noted how many doors it had and how they were placed, how many steps there were, whether if they used getaway cars there was a place to park and whether there were traffic lights on the near corners which might hold them up, and where the nearest rail stations and bus stops were. Ensslin stalked about with her stopwatch. Distances were paced out, sketches were made from memory and compared.

Grusdat had the idea of using "crow's feet," spiked devices made from metal piping, to be thrown out of the escape car to puncture the tires of any following vehicle. Mahler approved, so Grusdat and Ruhland set about the necessary cutting and welding in the workshop, in the evenings when the apprentices had gone home. "I never thought a break-in would involve so much work," Grusdat groaned. They could only get four made in an evening, and they were to have thirteen ready for each bank.

On the day fixed for the job, Ruhland put on, as Mahler thought best, cord trousers and a rolled-neck pullover, "as if just driving into town to buy spare parts." He and Grusdat had an early and hearty breakfast of rolls, eggs, jam, and coffee. The Grusdat children came to join them, but their mother shooed them back to bed.

"Daddy's got a difficult job today," she said.

Grusdat and Ruhland met with the others near the bank. Two of the robbers went for a last look at it before the raid and found that building workers were swarming over scaffolding newly erected in the hall. This was an unforeseen complication, so they all went back to Bäcker's apartment. Mahler reassigned Ensslin's band (Gudrun, Ingrid Schubert, Bäcker, and Ruhland—the teen-ager had dropped out before the raid day arrived) to join his own (Baader, Goergens, Proll, Grusdat, and himself), and only three banks were robbed that morning.

The gang was armed mostly with pistols, but Ruhland was given a Landmann-Preetz small-bore machine gun and Grusdat a sawed-off shotgun.

Two by two the desperadoes went out into the street and got into the cars. Grusdat and Ruhland were driven by Bäcker to the building next door to the Berliner Bank in the Rheinstrasse. Its lobby was to be the assembly place. But Mahler, already on the scene, was pacing up and down in front of the bank, wearing a dark blue woolen cap. He explained that he had mistaken the time and arrived ten minutes early. His synchronized watch had let him down.

In the lobby Ruhland, feeling nervous, loaded his gun and released the safety catch. Baader and Irene Goergens, Ulrike Meinhof's protégée from a state home in Berlin, costumed in black trousers and a leather jacket, arrived next. They all got out their guns and balaclavas. Only Grusdat put on a long-haired wig and a pair of sunglasses as his disguise, since he was to stand at the door.

"Let's go!" Mahler said.

One after another they stepped out of the building into the street and marched straight into the bank, putting on their balaclavas as they went in. Baader put his on crooked, and it took him some moments to adjust it with the eye slot in place, so at first he couldn't see a thing.

The guns were raised and pointed.

Mahler shouted, "This is a stickup! Hands up and keep quiet and nothing will happen to you. After all," he added consolingly, "it's not your money."

Baader and Goergens jumped over the counter and waved the clerks back with their pistols. There were only three or four customers. All raised their hands in the movie-honored manner, and Baader and Goergens stuffed the briefcases with money.

Ruhland noticed that the clerks and customers were trembling, and he relaxed. His only fear then was that some "bloody fool" might press the alarm button. "All they had to do was to stay nicely away from their desks so that the police were not alarmed too soon and I would not have to start shooting."

Baader and Goergens jumped back over the counters, and they all started to withdraw, Baader and Goergens first, then Ruhland and Grusdat. Mahler stayed to say, "Don't call the police immediately or we'll have to throw a bomb." Then he lit a smoke bomb and dropped it in the hall before he turned and fled.

The whole raid had taken only three minutes.

They hurried into the next-door building, through the lobby, and out a back door, jumped over a wall, and crossed an empty lot, where they all discarded their balaclavas. Baader also threw away his jacket, in which he had left the keys of the Volkswagen car he had parked nearby, so its use was lost to them. The guns were pushed into two long cardboard rolls which had been put into the yard for the purpose by Proll and Schubert. The wire fence had been cut before the raid by Mahler, with a pair of cutters bought for the job by Grusdat and Ruhland, and so in a few more seconds they were on the Lauterstrasse, where three escape cars—all Mercedeses—were waiting, one with Astrid Proll at the wheel, one with Ingrid Schubert, and one with Gudrun Ensslin in it. They were not pursued and did not need the "crow's feet."

When they were all back at Bäcker's apartment, they listened to the police radio and gathered that the police were not on their trail. Grusdat and Ruhland drove back in the Volkswagen to the workshop, listened to the radio with Frau Grusdat, and heard, for the first time, where the other two raids had been carried out. They lunched, then worked through the afternoon. Customers told them how three banks had been broken into that morning. They expressed surprise.

The other two raids had also been brought off, between 9:48 and 9:58 that morning. From one of the banks DM 55,152 had been grabbed, but from the other Meinhof's band had got nothing very much: DM 8,134 was all. News bulletins later revealed that the raiders had missed a carton containing DM 95,000. The comrades taunted Meinhof over this failure. "Eight thousand marks—you could earn that much doing dirty work for *Konkret.*"

On October 6, Ruhland was to get his share of the loot. This time the gang met in the apartment of Jan-Carl Raspe and Marianne Herzog. (Prearranged signal: two rings—later made more particular with the "Ho-Chi-Minh knock": two short, one long.) Ruhland was very impressed with the place. "Real student digs . . . books lying everywhere, you had to clear them away if you wanted to sit down . . . walls covered with posters."

First came analysis. Mahler and Baader had criticism of the entry into the banks, and both said that the getaway had to be faster. More preplanning was prescribed.

Then came the moral-political lecture from Mahler. He explained to them that bank robbing was morally justified because it was the money of capitalists that they took. The "little man," he said, was not the loser by it.

Nor the gainer, as Ruhland was imminently to discover. For next came the moment for the distribution. Mahler had decreed that only a small amount was going to be distributed at first, so that, he reasoned, nobody would be able to splash it about and attract attention. "Later we could talk about more." Out of DM 217,469.50, Ruhland received DM 1,000. He was rather disappointed, but optimistic that eventually he could make a good living this way.

Two days after this, October 8, at a little past five thirty in the afternoon, the Popo—Political Police—arrived at the apartment in the Knesebreckstrasse of one "Renate Hubner," who purported to be an interior decorator. "Frau Hubner" let them in, and they proceeded to search the place. They discovered a Spanish pistol, some detonators, chemicals, crow's feet, stolen license plates, notes on the Berlin banks which had been attacked on September 29, and accounts of how DM 58,230 had been distributed; and that "Frau Hubner" was really Ingrid Schubert, whick they had suspected all along, having come there because of a tip-off. The police had been looking for Ingrid Schubert ever since the freeing of Baader from the Dahlem Institute of Social Studies on May 14. And more was in store for them. On a table, next to a copy of the "Minihandbook for Urban Guerrillas" by Carlos Marighela, lay some files, the property of the lawyer Horst Mahler. They sat down to wait. Pop music from the record player made a loud and normal noise.

At six o'clock the doorbell rang. The police told Schubert to answer it. There on the threshold stood a tall man with a freak-out hairdo and a beard. He stepped inside to find twelve policemen pointing their pistols at him. He pulled out identity papers to prove he was Herr Gunter Uhlig, but one of the officers grabbed hold of his hair and pulled his wig off.

"Do you still imagine that we can't recognize you, Herr Mahler?" he asked.

Mahler, with his sense of theater, accepted defeat gracefully. "My compliments, gentlemen," he said with a bow.

He was found to have a loaded pistol in his trouser pocket and thirty-five rounds of ammunition in the pocket of his jacket.

The police were also watching an apartment in the Hauptstrasse in the Schöneburg district, rented by one "Brigit Wend," an architect, whose real name was Monika Berberich—undercover name, "Nelli"— Mahler's assistant, who had arranged for Baader to "work" in the Dahlem Institute and had visited Jordan.

On the day of Mahler's arrest, she and Irene Goergens ("Peggy") and Brigitte Asdonk ("Clara") drove Ulrike Meinhof ("Anna" or "Rana") to the airport, to fly to West Germany and carry out a plan to spread the band's activities in the Federal Republic. On their return from the airport, the three women went to the "Hubner" flat for a prearranged meeting and were scooped in the same net with Schubert and Mahler.

Two days after that the remaining members of the gang met in the apartment of Jan-Carl Raspe and Marianne Herzog. They agreed that they had lost their leader. But Baader took control. "Now don't shit in your trousers," he said aggressively. "So the bulls have caught a few of us. That's no reason to lose your nerve."

He said he suspected Mahler had been betrayed. The others agreed, and their suspicions settled on Hans-Jürgen Bäcker—undercover name, "Harp." They recalled that he had excused himself from meeting Mahler in Schubert's apartment on the night of the arrest, saying that he was sick. And when their discussion was interrupted by the arrival of Bäcker himself, they questioned him suspiciously until he became angry and left. Baader said that they had better go on paying him because otherwise he might be more dangerous to them. But they would all change their addresses. And they swore vengeance. Astrid Proll ("Rosi") was to claim later that she shot at him from a car but missed.

Bäcker was known to Ruhland as a mining electrician from the Ruhr. He was supposed to be studying something in Berlin, but seems to have lived more in underground shade than daylight. He remained rather mysterious even to his fellow conspirators: a man who was, figuratively speaking, in a permanent mask; who had been most useful to them with his knowledge of how to get and handle firearms, and most bold in their service, at the time of the freeing of Baader from the Dahlem Institute.

The group went on to plan the rescue of Mahler. Grusdat said he would build a helicopter and rescue him from above; and if that failed they could try from below, through the sewer system. Neither plan was ever put into effect.

Then Ruhland ("Kali") was instructed by Baader ("Hans") and Ensslin ("Grete") to join Meinhof ("Anna"/"Rana") in West Germany and help her to find, borrow, or rent safe houses. They gave him a forged driving license and false papers for the car, and an identity card which bore his own name but with other details invented. He left at dawn and drove his own Volkswagen "bus" to Hanover to meet Meinhof in a café at the main entrance of the Zoo. He waited there for an hour over a cup of coffee, but she didn't turn up. The alternative was the first-floor restaurant in the main station, where he finally found her in the evening, sitting at the bar with a cup of coffee in front of her. She no longer looked like her pictures on the Wanted notices. Her dark hair had been cut short and dyed blond.

Over dinner Meinhof told him her plans for that night. They would drive to Wittlich in the Eiffel, near the Belgian border, to find quarters for the whole group from Berlin, which was to move into West Germany. Berlin was getting more dangerous every day, she said. Meinhof paid for the meal. To Ruhland it was a new experience to have a woman pay for him, though he accepted that she should be the one in control of the common purse.

They drove first to Rodenkirchen, near Cologne. Meinhof did not talk much. She turned on the radio and tuned in to the American Forces Network, or the British, because she preferred American music, jazz, or country songs.

They were to go on "many and long" travels together, "Anna" or "Rana" Meinhof and "Kali" Ruhland. (He usually called her "Rana," even when they were alone together.) She never said much to him, and always listened to the same kind of music.

In Rodenkirchen they drove the Volkswagen bus into a basement garage, and there, ready for them to drive away, stood a Volkswagen beetle. It was owned by the man who was making his weekend house at Wittlich available to Ulrike. He was an editor on West German Radio,

and Ulrike had written a piece for him in 1969 on the student movement.

They arrived at 5 A.M. in the street of the weekend house, in a fog.
They were supposed to get the key from a neighbor, but thought they
should not wake anybody at that hour. So Ruhland, the handy fellow,
picked the lock.

Ulrike was not only disappointed with the place, she was annoyed.
"What can he be thinking of, lending such a place to me?" she asked.

A high standard of living accommodation was always demanded by
the Red Army Faction. Very seldom did they live in a neighborhood that
was less than solid, bourgeois, respectable, expensive, luxurious. Often
they had fine views. And always central heating.

There were three rooms in the substandard weekend house which
the inconsiderate editor had lent them. In one of them they lay down on
the beds and fell asleep straight away. When they woke up, "Ulrike had
nothing against my getting into bed with her." From then on, Ruhland
was to remember her as "natural and human." He felt honored by her
willingness to sleep with him. "I am a worker; she has studied. But although she is intellectually far above me, she never reminded me of
that."

In the morning they left, since the place would not do for the gang.
And sometime later they found that they had broken into the wrong
weekend house, missing the right number in the fog. The right one, luxurious and well equipped, had been a few yards farther on. •

Now by the rules of the game as Ruhland knew it, he had a relationship with Ulrike in which he was dominant because he was the male.
When Ulrike lighted up a Gauloise after breakfast, he told her that he
didn't like women to smoke. He was taken aback when she only laughed
at him. She smoked whenever she liked, "which sometimes," he said,
"made me really furious."

They drove north to Neuenkirchen, near Ulrike's birthplace, Oldenburg. Ulrike had a key to an apartment, and they let themselves in. Nobody was home. They fetched food from the kitchen and went to sleep on
the living-room couch. They were wakened an hour later by the owner
coming in—a man over fifty, dressed in jeans and a colored shirt. Ruhland was surprised to learn that he was a Catholic priest. He was on familiar terms with Ulrike, whom he called Marie.

He complained that Bäcker had telephoned him from a Hanover hotel, and said he wanted only to be called from public phone booths. Ulrike
told him that Bäcker was now out of the group because they suspected

him of betraying Mahler. Then she asked the priest if any mail had come for her, and he handed her a large padded envelope. Inside was a book. It was hollowed out and contained about DM 3,000.

There was also a suitcase full of clothes left at the priest's apartment which had been picked up in Berlin and brought to this safe place to wait until Ulrike should fetch them. Ulrike still had many helpful friends and sympathizers out in the bright air of legality; among the most privileged and successful in the society she had declared war on, and in which they prospered so well that they could afford the most fashionable of everything, including opinions—especially the rather vague, but thrillingly extreme, and surely safely inconsequential view that such a society was worthy only to be undermined and destroyed. At the very least Ulrike could count on personal loyalties in her old circle for assistance and the cover of silence, and a need in her fellow bourgeois for vicarious excitement from the activities of her moralistic criminal band.

Many of the Schili, in Hamburg particularly, were excited by Ulrike Meinhof's going underground and would confide to each other in an agitated manner that they simply did not know what they would do if Ulrike turned up in the dark of the night at their doors and asked to be sheltered and hidden. But judging by the reaction of those who were asked for money, the inner struggle would not have been painfully prolonged. The owner of a house in Övelgönne, an acquaintance of the Rühmkorfs, got a telephone call from Ulrike Meinhof asking him for "a contribution to the defense fund for Gudrun Ensslin and Andreas Baader, who wanted to give themselves up if they were sure of being able to pay for a good defense." The man paid DM 100. Later the realization dawned on him that next time if he was asked for much more he'd be risking a lot if he refused—had he not aided and abetted wanted criminals, and could they not denounce him if they chose? Again (as in the "apprentice" days, when Baader and Ensslin collected money from many sources) it is unlikely that such threats were ever uttered. They didn't have to be.

Then there were such small problems as how to get their dry cleaning done. Some things just have to be dry-cleaned; they have to be taken and fetched again—two opportunities for a dry cleaner to recognize an outlaw. But Ulrike Meinhof had no difficulty solving that one, as she had only to phone a woman friend (so women friends later reported) and it was seen to.

Ruhland was to find that Ulrike's rich and important helpers were numerous and ubiquitous. After the editor and the priest there was to follow a long line of them. She had the key to another apartment, this one in Hanover. They let themselves into it at night. In the morning Ruhland met the owner, a professor with whom, Ruhland discovered, "we were also on intimate terms," though Ruhland would only introduce himself as "Kali." Several suitcases awaited them here, filled with Federal Army uniforms for a disguise attack on an army camp at Munsterlager to steal arms. They were to be helped in this by Heinrich Jansen ("Ali"), who knew the camp from his own illegally terminated National Service stint. To meet him they drove to Oberhausen in the Ruhr.

Meinhof went into the café where they were to meet and found Jansen very drunk. She and Ruhland got him into the car and drove him to the professor's apartment in Hanover.

The three of them stayed there for a couple of days, and Ruhland received a further lesson in middle-class mores. "We played records and then Ulrike and I went to bed together. Jansen was in the room but we had no alternative, since there was only one room available to us. Fortunately, Jansen went to sleep after drinking a lot. And besides, nobody in the group ever really cared if someone else was around when you felt like doing it. Relationships between couples were always expressed quite openly."

Meinhof found a holiday bungalow to rent, on a hill at Polle, a pretty village on the river Weser. The professor wrote to the rental agent on the letterhead of the Technical University of Hanover, saying that the people who wanted to rent the bungalow were students preparing for their exams. They took books with them as stage props for their act and moved in. There were three rooms and a kitchen and bathroom. Meinhof and Ruhland took the main bedroom, Jansen the child's room. But seven people could be accommodated, and it was intended that the West Berlin comrades should join them.

Keeping busy over the revolution was not easy. There were tedious hours when there was little to do but doze or watch the boats sailing up and down on the Weser. But a sense of urgency and purpose could always be worked up. Ruhland and Jansen chose to drive all the way to Bremen—much farther than either Hanover or Kassel—to buy a ladder and a pair of weak binoculars ("we were told they were good for seeing in the dark") for a hundred marks: equipment for the Munsterlager raid.

Then they thought of a way of getting authentic information about specific cars for document forgeries. The "students" became market researchers for a fictitious Hanover institute. They asked car owners whether they were satisfied with the cars they owned, and incidentally gathered the information they were after for the forgeries. Then they or-

KAMPEN

EAST GERMANY

HAMBURG

NEUENKIRCHEN
OLDENBURG
BREMEN
MUNSTER LAGER
OSTERBURG
BERLIN
WEST EAST

NEUSTADT
OSNABRÜCK
HANOVER

MÜNSTER

Weser R.

POLLE
GÖTTINGEN

CLEVES
OBERHAUSEN
GELSENKIRCHEN
WUPPERTAL
KASSEL
MELSUNGEN
HALLE
LEIPZIG

WEIMAR
JENA

Elbe R.

COLOGNE
MARBURG
BONN
WEILBURG
Lahn
LANGGÖNS

Rhine R.
COBLENZ
FRANKFURT
OFFENBACH
BAD KISSINGEN
BERNECK

WITTLICH
MAINZ
DARMSTADT

LUDWIGSHAFEN
KAISERSLÄUTERN
HEIDELBERG
NUREMBERG

WEST GERMANY

KARLSRUHE
STUTTGART

TÜBINGEN
Danube R.
AUGSBURG
MUNICH

TUTTLINGEN
LANDSBERG

FREIBURG

AUTOBAHNS ·····

MILES

0   50   100

dered license plates and attached them to another car of the same description "so there were two cars running with the same number, the real
owners who had the real logbook, and ours with our forged logbook."
Ruhland didn't do much of the questioning. He felt he was unconvincing
in the role of a student. Later they found a simpler method: they answered "for sale" advertisements in newspapers, went to examine the cars,
and copied down all the data they needed.

They went to Munsterlager to learn the guard system of the army
camp and found that a patrol passed a certain point near one of the arms
stores every two hours. In the dark, while Ulrike kept watch at the edge of
a wood, Ruhland and Jansen climbed over the fence by means of their
expensive ladder, and Ruhland examined the lock on the arms store. He
concluded that he could crack it in eight minutes. They returned to
Polle. Six people would be needed for the raid, and as soon as they were
assembled it would be carried out.

But it never was. Jansen, driving to the place for a last reconnais-
sance, smashed up the borrowed Volkswagen beetle. The sight of the
wreck so upset Ruhland that he hit Jansen in the face with his fist.
Ruhland's life had been full of violence, but he did not make a philosophy of it.

Then orders came from the Berlin contingent of the gang that the
army camp raid was to be called off and the three were to steal passports
and official stamps instead. So they drove about looking for municipal offices to break into. Jansen had to be Ruhland's passenger, and they quarreled until Ruhland discovered that Jansen had led one of the other
Berlin bank raids "as Mahler had led ours," and his respect for him rose.

For so much driving about they wanted a better car. "We preferred
Mercedes 220s or 230s because they could easily be started by short-cir-
cuiting and because the steering locks were easy to change." Ruhland,
equipped with the right tools, chose a suitable machine in Hanover in a
private parking lot.

"Come," he said to Ulrike. "Now you can learn something from me."

Getting into the car by pushing open the side window, reaching in
to unlock the door, and starting the car by short circuit took six minutes.
Then they drove the car off, stopped at a suitable spot, and changed the
number plates, putting any old plates on for the time being, but later the
number of a Mercedes of the same type and color.

At one o'clock one dark morning they drove about seventy-five miles
northward to the municipal offices at Neustadt am Rübenberg. It was in-

tended to be an inspection trip only, and though Ruhland had tools with him, he had not brought gloves. Jansen got into the cellar but couldn't get up into the building. Ruhland opened the back door with a screw-driver. "It only took about five minutes. In the porter's lodge the keys hung in beautiful order." He showed the others "the simplest method for breaking in" when there were locks without keys and went outside to wait, because he had no gloves, and he remembered how the police had published the fact that Ingrid Schubert's fingerprints had been found in the escape cars after the bank robberies.

Jansen and Meinhof spent half an hour gathering what they needed: passports, official stamps, and one partly completed identity card. They got back to Polle at about four o'clock. They found nothing in the papers next day about the burglary. (Any disappointment at lack of publicity was, however, to be amply compensated in the future.) Ulrike called Berlin and was given a coded address, which she decoded wrongly, and they dispatched all the passports and cards and stamps to it. When they found out that it was the wrong place, Meinhof said, "What's happened has happened. We shall simply have to find another passport office." She had not, so far, shown herself a very efficient bandit.

So off they drove again, some eighty miles in a different direction, to a town near Kassel called Gelsungen by Melsungen. They were standing at the door, and Ruhland was about to examine the locks, when the mayor passed by and asked them what they were doing there so late.

"Oh, you see, we have a historical interest in old buildings," said Ulrike Meinhof, who had once sat up late over art books, and had ear-nestly inspected old churches in England, "and we particularly like the look of this one."

The mayor felt complimented and walked on.

The next successful raid was on a town hall in Lang-Göns near Frankfurt. It stood on the edge of the town and was not overlooked by other buildings. They had to break open a number of doors to get into the mayor's office. Then they had to break open cabinets. Jansen waved the torch about, "across the windows, as if he wanted to signal to the village inhabitants," according to Ruhland, who got mad at him but had to keep his voice down. He calmed himself with a big swallow from a bottle of cognac which he found in one of the cabinets. The robbery took about an hour. At last they found a pile of identity cards and passports, and official stamps, and they left.

Jansen had found some money which he kept for himself; and he said nothing about it until much later when he had spent it all.

Ruhland was "half drunk," and Meinhof had to drive. She wanted to go right ahead and break into another town hall, but Ruhland "exploded" at her.

"You're not all there," he said. "You've got delusions of grandeur."

She drove on nervously. After a while Ruhland ordered her to stop. "And when she wanted to say something, I told her to shut up."

He took over the wheel and drove on rather woozily for about two hundred miles to Hanover. Ulrike was subdued at first by Ruhland's anger; then she tried to regain his approval. Besides, she was excited over their haul. This was her first distinct success as an urban guerrilla. She laughed, fooled, and pinched Ruhland playfully.

But some failures followed.

Their next task was to get weapons. Another book of money was fetched from the priest's apartment, and Ruhland and Jansen were given DM 300 to go and inspect a weapons depot near Cleves, on the Dutch border. They found it unsuitable for breaking into; with only one road leading up to it, it was too risky. An attempt to buy submachine guns in Hamburg also failed. They met Grusdat there, who had brought more money from Berlin, and they bought a large laundry basket for transporting the guns. But the dealer inexplicably failed to deliver the goods.

Every day Meinhof telephoned Berlin, at 11 A.M. or 6 P.M. or 10 P.M. One day, when several projects for getting weapons had failed and the talk was again of robbing banks, she gave Ruhland the Berlin telephone number and the code word, "the name of a town which changed every day," and told him to find out when Jan-Carl Raspe was due to arrive. He called the number at 6 P.M. from a public telephone, gave the name of the town, and asked when "Fred" would join them. He was told that he was on his way. Later that evening "Fred" did arrive, by car, wearing collar and tie, Ruhland noticed. "He always kept very correctly to the bourgeois clothing that had been arranged" (presumably by Mahler, who had been the first costume designer of the show).

Raspe brought some electronic equipment with him: an oscilloscope and a VHF signal generator, both made by the American company Hewlett-Packard, exactly the same as had been recently stolen from the physics department of the Technical University of West Berlin. They were to be used to modify radio equipment to receive messages on frequencies used by the police.

Almost as soon as he arrived at Polle, Raspe drove off again with Meinhof, over a hundred miles to Bremen. Ruhland was left alone in the bungalow, feeling that he had been abandoned by Ulrike and ousted by Raspe, and he began to think about getting out of the game. When

Meinhof and Raspe returned, "Ulrike gave me not a single word of explanation." Ruhland was hurt.

They all three drove off to look at banks in Oberhausen. In Gelsenkirchen, near Oberhausen, they were put up by a family who, Ruhland was sure, had no idea who Ulrike was, only that she was a friend of friends, a Frankfurt couple Ruhland was soon to meet. They sat talking with their hosts, who brought up the subject of the Baader-Meinhof Group (as it was now called in the newspapers), and the wife mentioned that she had seen the "Wanted" pictures of Ulrike Meinhof. "Ulrike moved not a muscle," Ruhland observed. "It seemed as if she even enjoyed this game of hide and seek."

During the day Ruhland and Raspe filled in time by driving about and looking at banks. At night Meinhof slept with Raspe in one room, and Ruhland slept in another. Ruhland became increasingly resentful at being abandoned by her. But he lingered on with the other two in the apartment.

When the next bookful of money arrived, Meinhof announced that they would go to Frankfurt and buy pistols.

Ruhland and Meinhof set out together. Ruhland was glad to be alone with her again, "driving through the night, listening to American music. I didn't mind at all any more about her smoking.

" 'Rana,' I said to her. But I cannot talk sweet nonsense. She just stared out of the window. Then I made another start. 'It can't go on like this. Don't you understand? I simply can't go along with it. You have got to know me a bit. O.K., I'm very uncontrolled, hot-tempered, but I don't quite mean it like that. If you've had enough of me, let me get out of the whole thing.'

"She said, 'No!' quite harshly. I still don't know whether she wanted me to stay in the group because I was useful to it or because she liked me."

He let her off at the café where she was to meet some members of Al Fatah to buy the pistols.

She bought twenty-three 9-mm Firebirds—the kind she had learned to handle in Jordan—for DM 450 each. The normal trade price in Germany then was DM 127, to the buyer with a license.

Pistols were distributed to the others at the apartment of the Frankfurt couple Ruhland had heard about. (The man was an editor who worked for the German Press Agency, and his wife was also a journalist.) Raspe and Ruhland each took one. Five pistols were left in the apartment for other comrades who were soon to arrive, and the rest were mailed in two parcels to Berlin.

"From that time onwards," Ruhland related, "I was always armed. I wore it on my left side in my belt, always fully loaded, with the safety catch off, as was customary in the group."

Meinhof (who had had a pistol for some time before this) and the other women carried their guns in their handbags. Firing practice was held in a wood near Frankfurt airport, where the sounds of shooting were covered by the noise of aircraft taking off.

The bungalow at Polle was now to be given up. It was Raspe who drove the Frankfurt editor and his wife to fetch the things the gang wanted, Ruhland remembered, though the couple were to deny that they ever saw the bungalow. Ruhland's poverty-conditioned outlook was offended by the prodigality of leaving the place when the rent for some time yet had been paid in advance—in cash, by "Sabine Markwort"— and the refrigerator was full of food worth 150 marks. They also abandoned some black underwear left soaking in a washbasin, "Sabine Markwort's" property.

Soon four more comrades joined them in Frankfurt. Ruhland had not met them before: Ilse Stachowiak ("Tinny"), who was only seventeen, and Ulrich Scholtz ("Uli"), who were to pick out some banks in Nuremberg; and Beate Sturm ("Jutta") and Holger Meins ("Peter").

There were too many to fit into the journalists' apartment, so Raspe went over to the Seiferts'—Meinhof's old friends Monika (Mitscherlich) and Jürgen. Raspe had known them for some time. (Monika Seifert later maintained that neither of them knew that he had any connection with Ulrike Meinhof or the group.) Meins and Beate Sturm also found accommodation with friends and acquaintances. But more comrades from Berlin were expected, and Meinhof had to find hideouts.

She rented a little bungalow at Fürth, a village near Darmstadt, about forty miles by road to the south of Frankfurt. And she went to a top-floor apartment in a small apartment house on the other side of the river Main, asking for a writer who she thought lived there. He no longer did. The present owner was another writer.

"Come in, I'll give you his new address," he said. They quickly became very friendly: intimate, even. What she wanted, she revealed, was accommodation for leftist friends. She asked her host what he thought of the Baader-Meinhof group. He replied that he did not think much of them. When she told him that she was Meinhof, he was not in the least put off and let her stay all night. Next morning she had breakfast and a bath and went away, and returned later with her leftist friends.

Baader and Ensslin arrived together from Berlin on December 12 and were brought from the station to the writer's apartment by Meinhof. Baader's hair was cut short and bleached almost white, and he wore rimless spectacles for disguise. Ensslin's long blond locks were replaced by a mass of short dark curls.

The gang now assembled in Frankfurt: Petra Schelm, Ulrich Scholtze, Beate Sturm, Holger Meins, Astrid Proll, Marianne Herzog, and Ilse Stachowiak arrived. Some were to be accommodated at Fürth. Meinhof drove Ruhland, Scholtze, Sturm, and Raspe to the bungalow. But when they got there she refused to stay in it herself. She said it was too small and she found it unbearable. She flounced off and drove back to Frankfurt to the writer's apartment.

All the writer's belongings except his bed were used as the common property of the group. The bed was nearly lost too: Astrid Proll told him he should let her have it because she was sick of sleeping on an air mattress. The writer claimed later that he tried but failed to get rid of them. He did not like Baader, who took books from the shelves and tore their covers off and used the backs of them for notes. Baader also stole one of his coats, but it was later paid for by the group. He found Ensslin naïve, Petra Schelm a child, but Raspe a fine sensitive person. Raspe, he said, would sometimes drink beer—the rest of them drank only fruit juices. They despised his library for containing too little leftist literature, and his record collection for being only of classical music. Eventually he fled from his own apartment. In February 1971 the police arrested him for aiding the Baader-Meinhof gang, and he spent two weeks in prison.

But before Christmas, the gang had found a place big enough to house them all. Raspe had obtained the key of a sanatorium owned by the Mitscherlich family, at Bad Kissingen. ("We always gave the key to anyone who wanted to stay there," Monika Seifert explained. "Anyone who wanted to could get in without a key anyway through the basement windows. We were always having to repair them.") Ruhland and Proll were to go there ahead of the others and get it warm and ready. Ruhland bought oil stoves and tried to heat the big rooms. But when the others arrived they were still cold, and nobody wanted to stay there very long. Baader swore.

"How's one expected to do any work here?" he demanded, who had given no warning that he intended to do anything so unprecedented. "It's like a fridge."

And Ensslin thought it was too uncomfortable for her to put up with. So Baader, Ensslin, and Meinhof drove back to Frankfurt to wait in comfort while the sanatorium was well warmed. They returned after a while. Ruhland found it a full-time job, warming up the sanatorium and getting it in order. He even had to rewire the place. He had no time to listen to the discussions. Meinhof gave him political education, to keep him clear on the purpose of what they were doing. "The ruling classes have to be made to feel insecure. Classes have to be abolished to lighten the living conditions of the workers." Ruhland "let this stuff pour over him" as he worked on the wiring and refilled the stoves.

Baader was in a state over another accident he'd had driving into a ditch. The members of the gang had frequent small accidents, and Baader had the most, though he would contemptuously explain and demonstrate how he would never have this or that sort of accident such as the one someone else had just had. The wonder of it was that they were not worse, that lives were not destroyed by sheer recklessness, and that the police never stopped them or found them at the scene of the accidents.

Now Baader had to give his attention to the big new plan: to kidnap some prominent person and release him in return for Mahler. Axel Springer? Well, they might get the money for him, but not the release of "political prisoners." CSU leader Franz Josef Strauss? "Nobody would give anything for him." Then Baader said it would be easy to kidnap the Chancellor, Willy Brandt, who always went out for his evening walk with only one security officer. But the idea was not taken any further.

There were also bank robberies to plan. And more cars to be stolen for the getaways.

On December 19, after a supper of bread and sausage around a big table (" 'Tinny' [Ilse Stachowiak] and I," Ruhland recalled ruefully, "had got ourselves a family-size bottle of Coke and some cognac, but the bandits took them from us and drank it up"), they all went into the living room. There was an odd collection of ramshackle furniture—mattresses on the floor, various chairs brought from other rooms, and a radio. A joint of hashish was passed around. They talked dreamily of the riches they were about to obtain. Ensslin hoped for half a million. It was just before Christmas, money's season. Baader said that the organization must be built up. They needed more safe houses and material. Afterward Baader and Ensslin chose a room for themselves, Meinhof and Raspe another, and the rest bedded down as best they could. It was Ruhland's last night with the gang.

The next day, December 20, he was driving with Beate Sturm, Jansen, and a friend of Jansen's through a small town near Oberhausen on a car-stealing mission when a police car stopped them. Ruhland showed his papers, and the police asked him to come to their car while they radioed for a check on their information. Surprisingly, something did not tally. They asked him politely if he would come with them to the police station. He agreed, but said he'd like to fetch his car keys. He walked over to the car where Jansen and Beate Sturm and Jansen's friend were standing. A policeman followed him.

"Scram!" Ruhland hissed at them.

As he returned to the police car, the other three walked off into the darkness. More police arrived.

"I've got a weapon on me," Ruhland confessed, and handed it over. He wanted to get out of the gang and he simply took the opportunity that presented itself. He had known for some time that the gang would never make him rich, what with Meinhof doling out fifty or a hundred marks at a time and no fair sharing of the loot.

Beate Sturm fled in a taxi with Jansen's friend. She too was to leave the gang soon of her own accord, and was to tell the story of her association with the RAF with candor, and also with some interesting insights. As a physics student in Berlin she had become involved with student political groups. She and Holger Meins (a student of film making), a girl named Ilse Stachowiak, and Ulrich Scholtze (a fellow physics student), Beate Sturm reported, wanted to take part in some political action "as a kind of happening like the actions of Fritz Teufel," as a continuation of student "happenings," only with arms. "A very naïve idea," she was to see in retrospect. Then they read Carlos Marighela. "There you find quite concrete instructions: the urban guerrilla must be fit, and must read this and that, and learn to do this and that." So they went swimming for the revolution, once a week. Then they thought they must get the technical know-how and wherewithal. And when they thought about where to get it from, the only answer seemed to be: from criminals. "Not difficult in Berlin if one knows certain bars." It was as a professional car thief that Andreas Baader first became known to them. He asked them whether they wanted to know about the ideology of his group or how to steal cars. They said they only wanted to know how to steal cars, and he was "very happy that he did not have to talk about anything political," Beate Sturm said. He told them about "lice"—bugs which can be hidden in cars—and how if the car is moving the "louse" won't work. "It was all like American crime fiction, and that's how Baader managed it"—to supplant their "heroic political ideas" with the excitement of being "really involved in a crime story."

"It was extremely fashionable and up to date in Berlin at that time to say that all connections [relevant political theory] are very simple, and one could find them out in one week and then immediately one had to act. 'Destroy what destroys you. . . .' Then everything was to be much better. But there were no concrete ideas, really none at all. Even the big leftist chieftains in Berlin had none. There was simply a desire to do things so that things should become different. This arises probably from the bourgeois parental homes of the students. . . . If, however, at fourteen, you are already working in a factory and have to look after your own skin, then it is not so easy to believe that you can do something for others. Well, one simply slides into something like this [the group]. . . .

"And then there was this conspiratorial air about Baader. If he was coming he'd say he'd be there at seven, and at seven sharp the door had to be opened, and he'd walk in, and the curtains had to be drawn. He invented this whole crime atmosphere, and he pulled our semipolitical beginnings down to his level. He really sent us on some kind of trip. . . . 'Either you come along or you stay forever just an empty chatterbox.'

"One comes along as a totally impractical student idiot and never having done anything with one's hands, and one is pulled along by something like this. Like Ulrike—the only thing that she has ever done with her hands is what she has written. One only has to explain to her that action is more important than her scribbling and that is sufficient for her. . . . It is Baader's great idea that criminal action is in itself political action. It appears complete nonsense to me."

She observed that "the solidarity of the group was forced upon it by the illegal situation; everyone had made his own fate."

She liked "Ali" Jansen and "Kali" Ruhland best. They were "real children." She didn't agree with the way Ruhland was judged in the group as "not a cadre." (The word "cadre" is used as a singular to mean a correctly-politically-minded-member-of-our-particular-leftist-organization. In Mao Tse-Tung's *Thoughts* the word is used in the same way. But what the B-M middle-class members implied when they called Ruhland "no cadre" was, unconfessably, that he was not their class equal.) Baader also dismissed anybody who was not "politically active" in his approved sense, including any of their hosts who put them up or provided them with long-term accommodation, as "stupid" and "not worth considering at all." Ulrike, Beate Sturm said, would talk to the journalists, political scientists, and professors of this and that about political theories in a way they were used to. But "she never represented the ideas of the group as being political ideas to these sympathizers. She couldn't do that because there were no ideas at all."

Once Ulrike declared that all the rushing about without any plan was nonsensical, and wanted to discuss what they were doing and what mistakes they had made. But "Baader was afraid and started his well-tried tricks. He shouted, 'You cunts! Your emancipation consists of shouting at your men.'

"He brought that out in a tone that is just indescribable. He was always raving.

"Gudrun said to him, 'Baby, you can't really know anything about that.' And that was the only moment when he really shut up."

Astrid Proll tackled him too, but she was "always a red rag to him." Marianne Herzog said that she would not be able to put up with this sort of thing. Baader replied that they "had to be hard," and that the "pressure of illegality built up aggression" which could only be "let out within the group," so there were bound to be rows occasionally.

Beate Sturm found "Baader's outbursts of fury quite senseless." She "could only shout back." She felt unhappy all the time in the group.

Holger Meins stayed out of the quarrels. Beate Sturm said of him that he "wanted to have authority. The authority that Baader represented fascinated him, he bowed down in front of it, he was prepared to do anything."

The women, she said, were "truly emancipated. We could do many things better than the men. We felt we were stronger, for instance, and much less anxious than they. We were also far less aggressive and we never quarreled." But there were inequalities. "In comfort, for instance. When we were in Stuttgart we had a whole series of apartments, and the question was who lives where. There was one place with a bath and it was quite clear that Andreas and Gudrun were going to have it. Why should they have it? Well, that was clear enough: Andreas had once been in prison and therefore you can't expect somebody who has suffered so heavily in prison to do without a bath, and of course Gundrun had to share with him because they were so happily married."

Beate was the one who was most often sent into the shops to buy things, because "I was best at pretending to be bourgeois." (Whereas the others were good at pretending to be revolutionaries, perhaps.)

She felt that the kidnapping plans were not serious, but that the group took the bank robbing very seriously. Baader once told her that he found the gathering together of money robbed from banks a "particularly pleasing experience."

She had not been with the group long when she confided to Ruhland, as they were tearing along the autobahn between widely spaced banks, that she was homesick and wanted to leave the group. Ruhland said he did too, and he made a (very wide) detour in order to take Beate past her home. That night Ruhland was arrested by the police and Beate Sturm fled with Jansen's friend in a taxi. She called Baader at the writer's apartment from a public telephone. She had no money, what should she do? Borrow some from "Ali's" friend, Baader ordered, and then go to the family in Gelsenkirchen for the night.

There, the next day, Raspe and Meinhof arrived in a high state of excitement because they had been stopped in their (stolen) car by the police and, after handing them her forged papers with her photograph in them, Meinhof had suddenly put her foot down and sped away. So the police had a recent picture of the blond Meinhof.

The police by this time were almost treading on the heels of the gang. They arrived to question the family in Gelsenkirchen four days after Ruhland's arrest. And a few days after that, both the Frankfurt journalists' apartment and the apartment of Monika and Jürgen Seifert were searched.

Jansen and Scholtze were arrested in Nuremberg after they had tried to steal a parked Mercedes. When the owner heard them trying to start it, he shrieked. They fled but were pursued and caught by the police. Meinhof, who had also come to Nuremberg along with Jansen, Scholtze, Proll, Meins, and Beate Sturm in order to rob a bank, telephoned the news to Baader. Baader told her that in Frankfurt too there was confusion. He had had another accident.

When some days later the group heard that Ulrich Scholtze had been released from custody, Beate was sent by Baader to get Scholtze to "work" with them again. If he would not, she must demand back the thousand marks he had been given from the gang's cash box. After all, what right would he have to keep it? It would be shameless daylight robbery.

Beate saw Scholtze in his mother's flat in Nuremberg on December 30. He refused to consider doing anything illegal again. His studies, he said, came first. And Beate forgot to ask him for the money back.

In Nuremberg, Ulrike Meinhof was given the keys to an empty apartment by an acquaintance, a political scientist and economist who insisted later that he never recognized Meinhof but was prepared to let her use his apartment all the same. Beate thought it was a beautiful place, but Ulrike poured contempt on what she called the "Röhl type of furniture."

On Christmas Eve the whole (remaining) gang was reunited in Stuttgart, where Marianne Herzog got them the use of a basement apartment in the house of an art teacher to whose brother she had once been engaged. It was a big old house, on the side of a hill. There the revolutionaries celebrated Christmas in a traditional way by feasting on goose. Baader got drunk and swore at the women. He quarreled with Meinhof over the definition of a guerrilla.

After Christmas, Astrid Proll suggested that they should rob some banks in her home town of Kassel. Everyone agreed about that and drove off along the autobahn to look over all recommended banks. They later sent Beate Sturm to two of them to make further detailed observations. She noted this and that, made a sketch or two, and thought how if she took part in this raid she would have started on a criminal course, that in fact "no class enemy was being struck" but only perhaps some savings-bank employees who might be hurt or killed. Her final decision to leave the gang was strengthened unintentionally by Ulrike Meinhof, who woke her in the middle of the night and talked at her for four hours, accusing her of "lack of political motivation." It was more a grilling than a discussion. Meinhof did all the talking. The harangue concerned what Beate called, bluntly, murder, and also whether she should have pushed a car three times to get it started when she had only pushed it twice and then given up. The next day Beate telephoned her mother and said she wanted to come home. Her mother told her to come.

Two banks in Kassel were raided on January 15, 1971, both soon after half past nine. In all, DM 114,530 was stolen (about $35,000).

After the Kassel robberies the police raided apartments in Gelsenkirchen, Frankfurt, Hamburg, and Bremen. The hunters were in hot pursuit. And soon three more members of the gang were caught.

On February 2, Hans-Jürgen Bäcker was arrested—the "traitor" long since excluded from the gang but still a possible source of danger to them as a witness against any of the Berlin group who might be caught. On April 12 "Tinny" Stachowiak was arrested on the main station concourse of Frankfurt after being recognized by a policeman from her "Wanted" picture. And then Astrid Proll—for whose arrest there was a warrant out, since the police suspected her of taking part in the freeing of Baader—was caught on May 6, in Hamburg. A pump attendant recognized her when she pulled up in her Alpha Romeo at his filling station, and he alerted the police. They found her, and she drove her car into a wall trying to escape from them. She reached into her handbag for her Firebird, but they grabbed her before she could use it.

The RAF had been in existence for less than one year. It had lost fourteen of its factioneers: Homann (still in hiding); Mahler, Goergens, Schubert, Berberich, Asdonk; Ruhland, Grusdat (arrested on December 3), Sturm, Bäcker, Janson, Scholtze, Stachowiak, and Proll.

In addition, a number of helpers (whether they had given their help intentionally or unintentionally) belonging to the much-respected academic and professional classes, and the Church, had been implicated—to their surprise or fury or irritation or, in some instances, pleasure; had been provoked to outcry, protestations of innocence, confession, or boasts. Some had lost their jobs as a result, some their reputations, some their trustworthiness, some their naïveté, some their willingness to assist terrorists, some briefly, perhaps, their boredom.

With their ranks so decimated, the group needed new recruits or they would be hard put to it to carry on with the revolution. Only eight remained: Baader, Ensslin, Meinhof, Raspe, Herzog, Meins, Grashof, and Schelm.

But reinforcements were at hand: a whole platoon, eager and prepared to play urban guerrilla—a literal lunatic fringe of West Germany's nonworking classes.

Fritz Teufel (left) and Rainer Langhans (right) at an SDS conference, Frankfurt 1967.

Horst Mahler (holding white helmet) leading a student demonstration, Berlin 1967.

Thorwald Proll, Horst Söhnlein, Andreas Baader, and Gudrun Ensslin (left to right) at their arson trial, Frankfurt 1968.

Fugitives from justice Gudrun Ensslin and Andreas Baader, in a café in Paris, 1969.

Ulrike Meinhof (left) age 6, with her sister, Wienke.

Professor Renate Riemeck, foster mother of Ulrike Meinhof, 1950 (below, left).

Ulrike Meinhof age 15, 1950 (below, right)

Klaus Rainer Röhl and his wife, Ulrike Meinhof, with their twin daughters, Bettina and Regine, 1964.

Ulrike Meinhof (*left*) *and her protégée Irene Goergens at the time of the filming of Ulrike Meinhof's television play* Bambule, *Berlin 1969.*

Karl-Heinz Ruhland after his arrest, December 1970 (police photo).

Extract from a "Wanted" poster showing (left to right), top: Jan-Carl Raspe, Holger Meins, Irmgard Möller; bottom: Ilse Stachowiak, Ingeborg Barz, Klaus Jünschke, Ralf Reinders.

Police photos of Angela Luther and Astrid Proll (top, left and right); Ingrid Schubert and Rolf Pohle (middle, left and right); and Manfred Grashof (bottom).

Wide World Photos

Bomb damage to the officers' mess of the United States Army headquarters, Frankfurt, May 1972.

Bomb damage in the parking lot of USAEUR barracks, Heidelberg, May 1972.

Wide World Photos

Holger Meins arrested, Frankfurt, June 1972.

Andreas Baader arrested, Frankfurt, June 1972.

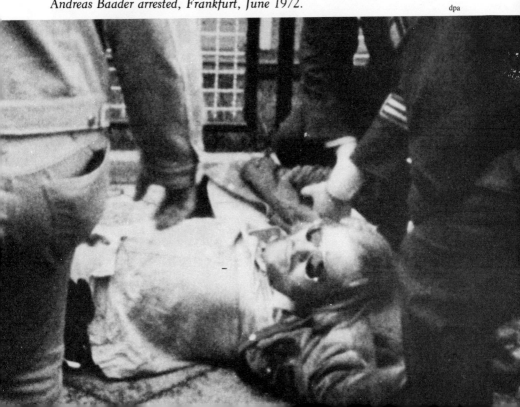

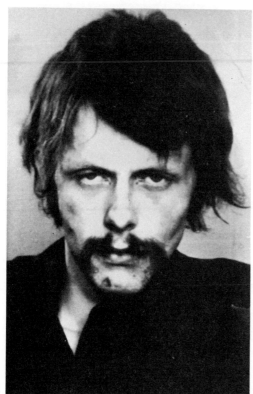

Jan-Carl Raspe after his arrest in Frankfurt, June 1972 (police photo).

dpa

Horst Mahler at the time of his trial in Berlin, November 1974.

United Press International

Gerhard Müller after his arrest,
June 1972 (police photo).

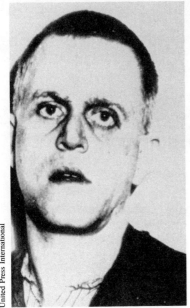

Hans-Jürgen Bäcker at the time of
his trial in Berlin, November 1974.

Ulrike Meinhof in prison, 1975.

Stern Magazine/Pixfeatures

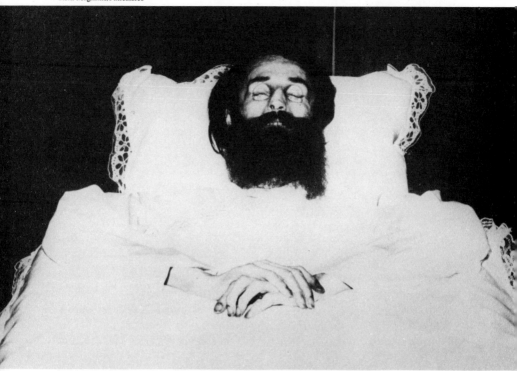

The laid-out corpse of Holger Meins, November 1974.

The German embassy, Stockholm, set on fire by the explosion of terrorists' bombs, April 1975.

Wide World Photos

Stammheim prison with, in the foreground, the single-story courthouse specially built for trying the Baader-Meinhof gang leaders.
Masked, placard-carrying mourners at the funeral of Ulrike Meinhof, Berlin, May 1976.

13

For Pity's Sake

Meanwhile, back in the real world, the seven-year-old girls, Bettina and Regine, who had been abandoned by their mother to the care of no doubt goodhearted people who might have felt deeply for the Vietnamese, had been moved on, at her instigation, toward another sort of life, among strangers in another country.

Perhaps Ulrike Meinhof, who had expressed herself forcibly (in her article on the Nirumand family) against families being torn apart, and on the indispensability and irreplaceability of mothers to their children, found the decision hard to make. But hard or easy, the decision she made was that the People's War came before her children's interest, or even their very lives, which she dedicated to the cause of Palestinian liberation. She arranged for them to be taken, by a devious route and several escorts, to those unwelcoming Arabs in Jordan who had taught her how to lift weights and fall out of a fast-moving car. The little girls were to live in a refugee camp and be trained along with Palestinian children to become "kamikaze" guerrilla fighters against Israel.

Their journey was to be made in stages. The last stop before their destination was Sicily, where for a couple of weeks they were in the care of a famous philanthropic social worker—who may have been misled about the children's circumstances—who then handed them over to a German hippie couple. The hippies housed them in a prefabricated hut near Palermo, in a camp for the victims of volcanic eruptions, empty at the time. Their furniture was a collection of fruit boxes.

They looked after the little girls unconventionally but conscientiously, on a diet of rice—they'd brought a large bag of it in their van— and vegetables. They smoked pot and let the little girls have a draw on their joints when they wanted to. They insisted that the children leave them in peace to sleep during the heat of the day, so Regine and Bettina went to the beach and swam in the sea and became brown and kept perfectly healthy and apparently perfectly happy too. And when their money and rice ran out, the hippies resorted to an unprecedented expedient and went to work—in a restaurant, which improved the variety and quality of their own and the children's food.

Meanwhile their father was searching frantically for them. Röhl asked Renate Riemeck whether she would have them to live with her if he sent a message to Ulrike that he promised not to take them himself. Renate Riemeck agreed. She saw that Röhl missed his children painfully and was deeply worried about them. "I saw such sadness in him," she said.

He sent his message, but no answer came. Perhaps Ulrike never got it.

Röhl made application to the Berlin courts for the transfer of their legal care and control to him. It was granted. He then drove through Germany, publishing their photographs in the local papers.

They were not with their Aunt Wienke (who had changed from the nursing to the teaching profession, had studied at the Weilburg College of Education after Professor Riemeck had left it, and was now married to a teacher who was against giving any help to Ulrike and her friends), and if she knew where her nieces were, she was not telling.

A Frankfurt commune told him that they were in Scandinavia; a women's commune on Sylt told him they were in Frankfurt.

After a while he learned that they had been sent to Bremen. Expecting that they would not be released to him, he got his brother Wolfgang and a friend to drive there. They made inquiries in the neighborhood and were told yes, the children had been seen in the house of Jürgen Holtkamp. But they had just missed them. Two hours before Wolfgang asked for them, two members of the Baader-Meinhof group had fetched them away.

Röhl wrote to a lawyer in Bremen who had been given a power of attorney to represent Ulrike at the care-and-control hearing in Berlin, but still he received no helpful news. And they had been missing for over two months.

He then employed Hamburg detectives to search for the children. They too could find out nothing.

In mid-August he suspended the search and decided to take a much-needed holiday in Italy, at a place called Ronchi near Viareggio, not far from Pisa.

For some time Stefan Aust (who was back from America) and Peter

Homann had had their minds made up that they must find out where the children were and somehow get them back to their father: not for Röhl's but for the children's sake.

One morning toward the end of August (about three weeks after Ulrike Meinhof had returned from Jordan to West Berlin), Aust came to the flat where Peter Homann was in hiding and found two people there, a young man and a young woman, who said that they did not like the plan Ulrike had made for the children and were prepared to tell Aust where they were, if he was prepared to go and fetch them. Peter Homann was still in hiding, had no passport, and under the circumstances was not going to apply for one. So it was up to Stefan Aust. He agreed, and they told him where they were, and that (subterfuge having its rules) there was a password which he must speak to the children's custodians before they would give them up to him. They told him what it was. And they stressed that it was only a matter of hours before the escort from Berlin would be arriving in Sicily to pick up the twins and take them on to Jordan.

Aust at once telephoned Lufthansa to find out the time of the next flight to Palermo, and the cost.

It was beyond his means.

He rushed off to see the nearest rich man who had both good sense and generosity and might lend him the money, an important liberal newspaper publisher. He gave it at once but told Aust not to make it known that he had. (In a story where pity, though made so much of, is in such short supply, it would be nice to praise by name everyone who showed he had it. But perhaps he was afraid of reprisal from the philanthropists of the RAF.)

Time was pressing. As much as possible must be saved. So again the two informants with Peter Homann came up with useful information: a Palermo telephone number of some trendy-leftist contact men. Aust called the number and stated that "on the orders of the group" the children were to be taken to a spot near the airport at Palermo, ready to be picked up. As this was the date which had been fixed for the children's departure for Jordan with an escort from Berlin, the order was not surprising, and the contact men agreed.

Aust bought his ticket and took the next flight to Palermo. The Italian radical trendies were there to meet him, and so were the two hippies.

First he had to give the password. "Professor Schnase," he said. It was the name of one of the children's dolls. (Though according to Röhl the doll's name was "Professor Schnake," so perhaps Aust got away with his coup more luckily than even he supposed at the time.)

They nodded. They took him to a nearby beach. And there he found the children.

They knew him well, of course, and were delighted to see him. They looked very healthy and happy, their blond hair bleached blonder, their skins deeply tanned.

Aust gave some money to the hippies for looking after them, as if it came from the gang. Then as fast as possible he drove the twins away from the airport, and the three of them got onto a train to Rome.

About two hours later the the gang's real envoys arrived and demanded the children.

Aust had friends near Rome to whom he could safely take them. But he had no passports for them, and besides it was time they were handed over to their father. From the house of a photographer friend in Ostia, the port of Rome, Aust tried to telephone Röhl in Hamburg, but he was told he was away and no one knew where. Aust left his number and said that everyone was to ask everyone and let him know as soon as they dug up the information. It was dug up. "Wonderful coincidence," Hamburg shouted down the line; "he is in Italy, near Pisa," and they even had the exact address.

Röhl had only been in Ronchi for three days when he received a telegram asking him to call, urgently, a free-lance photographer and occasional *Konkret* contributor living near Rome. No hint as to why. He did, and found himself speaking to Stefan Aust, who was saying something very extraordinary and incredible: "I've got the children." It wasn't possible, he said; how could Aust have the children with him in Ostia?

But he believed it at last when he heard their voices over the telephone.

"You must come quickly," Aust told him. "By now the B-M gang will know I'm here and they'll be after me."

Röhl hired a car and set out at once for Rome. He met Aust and his children in the beautiful Piazza Navona. But the happy ending to his search was delayed. The children had been given to understand in Berlin that their father was a monster. They would not go with him. They clung to Stefan Aust, who had to agree to accompany them to Pisa. On the way the children sang merrily, their German nursery songs interspersed with urban revolutionary ditties, about the Red Flag and Forward the People and Long Live Socialism and Liberty.

Aust had to leave them soon and go back to Hamburg. But first he told Röhl the story of the rescue, only leaving out Peter Homann's name, so that Röhl only discovered later that he owed the return of his children to Homann too.

After a while the twins understood that their father was not a monster after all. He kept them awhile in Ronchi, as he had to get passports for them, and then flew with them to Cologne. He was afraid that they would be looked for in Hamburg. But back to Blankenese they went, and to school in the neighborhood. In this upper-middle-class suburb there was no stigma on the child of a terrorist; on the contrary, being such a child carried a definite éclat. But they had lost so much schooling that they had to go into the class below their age group.

When Aust told Röhl that he had spent about three thousand marks on rescuing the children, and asked him if he would repay him so that he could pay back the money he had borrowed for the venture from the important liberal publisher, Röhl replied that he was quite hard up—look at the Porsche he had outside, he said, he had still to pay for it—and his roof had recently needed extensive repairs—"You should see the bills for that, so you can understand why I'm poor at the moment." But eventually he did agree to pay back what Aust had spent on saving the children, a little at a time—which he did.

A couple of months later, Aust got back to his home in the country after a horseback ride to find a message waiting for him that someone called Karl Heinz Roth was urgently trying to get in touch with him. Roth must speak to him; it was a matter of life and death.

Aust knew Roth as an SDS leader in Hamburg. He had been in hiding for some time, and when Aust went looking for him in Hamburg that evening he could not find him. He waited in his own apartment with a girl friend and Peter Homann, but heard nothing more, and eventually they all went to bed. They were wakened in the depths of the night by a long ringing of the front-door bell. Aust found Roth on the doorstep, almost hysterical, trying incoherently at first to tell Aust something, at last gabbling that Baader and Mahler were gunning for Aust and had forced him to show them where he lived.

"They say you know too much and are a traitor—they want to shoot you—three minutes to leave—because I told them I was working with them—if I'm not back in a couple of minutes more—"

So Aust and the others flung on some clothes, grabbed a few things, and fled out of a back door and down a back alley. They stayed away from the apartment for about a fortnight. For quite some time after that Aust kept himself armed.

Later he learned that Roth had gone down to the two avengers in the car below and told them that there was no one in the apartment, that they could come and see for themselves. They did, and were soon convinced that Roth was speaking the truth.

Röhl records that one day some swarthy men came to his door and demanded the children. They didn't get them, and they went away and fortunately did not come back again.

And the PFLP camp in Jordan to which the children were to have been consigned—that was bombed to rubble in a punitive raid by King Hussein's air force.

14

Killing

At the Psychiatric-Neurological Clinic of Heidelberg University there was a Dr. (of medicine) Wolfgang Huber, who had been appointed to his post at the age of twenty-nine, in August 1964. During 1969 he had been reprimanded several times by the director, Dr. von Baeyers, for refusing to collaborate with his colleagues. In December 1969 Dr. Huber organized his group-therapy patients to protest against Dr. von Baeyers in general and the management of the clinic in particular.

In his group therapy sessions, Dr. Huber propagated the view that "the late-capitalist performance society of the Federal Republic" was sick, and was therefore continually producing physically and psychologically sick people, and that this could only be altered by a violent revolutionary change of society.

On February 21, 1970, Dr. Huber was dismissed without notice from his position as scientific assistant at the clinic. His lawyer lodged a complaint against the instant dismissal. And on February 28, Dr. Huber got his patients to force their way into the offices of the administration director and occupy them, while Dr. Huber himself went to warn the Rector that some of his patients might commit suicide. A compromise was reached. The university administration agreed to continue paying Dr. Huber until September 30, 1970, and to provide him with four rooms in a university building.

Secure with money and headquarters, the mental patients and their doctor constituted themselves an organization which they named the Socialist Patients' Collective, SPK.

On March 25, 1970, four members of the SPK entered the office of the director, who was in conference with another doctor, and demanded that he sign and seal some blank prescriptions. The director refused. The frustrated patients therefore fell to abusing the two doctors, calling them "Nazi desk murderers." The director got the police to remove them.

Dr. Huber rejected the requirement by the university to do scientific work. He informed the Rector that "the SPK has no reason to prepare a scientific presentation of its views and actions, as it is already entirely legitimized by praxis." However, in July 1970 it put out a manifesto under the heading "Scientific Representation." Part of this document reads as follows:

The SPK must therefore take as its aim the retrieval [sic] of that sickness which has been turned into capital by the rulers, which in turn produces sickness and capital, so that the sick capital or the capitalistic sickness will disappear and the capitalistic utilization and cover-up process may come to a standstill, or start moving in the opposing direction. A movement in the opposing direction one calls by the foreign word "revolution."

The working circles of the SPK have among others the task of further strengthening the theoretical foundations for the aims of the SPK. Here for the first time at the University of Heidelberg the unity of research and teaching is manifest.

The "working circles" alluded to were officially designated:

Working Circle Dialectics
Working Circle Marxism
Working Circle Sexuality, Education, Religion

But within the group other working circles were distinguished by SPK members as:

Working Circle Explosives (led by Dr. Huber's wife, Ursula Huber)
Working Circle Radio Transmission
Working Circle Photography
Working Circle Judo/Karate

The jobs of the working circles were:

Explosives: to make explosives
Radio Transmission: to construct receivers and listen in to the police radio and to build transmitters to jam the police radio
Photography: to photograph all the buildings, vehicles, and personnel of the Heidelberg police
Judo/Karate: to become expert in these techniques

The Working Circle Radio Transmission achieved a success with a bug which Ursula Huber managed to install in the senate room of the university. It was soon discovered, however, stuck into an electrical socket.

The Working Circle Explosives achieved only qualified success. Ursula Huber and the other members, including two whose names were to become well known, Carmen Roll and Siegfried Hausner, started trying to make TNT in the laboratory of the University Institute of Physiology in mid-December 1970. They were only able to manufacture it in minute quantities. On the last day of that year, two others exploded a very small laboratory-made bomb by remote control, in a part of the Odenwald forest area. They took photographs of the explosion. The next day, the SPK celebrated the new year by trying to set fire to the State Psychiatric Clinic at Wiesloch, near Heidelberg.

In addition to all these activities, the group produced mimeographed pamphlets which they distributed in the town to the general public. They called them "Patient Infos."

Patient Info No. 1, which came out in the middle of 1970, proclaimed:

> Comrades! There must be no therapeutic act which has not previously been clearly and uniquely shown to be a revolutionary act. For this there are already criteria which we shall develop further. In the liberated rooms only that may happen which we know serves the struggling workers!
>
> The system has "made us sick." Let us strike the deathblow at the sick system.

The impermissibility of any therapeutic act which had not been clearly and uniquely(!) shown to be a revolutionary act proved a severe stumbling block to some who sought help of Dr. Huber. A Heidelberg couple who sent their mentally ill daughter to him for treatment had her returned to them after two weeks because in that time she had "made no noticeable political progress."

Patient Info No. 47 indicated that the SPK had found its emotional political home. Enraptured, it breaks into poetry to create the slogan:

> Mahler-Meinhof-Baader—
> Those are our cadre!

On Patient Info No. 51, dated July 12, 1971, every "SPK" was crossed out and "RAF" written instead.

On July 22, 1971, the SPK announced its dissolution and renamed itself IZRU, standing for Information Center Red [People's] University (Information Zentrum Rote [Volks-] Universität). They published an announcement to this effect, and then another asking for contributions. Soon after that, IZRU published a pamphlet announcing that they were supporting the formation of urban—and country—guerrilla cells.

Siegfried Hausner, Carmen Roll, Margrit Schiller, and Klaus Jünschke were some of the patients who brought their special purpose to the terrorist scene: violent attack on "society" in order to cure their personal mental disorders.

In September 1970 the financing of the SPK by the University of Heidelberg was due to stop, as agreed with Dr. Huber. But in fact the university continued to support the organization well beyond this deadline, not out of its normal funds, as hitherto, but out of its special "charity funds." In all DM 31,875 was made available by the "sick system" to those who planned to cure themselves by destroying it, from its inception to its dissolution, at which point the balance of the money was "distributed" to the private accounts of leading members.

The members were, however, incensed that the university should also oust them from their four rooms in a university building. In the pamphlet of July 22, 1971, which announced that the SPK was dissolved and that its successor was IZRU, the Rector was bitterly indicted for this cruelty.

Information Center Red (People's) University [is] temporarily without accommodation, as Rector Rendtorff, known throughout the town as a dirty sow of a parson, had the rooms of IZRU attacked by the autonomy storm troopers of the Heidelberg Perversity.

A second pamphlet gave an address:

IZRU—Black Help   Heidelberg
C/o AStA
Contributions bank account: Heidelberger Volksbank
No. 19964

And an explanation of IZRU:

IZRU is a legal organization at the University of Heidelberg, whose task is to inform the SPKs which are forming at various universities of the theory and praxis of the former SPK at the University of Heidelberg.

Several SPK members distinguished themselves in therapy work both before and after the B-M merger. In the middle of February 1971 a working party which included Siegfried Hausner were to treat themselves by means of a bomb which was to be placed in the special train of the president of the Federal Republic. The train passed through Heidelberg safely, however, because Carmen Roll arrived too late with the bomb—a small homemade affair.

Dr. Huber, having launched his crazy brigade on the too-authoritarian/too-permissive society, was pursuing his brain waves further at his house—or disguised sci-fi fortress?—in Wiesenbach. Coming or going in a car along a street in nearby Wiesental, several of the corps were stopped by the police on June 24, 1971. Two men named Ralf Reinders and Alfred Mahrländer, the police believed, were among them, and according to the police it was Reinders who pulled out a Firebird pistol and shot an officer named Brand clear through the shoulder. Both men escaped at the time, but both were arrested later.

About a month after the shooting incident, and one day before the SPK turned into IZRU, seven members, including Dr. Huber and his wife, were arrested on suspicion of having formed a criminal association and illegally buying arms and explosives. Two of those who managed to slip the net were Carmen Roll and Klaus Jünschke.

The B-M gang itself had meanwhile gained and lost more members. They had gone back north to Hamburg. There, on July 15, 1971, Petra Schelm and one Werner Hoppe were stopped at a police roadblock in the Bahrenfeld district while driving a stolen BMW. The police had become aware that the gang had developed a preference for BMWs and gave them special attention at roadblocks. According to the police, this is what happened:

At 2 P.M. on July 15, 1971, the woman driver of a blue BMW 2002 ignored a police stop signal on a main road. She drove on at high speed. A police car gave chase and overtook the BMW, which stopped, and the passenger, a man, got out and started shooting at the police. The woman driver then got out too, aimed a pistol, and fired. The police officer called out to them from the car to surrender. Petra Schelm answered by firing two more shots, but she missed. Then both officers called out to her again to surrender. Schelm's male companion, Werner Hoppe (a television employee and self-cured former drug addict), ran off. The police told Schelm to throw away the jacket she was carrying over her arm and to approach them slowly. She tore the jacket away suddenly and started firing again. One policeman threw himself to the ground and fired four shots; the other shouted to her to stop. (In the police report, the fairness of the officers is too scrupulous to be quite believable.) She stepped behind a car and alternately shot at each of the officers, one of whom then got out a submachine gun; a burst from that killed Petra Schelm with a bullet through the head. Her gun was found to be a Firebird Parabellum.

Werner Hoppe did not get far. A police helicopter which had been hovering over the roadblock soon found him. With the chopper over his head he threw his gun away and surrendered.

The nineteen-year-old Petra Schelm was buried in the Spandau cemetery of West Berlin. Her funeral was attended by her family, and fifty youths carrying a red flag which they laid on the grave, and sixty observing policemen, who saw to it that the red flag was removed.

When Hoppe came to trial, his association with the B-M gang could not be proved, but he was convicted of attempted murder in the shootout with the police.

On September 25, 1971, at the other end of Germany, two police officers, both named Ruf but not related to each other, walked toward a car wrongly parked in a parking lot off the Freiburg-Basel motorway. Two men and a woman jumped out of it and started shooting. Friedrich Ruf was shot through the hand only, but Helmut Ruf was seriously wounded. Friedrich Ruf identified two of the assailants, one as Holger Meins and the other as Margrit Schiller of the defunct SPK. The bullets found in the parking lot and surgically removed from Helmut Ruf were fired from Firebird pistols. In the car two underground publications were found, *The Concept Urban Guerrilla* and something innocently titled *Road Traffic Ordinances*, in fact another opus by the "RAF collective," which had the literally undercover title *Concerning the Armed Struggle in Western Europe*.

The Concept Urban Guerrilla began to circulate in May 1971, about a year after the freeing of Baader, and is regarded as a manifesto of the group. The style and tone, subject matter and treatment, and in particular an irritability over an article in *Konkret*, inevitably suggest the authorship of Ulrike Meinhof, though there are a few passages whose content and manner indicate at least one other hand. The language throughout is immoderate, emotional, at times incoherent. The notable points made by the authors are:

They urge the use of violence as the only means to change society.

They reject legal means of achieving that aim.

They reject parliamentarianism, and they maintain that most people do not know what they really want or what is really good for them.

"We are no anarchists," they state firmly.

"We are communists," they state equally firmly.

While they insist that "the question whether the prison rescue [of Baader] would have been undertaken if we had known that a certain Linke would have been shot can only be answered with 'no,' " they condemn the question as "pacifistic" (!). They accuse the police of having shot first on that occasion. (But that is untrue. Heinrich Böll accepted it as true in his article "Does Ulrike Meinhof Want Mercy or a Free Conduct?" but in fact Georg Linke was shot when the armed attackers were still two rooms away from the policemen who were guarding Baader.)

They laud Maoism and scorn the pluralistic society.

They argue that armed struggle against "American imperialism" can be carried out in Germany or anywhere else, thus: "If it is right that American imperialism is a paper tiger . . . and if the thesis of the Chinese Communists is right that the battle is being fought in all corners of the world, so that the forces of imperialism are splintered and have become defeatable . . . then there is no reason to exclude any country or region from the anti-imperialist struggle."

To this argument Renate Riemeck replied in an open letter to Ulrike Meinhof in *Konkret* on November 8, 1971, that the "ideological justification for the existence of the Red Army Faction rests on an 'if.' " And the "if," in Professor Riemeck's view, is a false assumption. The United States is not a paper tiger but a "superstrong superpower," and Ulrike Meinhof's "ghost gang" will only give reactionaries an excuse for reviving anticommunist witch hunts.

Concerning the Armed Struggle in Western Europe, commonly believed to be by Horst Mahler, advocates armed struggle and gives instructions for manufacturing armaments and forming commando groups. It asserts (like Marcuse) that "proletarian leadership can only be realized by the avant-garde" and names the students as that avant-garde. It insists on violence as "the highest form of class struggle."

Two other RAF publications, not found in the car with the others but worth a mention, are *Serve the People* and *The Action of the Black September in Munich.*

Serve the People, as well as covering the usual ground—class struggle, anti-imperialism, Vietnam—carries statistics of accidental deaths in industry, suicide, child murder, which might be accurate but are interpreted with a freedom that transcends even the confines of plausibility; as for instance: "1,200 people commit suicide every year because they do not want to die away in the service of capital; 1,000 children are murdered each year because the all-too-small apartments exist only to allow the landlords to collect a high rent." The idea was to suggest that the RAF was the server and guardian of the interests of multitudes. It was a wistful claim, like one made in *The Concept Urban Guerrilla* that the New Left had its history in the "workers' movement." The New Left was essentially a bourgeois-intellectual movement, and neither it nor its off-shoots, the bourgeois rebel terrorists of Europe and America, ever had a mass following (except briefly in France in mid-1968, when there was a short-lived alliance between workers and students).

The Action of the Black September in Munich (which appeared after the arrest of the "hard core" of the RAF) praises the terrorists who killed the eleven Israeli athletes at the Olympic Games in 1972. The authors say that the action was "antifascist" because it was "in memory of the 1936 Olympics." For the deaths of the Israelis, however, it blames Israel: "Israel has burned up its sportsmen as the Nazis did the Jews—incendiary material for the imperialist extermination policy." And the attitude behind that was characteristic of the RAF and all similar groups with which they came to cooperate or had already established links, both within Germany and outside of it. While they denied anti-Jewish prejudice, a virulent anti-Zionism was fiercely and frequently expressed in their publications. And whether or not a distinction between "anti-Jewish" and "anti-Zionist" is anything more than sophistry, it cannot escape notice that the "anti-Zionist" slogans of the seventies have served the propaganda purposes of the communist bloc in precisely the same way as the "peace" slogans did in the early sixties.

On October 22, 1971, Margrit Schiller was arrested. She came out of a suburban station in Hamburg at 10 P.M. As she started along the sidewalk she saw that a police patrol car was following her. .She turned into the basement garage of a shopping center and after a while came out again and walked on. But the police were trailing her again. So she hid in the garden of a prefabricated house, but came out to meet two comrades, Irmgard Möller and Gerhard Müller, late of the SPK, on the other side of the street. Again the police drove up, this time onto the sidewalk in front of her. She turned and fled into an adjoining park. The two policemen, Schmid and Lemke, got out and ran after her, leaving the ignition keys in their patrol car. Möller and Müller started running after Schiller too.

Schmid caught up with Schiller and grabbed her left arm. With her free hand she pulled a pistol from her shoulder bag. He shouted, "They're armed!" She broke away as her two comrades opened fire. Schmid fell, calling for help. Lemke was wounded in the foot. He shot back at the comrades, but missed. When he got to his fellow officer he found him unconscious. He limped to the patrol car, but it was not there. Someone had driven it off. By the time the two officers got to a hospital, Schmid was dead. Wounded by six bullets, he had bled profusely and died of his wounds. It was found that his own pistol had never left its holster. (In 1976, when Gerhard Müller gave evidence for the prosecution against leaders and members of the gang, Margrit Schiller's act of revenge was to make a statement accusing Müller of the murder of Schmid on that night.)

Police everywhere were alerted, and two plainclothesmen soon spotted one of the women they were looking for in a telephone booth at about 2:30 A.M. They waited outside the booth with their guns drawn, and when she came out they demanded to see her identity papers.

"Oh!" she exclaimed. "And I thought you wanted to fuck me!"

Her identity card gave her name as Dörte Gerlach. But in her bag was a fully loaded 9-mm caliber pistol, with the safety catch off, and a spare magazine with twelve bullets. They drove her off to the police station. As she listened to their radio she exclaimed from time to time, "Shit!" and "Shit bulls!" Later the keys of the stolen patrol car were also found in her bag. She was Margrit Schiller, twenty-three-year-old psychology student. There had been a warrant out for her arrest since the murder attempt on the two policemen named Ruf a month before.

Three days later the police raided an apartment in the neighborhood of the telephone booth. It was owned by an absent pop singer. There were signs that it had been left in a panic. It still contained foam-rubber mattresses, collapsible chairs, and the paperhanger's trestle table and dark blue curtains with peeping slits which had been found in other hideouts of the B-M gang and were clearly a part of their regular equipment.

Quite an arsenal was left behind: tons of explosive, 2,600 bullets of various calibers, and detonators with wiring. There were walkie-talkie sets, police uniforms and boots, numerous police magazines, and code sheets giving common radio-communication abbreviations. There was a book called *Church Black Book, Volume I*, and in the index thirty-two names of "progressive" pastors had been marked and annotated—by Ulrike Meinhof, according to the police, who believed that these men of the cloth were to be asked, or had been asked, for aid, probably accommodation. The gang could still find clergymen, doctors, professors, journalists, and others to help them.

. Loss of accommodation in Hamburg meant that the gang had to send vital equipment somewhere else to be stored.

In November a parcel labeled "Glass: Handle with Care," mailed in a small town north of Hamburg to the address of a potter in Berlin, broke open and bullets came dropping out. The police found six other parcels at the pottery, awaiting collection by a friend of a friend. They were found to contain fifteen hundred rounds of ammunition, two American rapid-fire guns, explosives, wigs, clothing, walkie-talkies, car license plates, false car papers, car ignition locks, medicines and anesthetizing drugs, articles of police uniforms, and various tools. There were thirty weapons in all, several silencers, and five thousand rounds of ammunition. The fingerprints of Holger Meins were found on some of them. Labels were said by experts to have been written by Baader, Ensslin, and Meinhof.

This was not the first B-M parcel to burst open in the mail. What with inadequate wrapping and misaddressing, the gang scored a number of failures with the postal service.

Many of the armaments had been bought by one Rolf Pohle, the son of a professor of law, who had failed his own law exams at Munich. He had joined the communards around Fritz Teufel in 1969 and had gone underground in 1971. He specialized in buying small arms from shops with forged papers and licenses. He was also responsible for acquiring the police uniforms found abandoned by the B-M gang, by the simple method of hiring them from theatrical costumers in Munich and Dortmund. Eventually his false papers aroused the suspicions of an arms dealer in Ulm, who informed the police, and Pohle was arrested.

Early in December Marianne Herzog was arrested. A letter from Astrid Proll, smuggled from Ossendorf prison in Cologne, was found on her.

Astrid Proll was not languishing forgotten. SPK veteran Rosemary Keser had made plans to get her out—with as much determination as Gudrun Ensslin had put into getting Baader rescued, but with less success.

It was on December 22, 1971, that the grisliest action was taken by the ex-SPK Bombers for Health, in Kaiserslautern, some thirty-five miles west of Heidelberg, when they attacked a branch of the Bavarian Mortgage and Exchange Bank and seized DM 133,987.

Twelve days before the raid, a young woman with long blond hair entered the bank and took an inordinate amount of time to fill in a lottery ticket for a charity called "Child-of-Woe Action." On the slip she gave her name as "Angelika von Zech" of (nearby) Mannheim, Herzogenriedstrasse 76. But there was no number 76 on the Herzogenriedstrasse. What there is on it is a prison, in which Alfred Mahrländer was locked up, the SPK member who had had a brush with the police in June. And on December 16 he was visited by the same young woman with long blond hair, accompanied by a man. The girl's real name was Ingeborg Barz, and the man with her, Wolfgang Grundmann. They had both recently come from Berlin to join the B-M gang.

Ten days before the robbery, an ultrasmart, new, supersnob RO 80 car rammed a truck on the autobahn (our heroes never did get very far from the autobahns) between Munich and Augsburg. The driver of the car got out and fled across the fields in a heavy snowfall. The car had been stolen in Hamburg, and the fingerprints of Holger Meins were found in it (it seems he never did wear gloves, even in the depth of winter, when there were heavy snowfalls), and false papers, and a pistol bought by Rolf Pohle. And the car and the people it pointed to came to be connected later with what happened in Kaiserslautern because the license disk was attached with a sticker from a car-accessory shop in that town; and the owner of the shop was to pick out a photo of Manfred Grashof (the B-M gang's forger, and lover of the late Petra Schelm) as a recent customer.

On December 22, at 8:05 A.M., a man casually entered a Bavarian Mortgage and Exchange Bank in Kaiserslautern and placed a tape recorder on a desk provided for the convenience of customers. He switched it on, and very loud pop music burst out. A moment later three people stormed in clad in anoraks and disguised in knitted balaclava helmets of various colors, with narrow eye slits.

"Raid, hands up! To the wall! Turn around!" They shouted several times. Then, "Silence!" they demanded.

One of them stayed near the door armed with a submachine gun. A second, also with a submachine gun, jumped onto the counter and threatened the employees. The third, armed with a pistol, jumped over the banking counter in front of the steel-shuttered cashier's cubicle and started filling a briefcase.

The fourth, who had put on the music, pulled out a pistol, jumped over the counter, and emptied the main cash box into his case. Then he forced the cashier to unlock an empty cashier's cubicle, and finally to start opening the safe.

Meanwhile, a red Volkswagen minibus was waiting in the no-parking zone in front of the bank, with two wheels on the sidewalk.

Opposite the Bavarian Mortgage and Exchange Bank stood the District Savings Bank. Their money carrier stepped out onto the street guarded by a police officer named Herbert Schoner. Schoner saw the illegally parked minibus and crossed to speak to the driver. As he went around behind the bus it was backed up suddenly. He jumped out of the way, and the minibus smashed into the pole of the no-parking sign. It went forward a bit but at once backed again, fast and hard. The policeman leaped out of the way just in time. One of the back doors of the minibus was open and swinging. Schoner took out his gun and went up to the driver's door and tried to open it. The driver shot at him through the window. With his face and neck cut all over by the flying glass and streaming with blood, Herbert Schoner staggered back. His cap flew off. A second shot hit him in the back and he fell, severely wounded. From the ground he aimed his pistol at the van, fired three shots, and then began to drag himself in great pain toward the nearest doorway—the door of the Bavarian Mortgage and Exchange Bank—for shelter. He reached it and managed to pull himself over the threshold and even further still, on his knees, right through the open inner door. But as he reached what he thought was safety, the robber who had emptied the first cashier's desk and was now sitting on the counter waiting for the safe to be opened took careful aim and shot him in the chest. Schoner collapsed and died. He was thirty-two years old, with two young children.

The robbers gave up the safe and ran from the bank. They jumped into the minibus and were driven off. The bus was later found abandoned. The police found they were unable to drive their vehicles straight out of either the Lauterberg or the Abensberg police station because the exits had been blocked, one with a Volkswagen 1300 and the other with an Alfa Romeo.

A witness claimed to have recognized one of the robbers as Klaus Jünschke, the former SPK member who had been wanted since the arrest of Dr. Huber and others on July 20, and whose picture had appeared in a Kaiserslautern paper.

Six days later, on December 28, the police found a hideout in Kaiserslautern. The usual B-M paraphernalia was found in the house: foam-rubber mattresses, blankets, the paperhanger's trestle table. They also found the fingerprints of Ingeborg Barz, Wolfgang Grundmann, and Klaus Jünschke. And the lottery ticket for the "Child of Woe." Finally a cryptic note, "Fat One 1330," written, the police claimed, in the handwriting of Ulrike Meinhof.

The Cologne edition of the Springer paper *Bild* came out with headlines on December 23, 1971: "BAADER-MEINHOF MURDERS ON."

This provoked a protest from Heinrich Böll, published in *Der Spiegel* on January 10, 1972. "Where the police are still investigating, making assumptions, conjecturing, *Bild* is already further on: *Bild* knows.

. . . I cannot suppose that the police or the minister responsible can be happy about helpers like *Bild.*" Every suspect, he said, had the right to be called only a suspect. It was true that evidence against the B-M gang had not been collected by the police when *Bild* came out with its accusation, and Böll's point against trial by press would of course have been valid even if they had. But his article, entitled "Does Ulrike Meinhof Want Mercy or a Free Conduct?" provoked a storm of controversy. Letters and articles poured in to the newspapers to support, agree with, criticize, or contradict Böll's and each other's point of view. (But the fair-minded intellectuals who protested now, where were they when the students and the APO took justice into their own hands and launched into trial by lynch mob of Axel Springer? Did the unleashing of violence against his organization because it published views which the students, the APO, Leftists, and liberals did not like—and with good reason did not like—accord with those same ideas of freedom, tolerance, and the rule of law?)

On February 4, 1972, Chancellor Willy Brandt addressed the nation on television to answer the question "Are we doing enough to contain the violence in our country?" He said that violence cannot be tolerated. "The free democracy which we have built from the ruins of dictatorship and war must not be understood as a weak state." He warned individuals and groups bent on using violence that "we are obliged and determined to stop their activities by legal means." He further warned that "no support may be given to those who do or preach violence." He asked for understanding and consideration for the police so that they could he helped in their frequently onerous duties. He went on: "I want to say very clearly: blind hitting out is no politics which corresponds to our constitution." He pointed out that "only factual information, cool evaluation, and appropriate action" help against violence and hatred, not "sterile excitement" (which could have been interpreted as an oblique rebuke to the Springer press). He also said (and it could be taken as an answer to Heinrich Böll's insistence that Ulrike Meinhof should be allowed mercy or a free conduct): "Nobody who has chosen to live outside the law should be prevented from returning to legality and reason."

Before Böll's article had actually been published, evidence had been gathered by the police which implicated people of B-M affiliation in the brutal and cold-blooded Kaiserslautern crime.

There was a mysterious and possibly even more brutal and gruesome aftermath.

Three weeks after the raid, Ingeborg Barz rented an apartment in the

Rhine town of Ludwigshafen near Kaiserslautern, under the name of
Petra Roetzel. In this apartment another bank raid on another branch of
the Bavarian Mortgage and Exchange Bank was planned. (It took place
on February 21, 1972, and the proceeds amounted to DM 285,000.)

Ingeborg Barz had been a secretary with the Telefunken Company
in Berlin before she and her boyfriend, Wolfgang Grundmann, had
gone south and joined up with the urban guerrillas. They had both been
members of the "Black Help" organization in Berlin, one of a number of
mushrooming revolutionary organizations, this one of anarchist leanings.

In early January she had rented an apartment in Hamburg under the
name "Angelika von Hassow, Photographer." The apartment was to be
the scene of a shootout between the police and two B-M gang members,
Grashof and Grundmann, some weeks later.

From Ludwigshafen on February 21, the day of the Bavarian
Mortgage and Exchange Bank raid, Ingeborg Barz telephoned to her
mother in Berlin. Like Beate Sturm, she had been with the gang just
about three months and had had enough. She told her mother she
wanted to come home. Her mother at once offered to send her some
money so that she could travel to Berlin. But Ingeborg said no, it
couldn't be done that quickly. But she added that she "really" had "nothing to do with them here."

Soon afterward she disappeared. According to police information,
apparently from Gerhard Müller, whom they captured four months after
her disappearance, she had decided to leave the group "because of its violent acts," and as a result was summoned by telephone to a meeting with
Ulrike Meinhof. She agreed and was driven to a remote spot near Ludwigshafen on the old Rhine riverbed where there were some gravel pits.
There she was met, so it is said, not by Meinhof but by Baader, who, so
the story goes, shot her dead. She had been "sentenced to death" for
wishing to leave the group. (Ruhland, in an interview with *Der Spiegel*,
made a statement to the effect that the "agreed policy" of the group was
to "liquidate" anyone who tried to desert them.). For a long time, however, no body was found. Then in July 1973 a party of people out for a
walk in a wood southeast of Munich, near the autobahn, came upon a
corpse virtually reduced to a skeleton. A police identification expert pronounced it the remains of Ingeborg Barz. But the dead woman had not
been shot. She had died from a severe blow on the head which had probably caused a brain hemorrhage. And she lay very far from the old Rhine
bed. So the police were not convinced that the body was that of Ingeborg
Barz. Gudrun Ensslin vehemently denied that Baader killed her, and insisted that they could prove it if ever they had to.

Ingeborg Barz's boyfriend Grundmann was in Hamburg early in March 1972, putting up in an attic apartment with Manfred Grashof.

At 10:45 P.M. on the night of March 2, the two men came together to the top of the building and opened their front door.

There were five policemen waiting in the apartment. One of them, the officer in charge, faced them with drawn pistol.

"Hands up—police!" he demanded.

Grundmann shouted "Stop! Don't shoot! We're unarmed!"

But at that moment Grashof fired from behind Grundmann's back. It was, the police discovered, a dumdum bullet, which exploded in the officer's body. The other policemen fired and hit Grashof. The officer in charge was terribly wounded but stayed alive for three weeks, unconscious all the time, and then died in the hospital. Earlier that night he had been wearing a bulletproof vest. But he was not a young man and was rather stout, and the vest had been chafing him uncomfortably, so he had taken it off just before Grundmann and Grashof turned up.

On that same day, an urban guerrilla was shot dead by the police during an exchange of fire in Augsburg. He was Thomas Weissbecker— and with him was Carmen Roll, ex-SPK, whose bomb had just missed the President's train in Heidelberg a year earlier. She was arrested this time.

But Holger Meins, who had left his fingerprints all over the place, and Jan-Carl Raspe, and Baader, Ensslin, Meinhof—the old crowd—had disappeared, although the police had been breathing down their necks in Hamburg.

Meinhof stayed mostly in the north. She and Baader had never found it easy to agree, and their quarrels finally split them apart. Meinhof hoped to win a number of the gang over to her side (including Gerhard Müller, who testified to this division) and eventually to form her own breakaway organization.

Baader and his adherents moved south, and there was one person who was sure he had seen both Meins and Raspe.

Toward the end of 1971 a young man came to a door in Frankfurt's West End on which there was a small sign: DIERK HOFF—*Studio Metall*.

When he was admitted to the "metal studio" the caller gave his name as "Erwin." This was a workshop for special requirements, was it not? Well, he wanted Herr Hoff to do some special metalwork for him.

Dierk Hoff was a sculptor extraordinary. The Frankfurt judge at the trial for arson of Ensslin, Baader, Proll, and Söhnlein, who did not believe that people of artistic inclinations could assemble a bomb, might have been surprised to learn, when Hoff was called as a witness to Stammheim in late January 1976, that it was this artist who had made bombs to the order of the B-M gang—and very ingenious bombs some of them were, and potentially very damaging too, even if a few turned out to be duds.

At the time that "Erwin" called on him, Hoff, in his mid-thirties, was smithing tubular chairs, steel doors, copper fireplace hoods, and brass bed frames, having trained as a fitter and turner (as well as a potter). His metal studio was very near Frankfurt's bombed-out Opera House and the Club Voltaire, where he was often to be seen.

The graffiti on the walls of the men's room had by now, in the winter of 72–73, begun to concern themselves with the RAF:

If the Jews didn't exist one would have to invent them. If the RAF didn't exist one would have to . . .

An arrow from "RAF" indicated three words written by a different hand: *Royal Air Force.*

And some old pacifist who had not moved with the times, and therefore perhaps eschewed the Club Voltaire, had written in English in a nearby telephone booth: "Killing for Peace is like Fucking for Chastity, man!"

Dierk Ferdinand Hoff, whether he did or did not think much about the RAF or peace or chastity, was well known in leftist circles in Frankfurt. As soon as he was arrested in July 1975, his father, a famous surgeon and erstwhile director of Frankfurt's University Hospital, obtained the services of a lawyer who had no connections whatsoever with the Left.

But Hoff's own friends were many of them decidedly of the trendy Left, the radical chic, the Schili. And to them he seemed an eccentric. When long hair was fashionable, he wore his very, very short. He was known as "Stubblehead." But he did smoke hash and frequent places like the Club Voltaire, so he wasn't a square.

He liked tinkering and inventing things, like a submachine gun driven by liquid carbon dioxide which shot peas.

What "Erwin" wanted him to do was not made clear at first. "Something for a film project," the caller said.

He went away and returned a few weeks later with a friend called "Lester." They smoked some hash together, and then Hoff was given an order to make some "props" for a film about revolution in South America. First a dozen or so upper (explosive) parts for hand grenades. He was to do the metalwork only, not put in the explosive: then other things, such as hand-grenade covers and car ignition-key removers. He was also asked to convert a shotgun into a machine gun, but he didn't think it would work. Besides (he told the court at Stammheim) he was beginning to get suspicious. Not surprisingly. When he expressed reluctance to do what "Erwin" wanted, a Colt .45 was waved under his nose and he was told that he didn't stand a chance of backing out of the deal now. And he didn't think "Erwin" was fooling because he knew he was Holger Meins and that the quiet "Lester" was Jan-Carl Raspe. And Baader, still blond, turned up one day to inspect the workshop. He sauntered through the place, hardly said a word, nodded a couple of times, and stalked out.

So Hoff did what they asked of him. He altered the grip of a submachine gun for Raspe—"personalized" it for him. He made the metal outer covers for about twelve bombs, out of 7½-inch sections of steel pipe 6½ inches in diameter. Each of these had a bottom plate welded onto it and a top plate with a narrower pipe sticking out into which a screwing thread was cut. Hoff screwed hexagonal pipe-terminating nuts into them, but someone else apparently replaced them with octagonal nuts. (He said in court that he had not supplied these and did not know they were on the market at all.) The detonators were fitted into these nuts and connected on a circuit to a 50-volt dry-cell battery via an egg timer, giving a maximum delay of sixty minutes.

The bomb cases were fetched away in early May by someone called "Harry" (Gerhard Müller).

Hoff was further ordered to weld handles onto army water bottles, also used as bombs. His customers objected to his taking the time he did. He must, they said, drop his exacting standards of workmanship; it wasn't for him to worry about whether the water-bottle bombs were the right sort of dummies for the alleged film.

Hoff's imagination, however, produced some extraordinary devices for his impatient clients. Like the "baby bomb." This was in the form of a half sphere which a woman would put under her dress so that she looked pregnant. It was held in place by shoulder straps. But what if a woman walked into a public building pregnant and walked out again a few minutes later delivered? Hoff solved the problem neatly. Under the "baby bomb" was a flat balloon. All the lady bomber had to do, when she had taken off her bomb and put it where she desired the explosion to take place, was to blow up the balloon before she walked out again.

Hoff bought the webbing for the shoulder straps at the Schneider department store, that decadent palace of consumption terror punished by Baader and Ensslin in 1968. His girl friend sewed them for him. She was an American who worked at the U.S. Army headquarters in the I. G. Farben building, a few minutes' walk from the metal studio.

When all his work for the RAF was completed, the two of them packed up, put their things into his camping car, a converted Volkswagen minibus presented to Hoff by his father, and on May 11, 1972, set out for St. Tropez. Just as they were driving off from the house in the Oberlindau, they heard an explosion quite nearby. It was a bomb going off in the U.S. Army headquarters.

That day three bombs went off within minutes of each other in the I. G. Farben building. They were homemade "pipe bombs" of the kind made by Hoff and, according to Gerhard Müller's later testimony in court, placed in a telephone booth by Baader, Meins, Raspe, and Gudrun Ensslin, who had wrapped them in pretty gift-wrapping paper and added flowers. They destroyed the entrance and the officers' mess of the Fifth U.S. Army Corps. Thirteen people were injured and one was killed, Lieutenant-Colonel Paul Abel Bloomquist, thirty-nine, of Salt Lake City. He was hit as he walked to his car by a fragment of an exploded bomb and bled to death. He was a highly decorated veteran of the Vietnam War who had served two tours in Vietnam and was survived by a widow and two children. As a direct result of the bombings, U.S. commanders everywhere in Europe were instructed to take precautionary measures, including checking license plates and identification cards of all persons entering bases.

Damage to the building was estimated at DM 1,000,000 ($310,000).

Three days later the German Press Agency received a letter from the "Commando Petra Schelm" in which responsibility for the Frankfurt bombing "on the day when the bomb blockade against North Vietnam was started by the U.S. imperialists" was claimed for the RAF.

On the morning of May 12, two people carrying suitcases were able to walk into the police headquarters in Augsburg, climb to the third and fourth floors, find empty offices, place three pipe bombs fitted with batteries and timers on top of filing cabinets, and walk out again. The two, according to Müller, were Irmgard Möller and one Angela Luther. A little after 12:15 P.M. explosions wounded five policemen and brought down the ceiling of the fourth floor.

On that same day a Ford car in the parking lot of the State Criminal Investigation Office in Munich blew up. Sixty cars were destroyed, and most of the windows of the office and of many neighboring shops were blown out. A few days later, responsibility for both bombings was claimed for the RAF by a "Commando Thomas Weissbecker"—Baader, Meins, and Ensslin, so Müller was to disclose.

On May 15 at 12:40 P.M. in Karlsruhe, Frau Gerta Buddenberg got into her red Volkswagen in the Klosestrasse, turned on the ignition—and her car blew up. Miraculously she did not die, but she was severely crippled by injuries to both her legs. Her husband was Federal Judge Wolfgang Buddenberg, who had signed most of the warrants for the arrest of B-M members and the search of B-M hideouts. The avengers were (said Müller) Baader, Raspe, and Meins.

On May 19, two bombs exploded, at 3:41 A.M. and 3:46 A.M., in the lavatories of the Springer building in Hamburg. Three other bombs were found unexploded (one because it had not been set to go off, another because the hand of the egg timer was bent and failed to make the necessary contact). They had been put in different places: one on the directors' floor, one in a cleaning closet, and one near the rotary presses. Seventeen workers were wounded, two of them severely.

The idea of this target (so Müller plausibly asserted) was Ulrike Meinhof's: an old grudge paid off at last, and this time in no uncertain manner. She was apparently aided by Siegfried Hausner, Klaus Jünschke, and Ilse Stachowiak. Meinhof's characteristic inefficiency and Hausner's persistent bungling prevented more casualties and perhaps some fatalities too.

On May 24 somebody—a woman, some say, but they did not notice whether she was pregnant—drove a car into the Campbell Barracks of the U.S. Army in Europe's Supreme Headquarters in Heidelberg. It was not hard to get through the checkpoint at the gates because cars with the USA EUR green number plates were waved through. The number plates were easy to steal. U.S. Army cars were parked all over the city every day and every evening.

The driver of the car with the stolen green number plates parked it in a space next to a new bright-yellow Ford Capri in the large parking area in front of the creeper-covered clubhouse in the late afternoon. On the balcony there were bright umbrellas and tables and chairs where people would soon gather to eat and drink. Between the parked cars and along the grass verges came and went the soldiers, their wives, their children, secretaries, gardeners, waiters, cooks, visitors.

At about 6 P.M. Clyde Bonner, a twenty-nine-year-old captain in the U.S. Army (a married man with two young sons, one nearly seven, the other two), invited his friend Ronald Woodward (of Lansing, Michigan, who had a five-year-old daughter and two sons aged three and two), to come with him to the parking lot to see his brand-new bright yellow Ford Capri.

At two minutes past six a car beside Clyde Bonner and Ronald Woodward exploded and blew the two men into fragments. Debris was hurled hundreds of feet. The door of the club and part of its walls blew in, falling on twenty-three-year-old Charles Peck, a specialist fireman. "Lie flat and don't move!" some voices ordered when the noise had stopped. People in the grounds, on balconies, at windows, and in all the buildings round about fell flat and lay still. After about fifteen seconds there was a second explosion as a car blew up which had been parked outside a smaller building nearby, which housed the computer.

They were fifty- to sixty-pound bombs, and they had been planted where, of course, they could have killed children, visitors, "guest workers," anyone within reach. But from the point of view of the terrorists who left them there—who, it must be remembered, were the self-appointed knights errant to the peoples of Southeast Asia—the murdered men were exactly the sort they wanted to punish: all of them U.S. soldiers, and one, Captain Bonner, decorated in Vietnam with two Purple Hearts and a Bronze Star.

Two days after the Heidelberg bombings, the "Red Army Faction, Commando Fifteenth July" announced that it had laid the two bombs as a protest against the "genocide" in Vietnam. (July 15 was the date on which Petra Schelm had been shot by the police.) The commando, Müller testified, consisted of Angela Luther, Irmgard Möller, Baader, and Meins.

The Ministry of the Interior offered a reward of DM 100,000 for information about the bombings. The Ministry of Defense and the Federal Chancellery were put under special police protection. And Springer offices everywhere introduced stringent entry controls.

And now there was a change of opinion among the ranks of the Left. The RAF was doing nothing but harm to its cause; the whole country would swing to the right as a result of these outrages. The terrorists began to find it harder to get help. They were afraid now, and some were extremely anxious. The fun was over.

On the other hand, they were feared. The police and the public expected more bombs and more killings, especially on June 2.

Somebody who is still anonymous—officially described as "an old-age pensioner," which might mean a young housewife or anybody else—telephoned the Frankfurt police headquarters and asked to be connected to the Baader-Meinhof commission—so the caller had already made his own deductions from noticing that "many gas cylinders" (such as were used for the making of bombs less ingenious but as effective as Hoff's varieties) were being taken to a certain apartment-house garage within his observation, and that "the young people" brought the gas cylinders in "ostentatiously big cars."

The police went to the garage in the north of Frankfurt near the cemetery, got into it, and found bombs and other armaments and equipment of terror. They substituted harmless substances for the explosives, and installed a bug.

On the last day of May, in the evening, a party of policemen disguised as gardeners drove a truck into the short street and unloaded large packs of peat and turf, as if the sidewalks were to be grassed. Actually, they were to be used as protective sandbags.

At 5:50 A.M. on June 1 a lilac Porsche drew up in front of the apartment house. Three men got out. One remained standing beside the Porsche; the other two went around the corner into the yard and approached the double doors of the second garage.

The man left standing in the street became aware (how could he not?) that several hundred men—police supported by officers of the special B-M security branch—were creeping and tiptoeing and surveying all over the place, around, behind, in, on top of, near, opposite, above, and beyond the apartment building. He suspected that what was afoot might be dangerous to himself, and he began to run. But out of cars and from behind cars and from behind bushes, walls, and trees, policemen leaped out after him. He fired several shots, but they tackled him and brought him down. Another young man had appeared in the street, and when the running and the firing started, he ran too. The police fell on him and made their second arrest. But he turned out to be a male nurse on his way to his early morning shift who had nothing whatever to do with the B-M gang.

The other arrested man, however, the one who had got out of the Porsche and had fired at his pursuers, was Jan-Carl Raspe, the "gentle" member of the B-M gang.

Later they found (Hoff's) hand grenades in the Porsche.

The other two had gone into the garage, second in the row from the street, and shut the doors behind them.

The police drilled into an air vent next to the garage. It took them about twenty minutes. Then they threw tear-gas bombs into the vent. But the vents also served the apartments; so although the tear-gas bombs got into the garage, most of the gas itself was sucked off into the apartments, and the effort to "smoke" them out did not succeed.

But what the police failed to damage them with, the two men in the garage inflicted on themselves. They opened a door for a few seconds and flung out some of the tear-gas bombs, and the gas floated back into the garage.

To prevent them from coming out and perhaps slipping past the few hundred men waiting for them—and the few more hundred spectators gathering at the edges of the cordon—the police pushed an Audi car right up in front of the doors.

Half an hour later—at about 7 A.M.—they dragged the Audi away again with a rope. At once the besieged men opened the door. Clouds of gas came out. The police hurled more gas bombs at the entrance. The men tried to bat them away with long planks.

"Come out one at a time," a policeman bawled through a bullhorn. "Nothing will happen to you. Think of your life. You're still young."

Some twenty minutes later an armored car turned into the yard and drove slowly up to the garage door to push it shut. But the overhang of the building above the garages stopped it from getting in close enough. It moved on toward the end of the yard, and just behind it the garage door opened again and the two men tried to escape in its cover. But they saw at once that the police were blocking them in every direction. They started shooting, but hit only a tire of the armored car. They crouched down and retreated into the garage.

By this time a television camera had been set up. A Frankfurt TV director, editor of a program called *Tagesschau* (Day's Show), had been on his way to see a world record attempt by a Diesel car on the Opel test grounds at about 6 A.M. when he saw a police troop carrier with flashing light, then a patrol car. He reached a colleague with his car telephone, and soon cameras were filming the live show.

So not just hundreds, or even thousands, but millions could watch the event. Eight times that day it was shown in the news programs, the dramatic capture of the two men who (everybody knew by then) were Holger Meins and Andreas Baader.

Baader stood near the slightly open door, and within sight of some of the police drew on a cigarette, changed the magazine of his pistol, and took aim through the door. But a policeman watching from the balcony of a flat opposite fired at him first. The bullet missed but ricocheted and hit Baader in the right thigh. Baader howled and staggered back further into the garage.

About eight minutes later Holger Meins appeared in the doorway and surrendered. He held up his hands, and the police shouted at him to strip. He took off all his clothes except his underpants. His left thigh had been grazed by a bullet. He advanced to meet the two policemen who were approaching to seize him. They twisted his arms behind his back. Meins also howled.

"Who is still in the garage?" the police asked him.

"Andreas," he said.

Another ten minutes or a little more went by, and again the armored car drove up to the garage doors. This time creeping up in its cover there were several officers wearing bulletproof vests and gas masks. They got to the door and they could see, inside the garage, an Iso Rivolta, a luxury car made in Italy costing, new, all of DM 55,400 to most people, but nothing to Andreas Baader; and Baader, blond, unshaven, wearing dark glasses, bleeding. Four of them went in and grabbed him by the arms and legs, carried him out struggling, and laid him on a stretcher.

"You swine!" he yelled, squirming on the stretcher while he was restrained and cameras popped and turned.

The officer in charge asked, "Have you searched him for weapons?"

Before any of them could answer, a pistol dropped over the edge of the stretcher and fell to the ground. All those who saw it burst out laughing—except Baader, of course. They took him to a waiting mobile hospital car, and he was given a blood transfusion.

So once again Gudrun Ensslin was without her Baby. One week after his arrest she wandered into a boutique in Hamburg, quite near the offices of *Konkret*, where Ulrike Meinhof used to work. It was about 12:50 P.M. on Wednesday, June 8. She flung her leather jacket carelessly down on a sofa and began to look over the shop's consumption-terror choice. She looked "slightly unkempt," a saleslady noticed. (Observant salesladies were a bane to Gudrun Ensslin in her life of crime/politics/knight-errantry.) She was wearing brown tight-fitting cord trousers, red-brown lace-up boots, a sweater, large horn-rimmed dark glasses, and a brown shoulder bag.

She took some time to pick out three sweaters, one red and two white, costing DM 59 each. She tried them on in a dressing room, leaving her leather jacket on the sofa.

One of the saleswomen picked up the jacket to move it off the seat of the sofa. It felt very heavy. It must have had something in its pocket weighing it down and no doubt threatening the shape of the coat. A hand professionally considerate of clothes, or guided by curiosity, felt in the pocket. What it found there was a pistol. She told the manager, who quietly telephoned the police.

"We have a customer with a pistol in her jacket," she informed them.

They told her to delay the customer in the shop. They would be there as soon as possible.

The customer came out of the dressing room wearing one of the sweaters with the price tag hanging out.

"Can I help you?" a saleswoman asked, and tried to interest her in more sweaters, in anything, in everything.

But Gudrun Ensslin had made up her mind. She had chosen what she wanted. She got ready to go. The saleswoman picked up her coat to hand it to her and she grabbed it gruffly. When she stood at the cash desk ready to go with two fifty-mark notes in her hand, the saleswoman asked her apologetically if she'd mind waiting just a moment longer, as she had first to attend to another customer. Gudrun Ensslin replied, patiently enough, that in that case she might as well look at some stockings.

At 1:26 P.M. the police arrived. One shouted, "Where is the person?"

Gudrun Ensslin jumped, but a second officer was standing behind her, and he grabbed hold of her. She struggled and they both fell.

"What do you want of me?" she shouted.

"I'm sure you know very well," the officer said.

She was flown in a helicopter to Essen. She would answer no questions. A second gun, a Belgian high-precision 9-mm, was found in her bag, and newspaper clippings on the arrest and wounding of Baader, an identity card in the name of Margaretha Reins, Hamburg, Hochallee 21—a smart address—a front-door key which did not belong to that address, and DM 830 in cash. She asked to have the money returned to her so that she could buy cigarettes and other such consumer luxuries in jail, but this was refused.

A search of Hochallee 21 led to the arrest of five members of a commune, all of whom were later released.

Again one week went by. Then a teacher named Fritz Rodewald, who lived in the Langenhagen district on the edge of Hanover, just off and in sight of the autobahn, was telephoned at half past twelve at night by a strange woman who mentioned a mutual acquaintance and asked if he could put up two people who would arrive later that day. He agreed without knowing more about his would-be guests. When they arrived he found out who they were. Then he could not decide what he ought to do. He was a Leftist, and he believed that the terrorist gangs were harming the Left. Also he had a position of responsibility as Federal President of the Young Teachers Division of the Trade Union of Education and Science. So he went and asked the advice of friends. When they agreed that he must inform the police, he did so. He telephoned them, told them who was in his apartment, and stayed away from it. (Later he donated the reward money to the defense fund for the terrorists, which was appealed for by the Red Help organization.)

At 6:50 P.M. one of Rodewald's guests, Gerhard Müller, came out of the apartment (which was above a bank) to use the public telephone on the sidewalk, right next to a police phone box. The police were already there. They approached Müller. He pulled his pistol from his belt, but they arrested him, and though he struggled and hit and kicked he was overpowered. There was no warrant out for him and no "Wanted" notice. The police did not know of his B-M association until his arrest.

He was the son (born 1948) of an unqualified teacher who had fled the DDR and reached West Berlin in 1956, then moved with his family—four children in all—to the Black Forest south of Stuttgart, where he took a job in a Mercedes-Benz factory. Gerhard was clever at school, firsts all the way. He went on to a *Gymnasium* and continued to collect honors. But his father took him out of school, because he thought he was growing arrogant, and apprenticed him as a telecommunications engineer. After two years or so Gerhard gave it up, and moved about Europe taking various jobs. For a while he worked as an assistant electrician in the American Army Headquarters at Heidelberg. In 1968 he was convicted of an offense under the homosexuality laws, and later of a minor theft. He had an affair with a girl student, and when it broke up in 1970 he got drunk and attempted suicide, more than once. His doctor advised him to seek help with the SPK.

When Müller was taken away, the police went into the building and up to the door of the Rodewald apartment on the second floor. A woman opened it. She was not armed.

They seized her. She demanded that they let her go, she called them "you pigs" and "shit-bulls," but she couldn't escape. They took her off. She was shocked and terrified, and she began to cry.

For hours she struggled hysterically, until her face was quite swollen, so that in the photographs taken for the records and the newspapers she looked quite plump, but in fact she weighed only ninety pounds.

(Her way of life had surely become difficult lately. It was hard to find accommodation or help of any sort. The gang had spent twice as much money as they had stolen. She must have known that she could not go on for much longer.)

Eventually she was persuaded to drink some tea. But she insisted that "a bull should drink the first half." A bull did. Then she took the cup and stirred about in it with her finger looking for "poison powder." The police said they were not sure of her identity. She was not recognizable, they said. In her bag she had a *Stern* article which showed an X-ray picture of Ulrike Meinhof's head with clamps inserted after her brain operation. So they took their captive to a hospital and had her head X-rayed, and clamps were revealed in the same places. She also had the scar of a cesarian operation. Then they were sure, they said, that they had got Ulrike Meinhof.

In her luggage were found three 9-mm pistols, one submachine gun, two hand grenades, one ten-pound bomb. Some of the weapons had been bought by Rolf Pohle.

A letter written in prison by Gudrun Ensslin was also found on her. It was mostly so cryptic as to be semi-coded. It gave an account of her arrest, in which she said she "had shit in her brain." It started with the name "Liesel," probably Meinhof's new cover name. Some sentences were indecipherable, such as: "Ha Ga . . . barrel," and "El . . . garden and job later." Some were suggestive rather than interpretable: "3i. pond . . . assemble in fourteen days (not earlier via brother at daughter. KER—shop [Gabi knows] via brother contact to little fatty new.)" ("Little fatty new" was Wilfried Böse, who was to help hijack a French airbus to Entebbe in 1976 and to die there when Israelis rescued the hostages; but this was only known after his death, when "little fatty new" was at last identified by Gerhard Müller.)

Some of Ensslin's sentences were clear enough: "Shut your trap and stay in the hole." Another, "Mac is on holiday, four weeks, to be spent there," was a possible reference to the apartment of a man named Iain MacLeod.

On June 25, police entered an apartment owned by MacLeod in Stuttgart. It was six thirty on a Sunday morning. They let themselves in with a key and were about to enter the bedroom when the door was opened suddenly and MacLeod stood there naked. He shrieked—as who would not—when he saw a civilian pointing a submachine gun at him, and he slammed the door. The police officer fired two shots through it. One of them hit MacLeod in the back and killed him.

English newspapers claimed that the German police had made a tragic mistake. They grumbled, not without justification this time, about German police methods, German police brutality.

In Germany it was rumored that MacLeod was a British secret-service agent. He had been in the army, later had worked for the British consulate, and then stayed on in Germany as an agent selling Squeezie mop buckets, an English product out of which he had apparently made a fortune.

The German police believed he was transacting arms deals for the B-M gang in Switzerland. An arms emissary from Switzerland had, they maintained, met Baader in another Stuttgart apartment which they said was also rented by MacLeod. And at yet another apartment of his they found a "typical" B-M radio with its button fixed to the police radio frequency and notes on police radios in the handwriting of Ulrike Meinhof.

The lease of this last apartment was in MacLeod's name, and his name was still beside the bell, but his mother in Edinburgh and the German lawyer she hired maintained that he had in fact given it up when he moved into the apartment where he was eventually killed. The key found on Gundrun Ensslin when she was arrested fitted its door.

PART FIVE
THE DEVIL TO PAY

15

The Game Is Up, the Games Go On

In 1972 the world was looking toward Germany, where the fierce national rivalries of the Olympic Games were to be on display in Munich come September. From the printing presses early in the year, the posters advertising the games began to roll out. And an unofficial one appeared too, of Fritz Teufel looking thoughtful in a track suit. If he was not posted up on the public billboards, he did appear on the walls of communes, student rooms, leftist bookshops, the offices of certain lawyers, journalists, and professors, and on the pin boards of the model nurseries of the Schili alongside Che.

So Fritz Teufel was back, or expected back. His name was in the air again like a little figure on a recorder. And in the very month when Baader, Meins, Raspe, Ensslin, and Meinhof were arrested and put into jail, Fritz Teufel was let out. He had been sentenced to two years' imprisonment for attempted arson endangering human life; he had tried to bomb out the Berlin Lawyers' Ball. He worked as a tailor and was well-behaved during his stretch in Landsberg prison, west of Munich, the very same in which Hitler had served eight months and a bit for high treason in great comfort and luxury, dictating *Mein Kampf*. Two days' remission were granted to Teufel for the special purpose of voting in the Munich local elections. But for all his civic conscientiousness, he was soon to drop out of sight again, underground.

The proper posters for the Olympic Games went up in the proper places. The Games began. On September 5 and 6, some Arab gunmen of "Black September," the military arm of Yasser Arafat's PLO, killed eleven of the Israeli athletes. And the Games went on.

By this time—mid-1972—other terrorist groups were making their names and gaining reputation in the Federal Republic. Members of one would drift to another. No single group had a fixed membership over any length of time. The most notorious (after the B-M) was the "Movement Second June," named after the date on which Benno Ohnesorg was shot in 1967, several of whose members were associated with the B-M gang and/or the defunct SPK.

The group included a few more proletarian members than the RAF, which might have incorporated the Movement Second June if it had agreed to expel certain members whom the RAF accused of "lacking ideological foundation," by which the RAF ideologists, Ulrike Meinhof and Gudrun Ensslin, most probably meant that those Second June members regarded themselves as anarchists and not communists. All the terrorist groups of West Germany had popularly been called "anarchist" because the forces of law and order were their declared enemies, but the RAF repudiated the description.

One of the Second June members who was both proletarian and lacking ideological foundation was Michael Baumann, cover name "Alex," also known as "Bommi." He came onto the terrorist scene through his liking for rock music and so through the clubs of Berlin. After a while he wanted to get out again, but was afraid that his comrades would kill him if he did. His picture joined the "Wanted" gallery, and eventually he persuaded the organization to help him leave the country. They gave him the means to get to Vienna, where he stayed a while in a commune, then sent him an air ticket to India, via Rome, so that he could find a guru. One of his tasks on behalf of the Second June was to journey to Italy to visit Giangiacomo Feltrinelli in his publishing office. As he saw him walk in, Feltrinelli would take out his checkbook, open it, and say "How much?" The amounts were never small. But this was not extortion. Feltrinelli gave money to the terrorists because he wanted to.

Members of the Second June who made headlines were Angela Luther, Thomas Weissbecker, and Georg von Rauch.

Angela Luther (who, according to Gerhard Müller, helped with the laying of Baader-Meinhof bombs in Munich and Heidelberg) is the daughter of a very rich Hamburg lawyer. Her family's mansion stands in Blankenese, one block from Ferdinands Höh, where Röhl's house stands. She was briefly married to a film director, Hark Bohm, and became a teacher. In Berlin she lived with Heinrich von Rauch, brother of Georg and son of a professor of history at Kiel University. In June 1972 a smart apartment she rented under another name burst into flames. It was found by firemen to be a bomb factory, and things belonging to the once-again fugitive Ilse Stachowiak were found in it.

Thomas Weissbecker, another professor's son, was shot by the police in Augsburg, and along with Petra Schelm and Georg von Rauch has become a martyr to the RAF, Movement Second June, Black Help, Red Help, Black Cross, and so on.

Georg von Rauch was shot by the police in a moment of panic and confusion after a gun battle, when he had already been disarmed and taken into custody.

On May 3 the newspapers reported that three student leaders had been executed in Turkey. The Second June decided to put a bomb into the Turkish consulate in Berlin. But a more reliably lethal kind was wanted. Ulrich Schmücker, who had joined the group in March 1972, had become friendly with an Arab, a member of the PFLP, who had instructed him in the making and laying of bombs. On May 5 Schmücker took one to the consulate. The bomb was placed in the back entrance, set to go off in fifty minutes. Another comrade telephoned a warning to the police, and the whole group settled down in front of their television set. Not a word about a bomb in the Turkish embassy did they hear. They telephoned the police again to lodge a complaint that they took no notice of telephoned bomb warnings. The police explained that although the spokesman had given the location in detail, the bomb had not been found. It never was.

Undiscouraged, the group planned to make another bomb and blow up the Turkish embassy in Bonn. They tried to steal a Mercedes for the job, but though they had been instructed by the B-M on how to do it, and though they followed the instructions carefully, they did not succeed. So they hired a Fiat, and four of them, including Schmücker, set off for a small town near Bonn, to make the bomb in the bedroom of a friend. They decided to stop over at Bad Neuenahr, Ulrich Schmücker's home town, to spend the night with his parents. But they got there at 4:30 A.M. and were too considerate to wake them up, so they pulled up in a parking lot and slept in the car. At five thirty on May 7 they were wakened by the police, who found explosives and timing devices in the trunk. They were arrested.

When Ulrich Schmücker came out of jail, he was accused by the rest of the group of having ratted on them to the police. They "tried" him and Schmücker's most intimate friend, Götz Tilgener, was ordered to kill him since, they said, he had "helped the pigs." They told Tilgener that he had to do it to prove that he was still a comrade, and also because he was the only one trained in "control shooting." The plan was that he should shoot Schmücker in a forest area near Bonn next to the police sports ground. The corpse was to be covered with plaster of Paris and stood up in the parking lot at Bad Neuenahr, where the four would-be bombers had been arrested, on the second anniversary of that occasion.

Götz Tilgener believed that "the game had gone too far." The comrades slammed the gun on the table and said, "Get on with it." Tilgener refused.

But on the night of June 4–5 somebody else "got on with it." Ulrich Schmücker, at the age of twenty-two, was shot dead in the Grunewald, the wild park on the western edge of Dahlem in Berlin where once Kommune I had tried out its confectionery bombs against the trees. The Movement Second June said they had "liquidated an instrument of the class enemy." They dismissed all criticism of their action with scorn on the ground that "morality is bourgeois."

Götz Tilgener was found dead some time later, of drugs and alcohol, after receiving threatening letters. Murder was suspected, but no evidence of it has been found.

A murder was actually claimed by the Movement Second June. It was apparently an act of vengeance for Holger Meins, who had been arrested with Baader and who died in a hunger strike on November 9, 1974. On the Sunday after his death, the president of the West German Supreme Court, Günter von Drenkmann, who had never tried any of the Baader-Meinhof group, was celebrating his sixty-fourth birthday. A party of young men came calling at his home, carrying bunches of flowers. The Judge himself answered the doorbell. The young men, bearing guns as well as flowers, fired at close range, and von Drenkmann was shot dead.

Then came a kidnapping, of the chairman of the West Berlin CDU (Christian Democrats), Peter Lorenz, a lawyer aged fifty-two.

A letter set out the kidnappers' demands: first, that those sentences should be annulled which had been passed on Berlin demonstrators who had protested against the death of Holger Meins; then, that six jailed terrorists should be released, including Horst Mahler. The letter further insisted that they had to be "accompanied to their destination by a figure of public life. This person is to be the parson and retired mayor Heinrich Albertz" (the very same who had defended the police action on June 2, 1967, on the occasion of the Shah's visit, and who had subsequently experienced a conversion.) The letter was to be published as an advertisement (paid for by the CDU) in about a dozen newspapers, many of them Springer-owned. And while Lorenz was imprisoned there was to be a "cease-fire" on the part of the police—no house searches, no arrests, no "Wanted" posters, and so on. "If all demands are precisely met the safety of the prisoner Lorenz is guaranteed. Otherwise a consequence as in the case of Chief Justice G. von Drenkmann is unavoidable."

Horst Mahler refused to go and stayed in his cell, but the other five were flown from West Berlin to Frankfurt, where a Boeing 707 was ready with full tanks and a crew of four, as demanded, to fly them to Aden with DM 20,000 each.

Peter Lorenz spent six days in a cellar, 10 feet by 7 feet, which had been made to resemble a prison cell, with bars, bunk, washbowl, table, and chair. He was watched at all times. His captors were armed and wore masks, coveralls, and gloves. He never saw the face of any of them.

On March 2 the Berlin elections were held, and the CDU polled over 1 percent more of the votes than the SPD (Social Democrats). In the 1971 elections, the CDU's share of the votes had been 12 percent below the SPD. Even radicals now accused the terrorists of being countereffective.

Lorenz was released at midnight on Tuesday, March 4, in the Volkspark.

In the summer of 1975, citizens of West Berlin found bus and U-bahn rail tickets dropping into their letterboxes like gifts from heaven, uncharged-for. On Wednesday, July 30, and on Thursday, July 31, two banks were raided, both branches of the Sparkasse der Stadt Berlin West. On the thirtieth, two men and two women, all masked, held everybody up with guns, and while DM 100,000 was being lifted, the five customers in the bank were offered a little refreshment, chocolate-covered cakes called *Negerküsse* ("Negro kisses"). The robbers left the box behind them for the employees to help themselves. The next day another box was left in the Breitestrasse bank (loot about DM 100,000 again, and four hundred bank-guaranteed Eurochecks) with a leaflet beside it which read:

THE REFLATION PROGRAM OF THE MOVEMENT SECOND JUNE
Where everybody says that the RUBLE has to roll again so that the CHIMNEYS can smoke again, our movement too, within its limitations—after all we're all sitting in the same SHITTY-BOAT—wants to make its contribution. Let's hope it all goes well, therefore; OUT WITH THE COAL [money]!!
Revolutionary Negerküsse from the urban guerrillas of the Movement Second June attached.

Free tickets and little cakes as gifts from bank robbers—these happenings carried the signature of Fritz Teufel (the magic flautist blowing again), so perhaps he, in person or spirit, had something to do with them. Again the question of what he had or had not done was being asked.

The search for the kidnappers of Lorenz and the raiders of banks who brought cakes with them went on. In the course of it the police became interested in a four-story house on the Birkbuschstrasse, in the working-class Steglitz district of West Berlin. It adjoined a bombsite not yet restored. Number 48 had once been a delicatessen. Its sign was still up when the police arrived to look it over because a garbage collector had noticed large quantities of pamphlets and some vehicle licenses in the bins. The pamphlets were found to be issues from the underground, and the licenses forged. The building was not entirely uninhabited. There was a neatly kept flower bed behind it. And somebody was apparently using the second floor as a printshop. A search of it was found rewarding.

It seemed that Ralf Reinders and his girl friend Inge Viett had been there, and they were soon found there again. Ralf Reinders was the supposed leader of the Lorenz abduction group and was later identified as one of the party who had called on Judge von Drenkmann. He and Inge Viett and one Juliane Plambeck were arrested on September 9, 1975. And one thing leading to another, a few days later two others, a man and a woman, were arrested. The woman was named Gabriele Rollnick, and the man, Fritz Teufel. He had DM 31,000 on him, supposedly from the recent bank raids.

He no longer had the company of his old comrades Langhans and Kunzelmann. Langhans was swinging among the chic. And Dieter Kunzelmann had withdrawn his orgasm from public concern and had settled down, short-haired, to family life.

Fritz Teufel went to jail again, to await trial for complicity in the Lorenz kidnapping and the bank robberies by bandits who left gifts of little cakes. It seems that he belonged to the Movement Second June, as did Ralf Reinders. A very long-haired prophet of the Romantic ideal of self-fulfillment through the maiming, blinding, killing, and tormenting of others, Reinders had once planned to bomb the Jewish House in Berlin (a new building incorporating the portico of the old Jewish House destroyed by the Nazis). Why? "In order to get rid of this thing about Jews that we've all had to have since the Nazi time."

16

Crocodile Tears

Three years were to pass before the hard-core members of the Baader-Meinhof terrorist gang were brought to trial for murder, attempted murder, robbery, and forming a criminal association. During that time the courthouse was built in which the four were to be tried.

Ulrike Meinhof was put into Ossendorf prison in Cologne. She was alone in her cell, was allowed visits from near relatives, books, and a radio. She received and sent letters. Her sister visited her at first, and brought Regine and Bettina. No doubt their mother was glad that they were alive and safe. She wrote them, saying that she thought about them often; imploring them to visit her again; asking them to make things for her, to send paintings and drawings. And through them she sent messages to others: to their grandmother to write family news to her; to their father that she believed he wanted to be thought highly of by "communism" again. She advised them where to go for their vacations—to Kampen, or their Aunt Wienke, which, she added, would be very pleasing to Renate.

But when Renate wrote to Ulrike, the letter was returned unopened. Renate Riemeck understood. Much as she would have liked to visit Ulrike, she did not apply to do so. And she was afraid that if she was asked to give evidence at her trial it would be deeply disturbing to Ulrike, and she hoped it would not happen. "I don't know what Ulrike would do—I'd bring back to her all her real life," she said.

During the initial period of imprisonment, the solitary confinement was also relieved by the lawyers and priests whom all the prisoners saw, and representatives of Amnesty International.

Then the lawyers launched a campaign to protest against what they called the "isolation torture" of the B-M and other terrorist prisoners. They complained loudly that several of the prisoners were being kept in isolation to a degree that amounted to torture, that they were being subjected to "sense deprivation" in silent cells painted entirely white, that their lights were being kept on all night, that doctors of their own choice were not allowed to examine them to give an independent opinion as to the effects of such treatment on their mental and physical condition.

Astrid Proll, also in a single cell in Ossendorf, was examined by an "independent" doctor (that is, one not chosen by the court; the demand for him implying of course that any officially appointed doctor was likely to be untrustworthy), who said that she had suffered both mental and physical damage. She was sent to a clinic in the Black Forest, from which she escaped, and she has not, at the time of this writing, been rearrested.

The Ministry of Justice said in answer to these accusations that all prison cells were painted white; that the light was left on if the authorities had reason to fear that the prisoner might commit suicide, and the guard had to look in at intervals through the night. They denied isolation torture or sense deprivation. Meins and Raspe, they pointed out, were both allowed to join the other prisoners, but of their own accord did not. They did say that conditions could have been better for the B-M prisoners in the early days, but that it took them time to learn how to provide better conditions which were nonetheless secure.

Whether because of the campaign or because the ministry was learning better ways, conditions did improve. Ulrike Meinhof got the company of Gudrin Ensslin at Ossendorf. And at once she stopped the family visits—on the grounds that there was always a guard present, and she could not talk freely—and no longer wrote to her children. After a couple of years had gone by without another letter from their mother, the twins said sadly to Renate, "Mommy never writes to us any more, not even for our birthday." The guards had been kind to the children and tried to be friendly with Ulrike. But she rejected or ignored their approaches.

In September 1974 Meinhof was moved to the Moabit prison in West Berlin, where she was tried for her part in the freeing of Baader. She was sentenced to eight years' imprisonment, but until January 29, 1976, when she became officially a convicted prisoner, she lived like the others in the conditions of awaiting-trial prisoners at Stammheim. These conditions were by no means bad: the prisoners could have their lights on as far into the night as they wished, provided they paid for it. Pay for it they did. Or they could have candles. They were allowed portable television sets—Baader and Meinhof each got themselves one. Their daily walk was extended from the usual sixty to ninety minutes. On four days a week they were allowed to spend two hours together. They could have gymnastic equipment for the asking. They could play table tennis for an hour on Saturdays and Sundays, but did not do so. Ulrike Meinhof and Gudrun Ensslin could meet other women prisoners if they wished, but did not. They had about two thousand books and a special cell to keep them in. Their cells looked very like modern student rooms in a modern hostel, with bright blankets; tables, chairs, and shelves; records and record players. Some B-M prisoners got magazines sent to them free of charge, solicited from editors.

Eva Rühmkorf (Ulrike Meinhof's university and Hamburg friend) pointed out that the Stammheim four had extraordinary privileges. She could not get even one of their concessions for the boys in the juvenile prison of which she became governor. And even allowing for the difference between awaiting-trial and sentence-serving conditions, the four were unusually well off, and the other prisoners in Stammheim expressed resentment about it.

Gudrun Ensslin, when she was in Essen jail, went on a hunger strike from June 20 to July 10, 1972, in protest against an investigation into whether the lawyer, Otto Schily, smuggled letters from her to Ulrike Meinhof. She became worried about her health, her flaking skin and bleeding gums. Her own lawyer, Kurt Groenewold, was searched when he visited her. Her sister Christel came to see her and said, "We are simply sick of this Polit-Krimi" (political cops and robbers story).

Gudrun got very angry and shouted back that her true brother and sister were Thomas Weissbecker and Petra Schelm.

Christel said, "In comparison with the laborious, painstaking work of the Left, laying bombs is a simple matter."

Gudrun retorted, "You have no idea how difficult it is to lay bombs."

Ulrike Meinhof too went on a hunger strike over the Schily inquiry.

Baader, imprisoned in Düsseldorf jail, was laid up for a while with a smashed thigh bone. His mother could come and sit beside him. She reported that he was well fed and was reading *Uncle Tom's Cabin* (in German). He had cigarettes and other gifts from the Raspberry Reich, and devoured pudding with raspberry juice. He said of Gudrun Ensslin's hunger strike, "She shouldn't do it, she knows it keeps her from thinking clearly!" He was quite happy lying there with his bandage, his momma by his side, his pudding with raspberry juice and his tear-jerker book to read, so why should he go on a hunger strike? It was only when the influence of the two women, Ensslin and Meinhof, made itself felt on him again that he "continued the struggle in the only way left," threatening the callous authorities by endangering his own life.

There were a number of hunger strikes among the prisoners during the months and years that followed. The prison authorities preferred to provide fortified milk rather than force-feed. If the hunger strikers would not take it, after two days their water was withdrawn so that they would be compelled by thirst to take the milk.

The B-M gang members were imprisoned in several cities. Most of them chose lawyers they believed sympathetic to their views, largely from the Socialist Lawyers' Collectives; Christian Ströbele (who was to be excluded from the Stammheim trial) was a member of the Berlin collective which Horst Mahler had helped to found. In Frankfurt there were von Plottnitz and Riedel (who were to be Stammheim defenders), in Stuttgart Klaus Croissant (excluded) and Jörg Lang (who was to go underground), in Heidelberg Eberhard Becker (underground) and his wife Marieluise Becker (Stammheim defender), and in the Hamburg collective most notably Kurt Groenewold (excluded), who is the son of a property millionaire. It was he who had acted for Ulrike Meinhof in her divorce proceedings. He and Klaus Croissant led the campaign of protest against the conditions of imprisonment. And one of the weapons of the campaign was the hunger strike.

Some of the prisoners did not want to protest in this way. But when one of them, a helper of the gang named Kay-Werner Allnach, wanted to start eating again because he became very ill, his lawyer advised that he continue. Kurt Groenewold was this lawyer. But Allnach ignored his defender's advice and gave up his fast. So Groenewold stayed away from him. Allnach had to undergo an operation and was so ill that his recovery was in doubt. When the doctors thought there was no hope for him, Groenewold came to see him again. But Allnach did recover—and engaged another lawyer.

Another prisoner wanted to abandon her hunger strike, too, but was afraid of reprisals if the gang should get to know that she had so "betrayed" them. So the prison staff protected her by continuing to include her name on the daily report of those still refusing to eat. The defending lawyers did not find out that she was eating again. Nor did the other members of the gang. And the lawyers continued to try to rouse public opinion to indignation on behalf of the sufferings of the prisoners: the conditions of imprisonment, the so-called "isolation torture," "sense deprivation," and so on.

In addition to the charge that they acted as clients' couriers, some of the lawyers were investigated for other alleged offenses: Dr. Klaus Croissant and Dr. Jörg Lang, for instance, for "supporting a criminal association." Early in May 1972, the police had found out that Klaus Croissant was looking for an apartment for Baader and Ensslin. A woman police employee met Dr. Croissant in a restaurant and told him that they knew. ("She must be credited with a service to the revolution," he said.) But the police had been watching her, and when they confronted her with an accusation, she admitted everything that had passed between her and the lawyer. The next day Croissant's office was searched. And in August 1972 Jörg Lang (the son of a parson) was arrested. The occupant of a Tübingen apartment—which the police had found to be a complete forgery-printing workshop—alleged that Lang had employed him to forge papers for the B-M gang. Lang was released but went underground.

The Hamburg Lawyers' Collective, which included Kurt Groenewold, had powers of attorney from several of the arrested terrorists, but dated, if at all, from some day in the period during which they were still being sought by the police for serious crimes.

The solidarity of some of the lawyers with their terrorist clients was openly and unequivocally advertised in their offices, with posters displaying slogans about isolation torture, hunger strikes, the Red Help defense fund—along with the poster of that poor, clever, crippled Polish Jewess who failed to bring off her Spartacist revolution and was brutally murdered in 1919, the ubiquitous Rosa Luxemburg, purportedly criticizing the socialists now in power: "The SPD does not want socialism."

On February 9, 1973, seven lawyers, including Eberhard and Marieluise Becker, Croissant, and Groenewold, staged a four-day hunger strike themselves. Dressed in the lawyers' robes which they tried to avoid wearing in court, they carried banners in front of the Federal High Court (Bundesgerichtshof) in Karlsruhe, reading:

> BGH [Federal High Court]—brown Nazi gangsterband.
> BGH is reprehensive. One it's shit, and two expensive.
> Stop the murder of legally deprived groups.

In the testimony which Gerhard Müller gave at the eventual trial of Baader, Meinhof, Ensslin, and Raspe, he said of Klaus Croissant that he was a "traveling salesman in matters Ensslin"; that it was Croissant who brought Siegfried Hausner into the group and frightened him off again (but not for long) when Ensslin thought him unreliable and decided he should be liquidated. Of Ströbele and von Plottnitz he said that they "kept the B-M members in line with leadership policy"; of Haag that he passed on Baader's instructions to the other prisoners; of Groenewold, Croissant, Ströbele, von Plottnitz, and the Beckers that they did, as the State had alleged, carry messages between prisoners; and of Ströbele,

Haag, Croissant, both the Beckers, Lang, von Plottnitz, and some other lawyers that "they were to rebuild the RAF." In addition, he said, Ströbele had the task of getting formulas for explosives from Jordan.

Several arrested B-M members were brought to trial. Karl-Heinz Ruhland was sentenced on March 15, 1972, to four and a half years—six months more than the prosecution asked for. Horst Mahler was tried in Berlin on March 1, 1971, for his part in the freeing of Baader, along with Irene Goergens and Ingrid Schubert. Otto Schily defended Mahler. There was one surprise witness: Mahler's old friend and accomplice who had helped with his dig-for-arms project in the cemetery, Peter Urbach, stepped up before the judges to give evidence against him. He had been spying for the police all along. Dieter Kunzelmann appeared as a witness to discredit Urbach. When asked what his profession was, he answered, "Victim of class justice." On the night before the judgment APO groups threw Molotov cocktails into a Berlin police station. Shop windows on the Ku-Damm were smashed. The police made a hundred arrests. Several Marxist groups insistently dissociated themselves from the demonstrations. The verdict was: Horst Mahler, not guilty; Ingrid Schubert, six years for attempted murder and freeing a prisoner; Irene Goergens, four years of youth detention for the same offenses. But the State appealed (as the Napoleonic Code permits), and on appeal the "not guilty" verdict on Mahler was reversed and the sentences on the two women upheld.

In the autumn of 1972 Mahler was tried for bank robbery along with Asdonk, Bäcker, Berberich, Goergens, Grusdat, and Schubert. The defending lawyers included Ströbele, von Plottnitz, Riedel, and Eberhard Becker. All the accused were found guilty. Mahler was sentenced to fourteen years.

In November 1974, when Ulrike Meinhof was sentenced for her part in the freeing of Baader to eight years' imprisonment, Mahler was tried with her for forming a criminal association. He was sentenced to twelve years (to run concurrently with the earlier sentence of fourteen years). And Hans-Jürgen Bäcker, also tried with them, was found not guilty. There was tumult in the court when the sentences were announced. Meinhof addressed the Berlin court. Her speech, claiming exclusively political motivation for the freeing of Baader, was involved, ponderous, obscure.

By this time, however, Mahler had had a change of heart. He declared that the RAF's way was, after all, the wrong way. It had no support from the masses, and without it armed insurrection was impossible. He joined the Maoist DKP (Communist Party of Germany—the new, legal one.) So the RAF expelled him. Monika Berberich declared him, in September 1974, to be a dirty bourgeois chauvinist, a cynic, a mandarin now openly in league with the state protection officers. She said that he was and had always been arrogant, and had promoted a personality cult for his own person even way back in 1967; and furthermore he was politically irrelevant and ridiculous.

Meinhof and Mahler both appealed, but their sentences were upheld. The state prosecution did not appeal, so Bäcker's acquittal stood.

In September 1974, the terrorist prisoners drew up a list of demands:

Free self-organization

Payment on a par with those outside doing the same job, shop stewards, and the right to strike

Free choice of doctors

Self-administration through elections

Unrestricted visiting, without guards

Freedom of assembly without guards, and sexual contacts outside working hours

Mixed (sexes) institutions

The authorities did not grant these reforms.

Complaints from the prisoners pelted the judges. Marianne Herzog complained, "During my exercise time an officer had a gun in his pocket. On July 3 he even had his hand in his pocket"—this to Federal Judge Wolfgang Buddenberg, whose wife had been terribly injured by a bomb in her car which exploded when she turned on the ignition.

Complaints of "isolation torture" and the hindering of the defense continued. They were taken by Croissant and others of the lawyers to the European Commission of Human Rights. The plea was that as "political prisoners" their clients were cut off from contacts both within and outside the prison, and that it was being made difficult, if not impossible, for their defending lawyers to protect the rights to which they were entitled by the West German Constitution or the Convention of Human Rights.

The commission pointed out that the lawyers of the complainants were obviously not being prevented from lodging these complaints in detail. Further, the commission found, they did not prove their allegations, although repeated applications for extensions of time were granted to them. And their failure was never attributed to any attempt on the part of the accused government to prevent them from replying. So the government's version of the events not having been contradicted with evidence, the commission accepted it as factual.

The commission rejected the claim of the complainants that they were "political prisoners," since they were imprisoned not for their political convictions but because they were suspected of severe common crimes. The conclusion was that "the commission declares the complaint to be impermissible."

So the prisoners were not being tortured. That was surely good news. But there was no expression of relief from those who had cried out against their alleged sufferings—and supported their hunger strikes from which some suffered severely and one, Holger Meins, eventually died, his death thereafter being consistently blamed on the judiciary and the state authorities.

Still the lawyers continued to insist that their clients were being subjected to inhumane treatment and fascist-type political persecution. Why then, if they were so sure, had they not been able to prove it?

Klaus Croissant gave an answer: "It took us another four months," he said, "to find the right medical experts who would have given evidence in our favor."

A little longer yet, and they might have tracked down a qualified doctor.

Soon after the death of Holger Meins in the hunger strike, and as part of the campaign against the prisoners' sufferings, Dr. Klaus Croissant contrived to get Jean-Paul Sartre to visit Baader in Stammheim. The famous novelist and existentialist philosopher was met at the airport by Croissant.

The philosopher and the man of action had an hour and fifty minutes in each other's company, in a cell, but not in direct communication with each other, as they had no language in common. Daniel Cohn-Bendit had been nominated as their ideal interpreter, but he had not been allowed. (He later interpreted Sartre and the German press to each other.) They had a dependable interpreter, however, from the United Nations. Croissant was not present.

At the press conference afterward it was Croissant who spoke first. He said it was the eighty-fourth day of the hunger strike, and menacing for the prisoners. Was the government just letting people die? It was fascism that was going on. Nonviolent resistance had not been understood. The prisoners would go on with their hunger strike, and it was the apparatus of the government that was to blame. The stage of hunger was now such that coma would shortly set in, crisis point was possible any day, and the end of their lives. In intensive care, in a twilight state, they lay there tied to their beds. This was the kind of violent treatment to which they were subjected. The authorities were not answering the demands of the prisoners (for free self-organization, the right to strike, etc.). The intensive care was only a pretense of care. The five wanted to start a thirst strike. Isolation must stop. The lawyers were demanding a change in the conditions of imprisonment.

Sartre then spoke. He said he had just come from seeing Baader, to whom his first question was about Baader's political convictions, and whether there was any relationship of the group with the mass of the people. Baader answered that his small group had counted on building up a relationship with the working masses, and that a long education was necessary to make clear to the masses that there are actions necessary to construct a new organization of the masses. And this organization was just temporary and provisional, because the German proletariat was broken by fascism. The group searched for relations with the Third World, the Arabs, and with Latin America, to make a political organization against the influence of the United States. This part of the fight was not certain; it was just at present confined to the Federal Republic as a fight of the masses against capitalism—a revolution for labor against the bourgeoisie. Baader defined the masses as the farmers and the proletariat. He said this fight would end in a civil war. And it was different in France or Italy because in those countries there was no fascism. As there was no fascism in France and Italy, there were other possibilities for the fight there. So this sort of fight was especially for the Federal Republic.

Sartre described Baader as very thin and light, having lost thirty-five to forty-five pounds, so he had lines on his face and around his eyes. His face was drawn, and you could see he was hungry.

Sartre had asked him, "Why are you on a hunger strike?"

Baader had replied, "To protest against the intolerable conditions in solidarity with the other members of the RAF."

Sartre then told the reporters, in answer to questions, that Baader lived in a white cell, and there was no noise at all, just three times a day you heard the footsteps of the warder who came with the food. The light was on for twenty-four hours, and this was intolerable. Had Sartre witnessed these conditions for himself? No. Did Baader say that these were his own conditions? No, Baader himself had his light off at 11 P.M., but he said the others had it on for twenty-four hours.

Did Sartre think that this was like Nazi prison conditions?

No, this was not reminiscent of the Nazi treatment of prisoners in Sartre's view, but it was a form of psychological torture to have no life around you, no sound, no footsteps. Other people are necessary to the psyche, and noise is useful, and to be able to look out of windows and see people passing by. The warder approached, knocked, retreated, and then there was silence again. This sort of thing could also cause nervous troubles and troubles of the circulation. There were three effects. One, it destroyed them psychologically so that they were unable to defend themselves. Two, it drove them mad. Three, they died.

The European Commission of Human Rights, he went on to say, was against any form of torture.

In Baader's case, furthermore, the lawyers were hindered from talking to him.

Then Sartre explained why he had made the visit. Many people saw Baader just as a criminal, but he, Sartre, had visited him because he had sympathy with the Left, even if he was not at one with this section of the Left. He enlarged on this. The unity of the masses, he said, cannot be achieved by the advent of the B-M group. He understood the Latin-American and Algerian struggles, where people started to fight to free themselves before they even had weapons. He was not at one with Baader, but he was sympathetic to the terrorists in the Algerian war. "We can say this about the politics of Baader: that the proletarians cannot follow him. And," he said, "it is not the principles of Baader which are wrong, but his deeds." [What principles could those be?]

A journalist asked: Can violence be excused?

SARTRE: In 1943 every bomb against the Nazis was legitimate because mankind had to be freed from the Nazis.

In answer to a question on prison conditions he said, "Simple cells, yes, but the same conditions for all prisoners and they should not be separated from the other prisoners." [Sartre had not been told that the other prisoners resented the privileges the terrorists were getting.]

JOURNALIST: How do you know there was isolation? They have been offered exercise with the other prisoners.

Before Sartre could answer, one of the lawyers said, "It's an old story, it's well known, we've been pointing it out for years, Baader in one corner, Raspe in another, and eight cells around them without anybody, creating an acoustical vacuum. Ulrike Meinhof had been in such an acoustical vacuum for eight months [the radio and the visitors excepted]."

Croissant asked the assembled skeptics of the press, "Do you want more people dying?"

Someone asked Sartre where he had got his information from. He had got it, he said, from a long article in *Temps Moderne* and documents he had received. One such document was, for instance, a demand by the lawyers that the solitary walks in the hospital yard should be stopped.

QUESTION: Why did you visit Baader in particular?

SARTRE: The group is called the Baader-Meinhof group, and Baader is the chief.

QUESTION: Did Baader talk well in his discussion?

SARTRE: He was weak, he had his head in his hands to hold it up, he had difficulty concentrating.

A month earlier, Baader "would have been a better partner in the discussion," the philosopher misconjectured.

QUESTION: Was the murder of Judge von Drenkmann right, and is murder a tolerable form of political struggle?

SARTRE: No, I do not think that that murder was right.

The lawyers spoke again. They complained that the state was trying to prevent the accused from having any lawyers to defend them. They said that the accusation that the lawyers were supporting violence had not been concretely proved, nor that they had smuggled material to or from the prisoners. They said that the accused wanted a political trial.

Sartre then suggested that Heinrich Böll should found a committee to find out what was true. (Böll did form a group to support committees formed to support the prisoners.)

QUESTION: Does a democracy need such methods [as the RAF use]?

SARTRE: This group endangered the Left. It is bad for the Left. A distinction must be made between the Left and the RAF.

QUESTION: Would a visit like this have been possible in France?

SARTRE: Probably not.

QUESTION: Whose idea was it? And why now, when Baader is at crisis point?

SARTRE: Now is the right time. I came to help—three months ago it would not have been possible. The initiative was that of Croissant. The reason for the hunger strike was the conditions of imprisonment.

QUESTION: Did you ask about the murder of Drenkmann?

SARTRE: There was no time. And we could not talk freely because a policeman was there and a warder.

QUESTION: Why not see Meinhof?

SARTRE: Because it is called Baader-Meinhof, not Meinhof-Baader.

In the *Stuttgarter Zeitung* the next day, a commentator wrote, "Philosophy, someone once said, is reason in a dinner jacket. But if what French philosopher Jean-Paul Sartre had to offer journalists after his visit to Andreas Baader in Stuttgart yesterday has anything to do with philosophy at all, one would have to say it was unreason in its old tweeds."

Early in 1975 the hunger strike was called off, gymnastic equipment was put to use, health and strength were assiduously built up by the prisoners, and the authorities wondered what kind of rescue bid was imminently expected. Helicopter? Sewers? Or was someone about to be kidnapped and held to ransom?

It was past mid-April when Baader issued the following cell circular, mostly in small letters.

> to g/u. [Gudrun/Ulrike, probably.]
> i no longer bothered about it: i had n radio + have the sequence + analyzed the reporting. that will still have to be done in the newspapers in the next few days: sequence of decisions, Fundamental decisions (important!) n diagram of the times they need be able decide: to become grand Crisis staff (state ministers, presidents, minister of interior, minister of justice, buback [Buback, Chief Federal Public Prosecutor]) air flight times etc. hanna [Hanna-Elise Krabbe] is to do it. that is very important + must go quickly. i will pass on the stuff from wednesday.

Nine terrorists imprisoned in Hamburg burned papers and got their belongings together. One joked to a guard, "I'm going out today."

On April 21 there was a flurry of visits by lawyers.

Then on Thursday, April 24, 1975, at 11:30 A.M. two young men came into the commissionaire's lodge of the German embassy in Stockholm, said that they had lost a passport, and were given a yellow visitor's card and told to go to the consular department on the first floor. The inner door with an automatic lock was opened for them, and they walked into the building. Two others appeared and said they wanted to see someone about student matters, and the commissionaire told them to go to the Goethe Institute. They argued aggressively, insisting they should see someone in authority and that the commissionaire was not someone they would take orders or advice from. While they were warming up their quarrel a young man and woman wearing black armbands asked to be directed to the department concerned with inheritance matters. The door was opened for them and they passed through, while the two students continued to complain. The social affairs attaché came out, and before the door could shut behind him, the young woman with the armband turned back and caught it, reaching out a hand to the students, who nipped into the building, and they all started up the stairs. A police guard rushed after them, but when one of the students turned on him with a submachine gun, he ran back to the commissionnaire's office shouting, "Alarm! They're armed!"

The four went on up the stairs and met a woman who was brave enough to argue with them when they began to give her orders. They pushed her back into a corner, and when another embassy employee appeared and remonstrated with them they ordered him at gunpoint to lie down on the floor. On this-floor, the invaders, obviously having inside information, found the key which would admit them to the higher floors.

Then the alarm went off.

The terrorists, six of them together, now rushed on up the building, firing as they went, deliberately driving people out of the building. Three took the back stairs, three the elevator to the third upper floor, where a civil servant in one of the offices heaved a large safe against his door with a strength he had not imagined he had. Soon the expected terrorists came along, banged on the door, and shouted, using their standard form of address, "Open up, you pigs!" When nobody obeyed them they started firing at the door, but were nonplussed when their bullets ricocheted off the safe's back.

The economics attaché tried to get out by coolly putting on his hat and coat and walking out of his room toward the stairs, apparently oblivious of the commotion, pulling on his gloves. But he was stopped at the head of the stairs. The invaders gathered hostages into the library, then drove them with others into the ambassador's office. The ambassador's wife came in from their living quarters and saw her husband at the window of his office, waving her back.

There were twelve hostages held at gunpoint: the ambassador; the economics, military, cultural, and press attachés; a couple of assistant attachés; the office manager of the embassy; a messenger; and three secretaries. The terrorists looked into closets—where they found the messenger—but missed another secretary who was hiding in Room 306.

All the hostages were made to lie down on the floor in a circle, their heads in the middle. Their legs were tied, they were ordered to put their hands on their heads, then they were searched for personal papers. When they found that the messenger was a messenger they said to him:

"Well, you are more one of us, aren't you?"

But the messenger was no terrorist. And later it was known that they were not messengers. They were former patients of the Neurological-Psychiatric Clinic of Heidelberg, former members of Dr. Huber's SPK. The crazy brigade.

The ambassador told them who he was and asked them to keep him as hostage and let the others go. But the six ignored him.

Police were swarming over the building. One of the raiders went to Room 306 (where the undiscovered secretary was still in the closet) and telephoned to those below.

"This is the Commando Holger Meins calling. Listen to me. If the police do not clear the building the military attaché will be shot."

Another took one of the secretaries to a room with a typewriter and dictated to her:

To the Governments of the Federal Republic of Germany and the Kingdom of Sweden.
On April 24, 1975, we have occupied . . .

The secretary was nervous. The Collected Socialist Patient looked over her shoulder to check her typing and saw that she had given all the nouns an initial capital letter, as is customary and correct in German. Furiously he tore the paper from the machine and ordered her to type everything in small letters. A would-be designer of a whole perfect world, naturally he had aesthetic sensibilities which could suffer over trifles.

She started again:

to the governments of the federal republic of germany and the kingdom of sweden!
on april 24, 1975, 11:05 o'clock, we have occupied the embassy of the federal republic of germany in stockholm and have taken prisoner the ambassador dieter stocker, military attaché andreas von mirbach, economics attaché heinz hillegart, and cultural attaché anno elfgen to free 26 political prisoners.
these are: gudrun ensslin, andreas baader, ulrike meinhof . . .

The secretary had not adjusted the tabulator to list the names vertically. Again the small-letterist tore out the sheet and ordered her to start again, this time remembering to tabulate the names into a nice column.

The twenty-six names, headed by the Stammheim four, included the nine in Hamburg.

The demand was that within six hours the twenty-six prisoners were to be assembled at Frankfurt airport, each with twenty thousand *dollars* this time, and there was to be a Boeing 707 ready to take them to a country yet to be named. Any delay, and one German official would be shot. All would be shot if the embassy was stormed. And if the terrorists were attacked they would explode fifteen kilograms of TNT in the embassy.

By this time the police had cleared the lower floors. They set up ladders to clear the second upper floor, but the terrorists fired on them from the windows. Again there was a phone call. The police must get out of the building, or the military attaché would be shot in fifteen minutes.

The police ignored the threat.

So two terrorists marched Baron von Mirbach to the railing at the top of the main staircase near the elevator, and Mirbach called out, imploring the police to withdraw.

"We wouldn't think of it!" the officer in charge shouted back.

Mirbach saw the consul looking up from the second floor, and he pleaded with him to persuade the police to go. "I'll be shot if the police haven't cleared out of the building by two o'clock."

At two minutes to two a terrorist phoned down again to give a final warning. Everyone in the building could hear Mirbach screaming for help.

Meanwhile the endless demand was still being typed. The small-letter dictator was fetched out of the room by a comrade, and a few moments later Mirbach was shot. They fired at him five times. They hit him three times, in the head, chest, and leg. Two terrorists carried him out and threw him down onto a landing of the main staircase between the second and third upper floors. For an hour he lay there bleeding. Then the humanitarians above permitted two policemen, stripped to their underpants, to carry him away. He died three hours later in the hospital.

The small-letterist returned to his dictating.

the responsibility for the shooting of the military attaché is borne by the police. they have not left the building in spite of an extended ultimatum.

The remaining hostages were still in the ambassador's room, guarded by the woman terrorist, Hanna-Elise Krabbe, erstwhile Collected Socialist Patient, who sat with her legs crossed, wearing a flower-embroidered jeans suit, in fashion just then, with the "hip" accessory of the submachine gun trained on her captives.

One of the men served water to the prisoners, scooped from plastic wastebaskets which they had thoughtfully filled earlier in case water supplies were cut off. He also permitted visits to the lavatories under guard. Everyone waited for the reaction to the ultimatum, finished at last and sent downstairs with a relieved secretary at 2 P.M. They fully expected the authorities to be as compliant as they had been over the Lorenz affair. The time limit was 9 P.M.

It was getting very close when the Swedish Minister of Justice, Lennart Geijar, who had installed himself on the ground floor and was in touch with Chancellor Helmut Schmidt and Swedish Prime Minister Olof Palme, telephoned up to the terrorists and told them that their ultimatum had been rejected, without any concessions of any sort.

The terrorists were dumbfounded. This was simply impossible! A

German official repeated the message. It was true. The German government was not going to meet their demands.

An all-party crisis committee had been in session in Bonn, and the decision was now irrevocably made.

The Swedish Minister of Justice offered the six a safe-conduct if they would let their hostages go. But the terrorists rejected the offer:

> our ultimatum stands. if our demands are not met we will shoot one member of the embassy staff every hour. our motto: victory or death!

At twenty past ten they fetched the sixty-four-year-old economics attaché from under Hanna-Elise Krabbe's guard into an adjoining room and stood him against the window.

"Hello! Hello!" he called. "Do you hear me?"

Then three shots were fired.

The old man shouted out once more, unintelligibly, and fell forward over the windowledge, where he was left half hanging out.

At a quarter past eleven three secretaries were released with a typed message repeating the demands and threatening more shootings.

The Swedish Minister decided to attack with gas. But before an attempt of the kind could be made, at about ten to twelve there was a terrific explosion on the third upper floor. Parts of the roof were blown off and all the windows were blown out. A person was blown up: he was one of the raiders—identified later as Ulrich Wessel, a millionaire by inheritance. He was the one who had dictated the letter of threat and demand, in which he proved himself an anticapitalist of sorts.

The other five were caught by the police as they crawled out of a smashed ground-floor back window. Two of them were so badly damaged that they had to be dragged by their colleagues: One was Bernd Maria Rössner, the other, Siegfried Hausner, of the SPK Working Circle Explosives. He never did learn to use them properly.

They were all sent back to Germany. Siegfried Hausner died five days later in the intensive care unit of the hospital of Stammheim prison. Forty percent of his skin was burned, and his skull was fractured.

The seven remaining hostages were wounded, but survived.

The four members of the "Holger Meins Commando" left to stand trial, Hanna-Elise Krabbe, Karl-Heinz Dellwo, Lutz Taufer, and Bernd Maria Rössner, were all members of Dr. Huber's Therapy-Through-Violence movement, or Bomb-for-Mental-Health, Kill-for-Inner-Peace.

The prisoner masses in Stammheim rioted when the news of the attempted freeing reached them. In Hamburg the nine's belongings were scattered about the cells again. Gymnastic equipment was left lying idle.

It looked, even to the Stammheim four themselves, as if the trial would start as scheduled in a month's time. Baader was in difficulties over finding counsel. Both Groenewold and Croissant were excluded from his defense, as they were suspected of distributing secret prison letters—Croissant had also been excluded in May from the Stuttgart Lawyers' Association, because he referred to the Stammheim judges, who by law were the guardians of defendants, as the "murderers" of Holger Meins—so Siegfried Haag of Heidelberg took over. But he was arrested on a charge of having transported arms for the B-M gang. He was soon released from custody, but went underground.

On May 21, 1975, the Stammheim trial began.

17
Judgments

In late April and early May 1976 there was a newspaper strike in West Germany. The four prisoners, always eager followers of their own press, lost this source of reassurance that they were still important to the outside world, which might well have had a depressing effect on their spirits. Drama was reduced if attention was withdrawn. But dramatic announcements could still reach the public through radio and television.

On Tuesday, May 4, Gudrun Ensslin claimed responsibility by the RAF for three of the lethal bombings with which they were charged. The other prisoners dissociated themselves from her confession.

Discord reigned among them. There were angry quarrels between Meinhof and Ensslin. Meinhof, from her cell on the seventh floor of the prison, which she regarded as a center of revolution, issued a stream of political tracts—which got at least as far as Ensslin, who covered them with notes of objection and correction and then passed them on to Baader, after which they returned to their author, whether or not they passed first under Raspe's upturned eyes. Meinhof, the practiced propagandist, was apparently irritated to the point of fury at this editing and censorship. She was not being respected as the oracle of her last little group. They did not prize and cherish her; they were rejecting her. Her old melancholy stayed with her and deepened. It showed in her appearance. She hacked off her hair carelessly, so that it stood in tufts all over her head. After the confession of Ensslin the hope that the verdict could be anything but "guilty" could not easily be maintained. Meinhof knew that she faced the high likelihood of a very long prison sentence. The chances of rescue, after the Stockholm fiasco, were low. So cause for hope of any kind was hard to find. If she had resented having been "ineffectual" in her days of being a journalist, ineffectuality must surely have weighed on her now, more heavily than before. If the RAF had had any effect at all on the country as a whole, it was only perhaps to have swung the electorate a little to the right. Time and the next election would tell.

In early May she was reading her ex-husband's novel *Die Genossin*. His pleasure there was to fictionalize Baader as a tool of the CIA. That aspersion was less likely to have troubled Meinhof than the irritation she would certainly feel at his relating facts about her own past. Her need to deny that personal feelings, character, or even individual opinions—for which, after all, one must accept individual responsibility—had anything whatever to do with being an urban guerrilla, apparently remained unshakable.

But though Meinhof might have wished most earnestly to shed her identity by joining the gang and changing her way of life, identities are not shed, nor is a melancholy temperament cured by living outside the law.

On the night of Saturday, May 8, she typed as usual, but it was affirmed by the authorities that she wrote nothing that could be read as any sort of statement of private feeling or personal message to any particular group or individual. Nothing like a farewell note, or an explanation of the action she then took.

At ten o'clock she stopped typing. Some time after that, in the silence of the night, she stripped her bed, which stood under the window of her cell, lifted off the mattress, picked up the bed, and set it against another wall. Then she put the mattress back on the floor against the wall under the window and stood her chair on it. She tore her towel into strips to make a rope. She made a noose at one end. The other end she was able to tie to the crossbar of her window, by standing on the chair. She put the noose around her neck and jumped.

At 7:34 A.M. on Sunday, May 9, the guard opened the door and saw the prisoner hanging facing her, the head drooping, the eyes wide open and popping, the face, neck, and arms mottled. The shins of the corpse were just grazing the edge of the chair.

The prison doctor saw her a few minutes later. He found that the body was cold, which meant she had been dead some hours.

Gudrun Ensslin, whose cell adjoined Meinhof's, was told about fifteen minutes later that she could not see Ulrike Meinhof, as she was dead.

At noon the postmortem was performed by two state-appointed specialists. Their finding was that Meinhof's death was suicide by hanging.

At 2:30 P.M. that day, Meinhof's sister, Wienke Zitzlaff, came with one of the defense lawyers and Klaus Rainer Röhl's daughter of his first marriage, Anja. They were not allowed to see the body until 5 P.M., when it was handed over to them.

On Tuesday, the eleventh, they had another specialist of their own choice examine the corpse. He agreed with the official findings.

Nevertheless, Klaus Croissant cast doubt on the veracity of the official account of the death by telling reporters that "there was no crossbar on her window." There was. Crossbars are plain to see on every cell window of the prison; and if the State were going to lie, it would surely trouble to make its lie credible. But the suggestion of foul play on the part of the State—something to hide, something vicious and extreme—was seized upon by the foreign press for its sensationalism. In some English newspapers the suggestion that Meinhof was murdered by the State, which then tried to make a clumsy cover-up, was aired as a perfectly plausible and even preferable alternative to the suicide.

On that Tuesday the trial continued. Presiding Judge Theodor Prinzing ruled that Meinhof's death was no reason for a ten-day adjournment, as applied for by the defense. That day there were student riots and demonstrations in protest against the "state murder" of Ulrike Meinhof, in several cities in Germany, most violently in Frankfurt, and also abroad, in France and Italy.

On Friday the body of Ulrike Meinhof was driven to West Berlin. On Saturday, May 15, she was buried in the Protestant Cemetery of the Church of the Holy Trinity in the Mariendorf district. Neither her foster mother nor her twin daughters were there. But four thousand others (some of them wearing masks) followed her to her grave. To them she was a martyr.

But what had her own judgment been?

There is good reason to believe that she had long dreamed of personal glory, of having a heroic role to play, since the days of her girlhood in Oldenburg; also, that she had not matured emotionally, so that adolescent extremism, "absoluteness," and dogmatic moral idealism continued with her into her middle age. Martyrdom was all that was left to her in Stammheim prison, and martyrdom was, after all, the highest form of heroism which her country in her formative years, as well as the religion by which she was deeply affected, had provided for her admiration and ambition.

Any idea that she condemned herself to capital punishment because she found, through loneliness, fear, rejection, and despair, the truth that she had brought herself to this through her own actions, and that she had been guilty of moral failure, is not likely. The sort of insight into self which makes moral absolutism impossible was not within her capability. If she could not see herself as morally superior to others, she might choose to call herself a much greater sinner; but if she had had a change of heart about terrorism, she gave no hint of it.

Apologists for her have said that she "thirsted for justice," and that it was a burning sense of injustice suffered by others that drove her to terrible punitive acts against an unjust society. But unless she is seen as some avatar of vengeance set above humanity to scourge it, it must be charged against her that she was neither just nor humane.

She was an ambitious, love-hungry child. Her education bred both a puritan and a rebel in her, the one never reconciled to the other. She was sentimentally drawn to utopian communism. Because she was unhappy and intellectually unsure, she was too easily influenced by those whose affection she needed.

But whatever the truth about her may have been, what people wish to believe she was is another kind of truth which must be reckoned with.

At her graveside, Pastor-and-Professor Gollwitzer delivered the funeral oration, as he had done for Benno Ohnesorg at the start of the story nine years earlier. He declared that Ulrike Meinhof was "the most significant woman in German politics since Rosa Luxemburg."

It would have been far more convenient for the RAF and its supporters if Meinhof had been killed (like Rosa Luxemburg), preferably under cruel circumstances, by a state which they cast in the role of the wicked so that their own activities against it could prove them to be the good. Disagreeably for them, the state was innocent of the crimes they wished it to be guilty of, and continued to provide no justification for the actions which the terrorists performed in the name of "antifascist resistance" (an expression they misapplied more mischievously than ignorantly) and which were in fact carried out for no cause but the gratification of their own egotism.

Notes

Chapter 1: Play the Devil

28   The Argument Club was founded in the early 1960s, chiefly to voice op-
     position to the atom bomb. It had a strong influence on the student move-
     ment, which it continued to support through the turbulent years, and after
     the strife died down it turned its sympathies toward the East German
     Communist Party. In the beginning it was pacifist; later it supported the
     ideology of violence. Its journal, *Das Argument* (not to be confused with
     any student journal of the same name), had a circulation of about 20,000.

32   "Horror Commune" . . . "Mao's Embassy . . . supplies bombs" . . .
     "Murder attempt": these headlines, all of April 6, 1967, were in *Der
     Abend, Bild,* and *Berliner Morgenpost* respectively—all Springer-owned
     newspapers.

Chapter 2: A Night at the Opera

37   *Der Spiegel* is Germany's equivalent and resembler of *Time* magazine.

39   "Persians . . . made the first violent attacks": It was the Vice-President of
     the Berlin Senate who made this statement to the parliamentary investigat-
     ing commission. He also said that in his view the police could have
     stopped the Jubilation Persians' aggression if they had wanted to. In fact, a
     number of Jubilation Persians were convicted of violence at the Shah
     demonstration and sentenced to two and three months' imprisonment after
     charges were brought by the "Humanist Union" (of which Hans Heinz
     Heldmann, later Baader's Stammheim lawyer and earlier an observer of
     trials in Iran, was a member).

40   "Official permission for a memorial cross to be erected there was refused":
     A procession to mark the first anniversary of Benno Ohnesorg's death
     marched on June 3, 1968. It was formed by about three hundred German
     students and unjubilant Persians. In later years his death was commemo-
     rated in more violent ways.

Chapter 3: Martyrs and Scapegoats

43   ". . . associated with the Marxist 'Frankfurt School' ": Some other members of the Frankfurt School—or the "Café Marx" as it was nicknamed at first—were notably Max Horkheimer, Walter Benjamin, Friedrich Pollock, Leo Lowenthal, and Erich Fromm. The school had to leave Germany in the 1930s when Hitler came to power, but was reestablished and flourished in the United States.

45   "Teufel explained the theft . . .": "*Mammonspossessionegalitätsapplanierungsexperiment*" (quoting the Austrian playwright Nestroy).

47f   "Left-wingers of all shades . . . members of the Argument Club, the Republican Club": The Republican Club of Berlin was formed by leftist liberals who had lost touch with the SDS and with each other and wanted to have a place to meet. When a number of them saw each other at the funeral of a friend, they discussed the matter. They wanted to make a kind of Establishment Left. So they founded the club in 1966. Horst Mahler was one of the founders. A member was once refused admittance on the grounds that he *was wearing a tie*. When the student revolt gathered momentum, the older group hoped to exert influence on the younger generation. But as the student membership increased and brought its extremism and talk of violence into the club, it slowly lost its conciliatory and moderate quality, and so disintegrated.

Chapter 4: For Theoretical Consideration Only

52   "Many of the nonaligned students . . . those who wanted to qualify": Many students who were not politically committed believed that the radicals were mainly wanting to make things easier for themselves academically, by demanding that exams be abolished and that students work in groups so that good students could carry poor ones through. The pressure to perform well, to succeed at studies and in society was, as everywhere, a source of discomfort to some. Several ex-students of the Free University and Technical University of Berlin in the sixties made the interesting comment to me that they were "not rich enough to be active radicals" even if they had wanted to be, because they had to work in the evenings and the meetings were almost always held at night, sometimes all night.

"Those who remained in the protest movement now advocated taking the initiative of attack": It may be thought that the students who were now practicing violence with idealistic fervor were not the same individuals as those who had preached pacifism in the late fifties and early sixties with fervor as strong. But many of them were the same, as in Germany it is normal for a student to take five to seven years to qualify, and to study at university level for ten years is not unusual.

56   "Burn, warehouse, burn": The phrase is in English in the original: Pamphlet 8 of Kommune I, 2/27/67. *Warenhaus* can mean "warehouse" or "store."

57   "In Marcuse's terms the students might see themselves as . . . in revolutionary uprising": Marcuse insisted in his lectures at the Free University

that he had never said that students and hippies were the new revolutionary class, but only that at some time they might be able to "play a role" with "other, much stronger objective forces."

59   "They have been called the 'fatherless generation' . . . because the fathers were preoccupied with making the 'economic miracle' ": A "fatherless generation" also because, in the view of Jürgen Habermas, they were raised by their mothers with a stress on sentiment rather than thinking—"affective" rather than "intellectual" stress. Whether or not the mothers were the chief misplacers of the stress, many of the postwar middle-class children in the prosperous societies which alone can afford these "hip" politics were educated to believe in compassion as a sentiment rather than in justice as a principle.

Yet that the students, being young, should be emotional does not seem to require special explanation. The emotion was no doubt sincere, but the causes of it may not have been the ones they flattered themselves by laying claim to. They got a regular stirring up from "the media"—pity and indignation roused on behalf of story characters, existent or not. Learning about wars, exploitations, oppressions in the same way as they learned about the fate of fictional victims, they felt strongly not because they were a generation of visionaries but because they were a generation of televisionaries. In fact, an abnormal *lack* of compassion and humanity among some of the loudest "haters of the unjust society" is amply demonstrated by the whole story of the terrorist avengers in action.

Chapter 5: Momma's Boy and the Parson's Daughter

65   ". . . to sit and drink in a local dive, where he encountered Andreas Baader": Baader would order his drinks—whiskey, usually, so he could not have been hard up—five at a time, by simply holding up a hand to the barman with his five fingers spread.

71   "They formed the Grand Coalition . . . with Kiesinger as Chancellor": Kiesinger had been a member of the Nazi Party. But then so had Karl Schiller. Just which ex-Nazi who had remained in politics after the war was forgivable by the leftist young and which was not seems to have been determined chiefly by whether he joined the Social Democrats or the Christian Democrats. Though both parties worked for the establishment of democracy, those who joined the Social Democrats, as Karl Schiller did, were regarded as making the more acceptable amends.

"To join with the party of Franz Josef Strauss!": Strauss, leader of the CSU, was Federal Defense Minister at the time of the notorious "*Spiegel* Affair." On October 26, 1962 (the time of the Cuban crisis), the Hamburg and Bonn offices of *Der Spiegel* were raided by police, and documents were impounded and editorial staff arrested. There was a warrant out for the arrest of the editor, Rudolf Augstein, and hearing of it he turned himself in the next day. The federal prosecutor's office claimed justification on grounds of strong suspicion that the paper was publishing state secrets, and referred to an article of October 10 by Conrad Ahlers, who was in Spain at the time of the raid. He was arrested there and put into a Spanish jail. He and Augstein were accused of "betrayal of country and treasonable falsification of information." Publishers, journalists, students, teachers, and others protested throughout Germany. There was a row in the Bundestag. Strauss admitted his personal involvement in the affair and had to resign from the cabinet.

73f   "Andreas Baader was swarthy as a gypsy. . . . Such was the pure simplicity of Baader": The speech quotations in this paragraph are taken from Erich Kuby's article *Faust und Kopf* in the June 5, 1975, issue of *Stern* and are reproduced here in translation by permission of the author. I found the excellent series in *Stern* on the four Stammheim defendants (dated between June 15 and May 18, 1975) most useful, especially for this chapter.

74   "Even his own grandmother said that he had no backbone": What Baader's grandmother said of him exactly was that he had no "spunk," but that was one thing which, in the literal sense, he did have.

Chapter 6: A Little Night Arson

82   ". . . and flattering posters of Rosa Luxemburg": Leader, with Karl Liebknecht, of the "Spartacist" (leftist) uprising in Germany in 1919, Rosa Luxemburg was born in Zamosc, Poland, on March 5, 1871. She was killed by army officers in Berlin on January 15, 1919.

85   "Next to her sat the three men . . .": From *Frankfurter Rundschau*, October 31, 1968.

86   "Neither on my person nor on the matter": He was mocking the expressions and legal procedure of the court, where evidence is heard first as regards the person of the accused and then the matter upon which he is charged.

Chapter 7: Fugitives

89   "But the SDS, which had invited his opinion, was on the whole against the arson": Shortly after the arson was committed and the arrests made, a spokesman for the SDS gave a declaration to the German Press Agency in which it was asserted; "The SDS is deeply perturbed that there are people in the Federal Republic who believe that they can express their opposition to the social and political state of affairs in this country with unjustifiable terror actions." It also denied that Baader had ever been a member of the SDS, as he had claimed to be when he was arrested.

91   "Gudrun's mother spoke more bitterly. . . . 'In any case, her life is destroyed' ": These words of Frau Ensslin were first reported in *Der Spiegel*. Frau Ensslin confirmed to me that she had said them, but added that they "seemed to mean something quite different when they were set down like that."

". . . which was a venerable anarchist view": The most gentle of nineteenth-century anarchists, Peter Kropotkin, wrote in his paper *Le Révolté* on December 25, 1880, "Everything is good for us which falls outside legality." But Kropotkin, like all his brother anarchists, was against all laws. Ulrike Meinhof and those who were soon to be her fellow gangsters were only against the laws of the Western democratic states and not against those, for instance, of Mao Tse-Tung's totalitarian China. In their underground publication *The Concept Urban Guerrilla* (see Chapter 14) they describe themselves as communists and deny that they are anarchists.

93   "They were to continue as the students had started them, in 'collectives' . . . .": To the surprise of the Youth Office, it was not hard to find apartments for the boys. Estate agents were actually delighted to have the apprentice groups on their books and quickly found them excellent apartments at low rents. The Youth Office knew that their boys were not the quietest, tidiest, most cooperative of neighbors, so they inquired further and found out that it was precisely because of their shortcomings that the boys were favored. Landlords who wanted to put up the rent, for instance, and could only do so if the present tenants moved out, would happily have the boys in their apartments to disturb the peace.

98   "Peter Brosch had a proper apprenticeship": Brosch later wrote a book of his own on the subject of the apprentice experiment (see Bibliography).

101   "Five times in May, Ulrike Meinhof came again, having much to talk to him about": He had sixteen visits in all in the first fortnight of that month. A prisoner tipped off the guards that there was a plan to free Baader, but no one believed him because he was thought to be a frivolous tipster by habit.

104f   "Did the pigs really believe . . . ? Build up the Red Army!": On June 5, 1970, the West Berlin anarchist paper *Agit 883* published a similar proclamation. The motto of *Agit 883* was:
         Be high! Be free!
         A little terror there must be!

Chapter 8: A Game of Sorrow and Despair

109   ". . . a Jewish professor . . .": Dr. Paul Frankl was forcibly retired by the Nazis on July 1, 1934. He moved to the United States in 1939.

118   "In 1961 she was awarded the Carl von Ossietsky medal of the DDR 'for her efforts to promote peace' ": In 1929 Carl von Ossietsky published, in his paper *Die Weltbühne*, information about the production of military aircraft in the U.S.S.R. in part fulfillment of a German-Russian agreement which went against the Versailles treaty. He was jailed for seven months, but later, in 1936, he was awarded the Nobel Peace Prize. The Nazis persecuted him. He died of concentration-camp ill-treatment in 1938. The "*Spiegel* affair" (see notes to p. 71) was likened by many commentators to the "Ossietsky affair." The Ossietsky medal was awarded to Bertrand Russell, who returned it when a letter he wrote to the East German Chancellor concerning a political prisoner was ignored. Russell once wrote to Renate Riemeck as a fellow peace crusader.

120   ". . . she would expound to the others her views on . . . religion": The tale cherished by some German and English newspapers that Ulrike Mein-

hof wanted to become a nun is wildly improbable. Renate Riemeck has denied it, and all evidence of her religious and other beliefs is against it.

120 " 'She conveyed a sense . . . of being for things that our parents and most of the world were probably against' ": Belonging to a small daring group who opposed, and were morally right to oppose, a majority and a regime which was morally wrong, was Ulrike Meinhof's earliest experience of politics. Perhaps it always felt emotionally right to her thereafter to be one of a few against many.

121 "One of her school friends recalled those days": This erstwhile school friend of Ulrike Meinhof's died shortly after she had written this letter to me. Her family have asked me not to name her. Her death was suicide by hanging, about one year before Ulrike Meinhof hanged herself in her cell at Stammheim prison.

Chapter 9: Becoming Engaged

126 ". . . he became one of the heroes of the New Left in the late sixties": Besides Wolfgang Abendroth and the Frankfurt School philosophers, there were some Trotskyite lecturers, mainly at the Free University of Berlin, who won students' hearts. Trotskyism enjoyed a revival among students in the sixties, particularly in France.

Chapter 10: A Lefter Shade of Chic

140 ". . . the 'goodwill of the leaders seemed unduly naïve . . . they did not show enough independence vis-à-vis the communist bloc' ": Alfred Grosser, *Germany in Our Time*, p. 267.

150 ". . . one of her fellow bandits": Beate Sturm (see chapter 12).

151 " 'It has been prepared systematically since Godesberg' ": The SPD adopted a new program at a special congress held at Bad Godesberg, near Bonn, on May 15, 1959, which was more liberal than left.

Chapter 11: Nothing Personal

157 "These tactics, wrote a commentator in the liberal newspaper *Die Zeit* . . .": This article of December 29, 1967, was by the well-known author and journalist Rudolf Walter Leonhardt.

Chapter 12: Going Places and Doing Things

179 "They were taught to handle pistols, particularly Firebirds . . .": The Firebird pistol is an excellent pistol with a very high velocity, and its bullet will go through car doors and thick wooden doors. It has a long and accurate range. It is a 9-mm Parabellum with a 9-bullet magazine, made in Hungary. It was originally called "Tokagypt"—from "Tokarev," the Russian army pistol, and "Egypt." The Hungarians manufactured this pistol cheaply and delivered it in large quantities to Nasser's army. As the pistol

turned out to be so good, and as no 9-mm Parabellum was being manufactured in the United States, American arms dealers contracted to buy it
from the Hungarians, and it was then named "Firebird." But the government of the United States rescinded the import licenses unexpectedly, so
the makers were left with a pile of pistols already stamped with the new
name. These were then sold illegally to Palestinian groups.

180   "His weeks with the conspirators had infected him with the fear which the
        wanted criminals among them had . . .": Reward offered for capture of
        Meinhof: DM 10,000. Total group capture rewards: DM 25,000.

190ff   "Then they ordered license plates . . . 'so there were two cars running
        with the same number, the real owners who had the real logbook, and
        ours with our forged logbook' ": If the owner of a car should wish to order
        new number plates, he can get them by sending as proof of his ownership
        the car's logbook—a document which includes such details as engine
        number, chassis number, make, year of make, registration number, etc.,
        as well as the name and address of its owner. A well-forged duplicate
        would secure the number plates for whoever orders them; and with these
        plates fitted to a car which in all other respects fits the description in the
        logbook, the driver stands a good chance of passing any police check. But
        of course for the description and numbers to match those on an official
        registration, there must already be a car in existence, duly registered,
        which is the right machine to which the data refer. Hence two similar cars
        with identical documentation, one genuine and one forged, would be out
        on the streets simultaneously.

193   "At last they found a pile of identity cards and passports . . .": Some of
        these found their way into the hands of "Carlos," who gave one of the
        passports to Wilfried Böse in Paris in June 1975 to take to an accomplice.
        The accomplice had been arrested, and when Böse came to his apartment
        he walked into the hands of the police.

203   "In all, DM 114,530 was stolen (about $35,000)": About one week after
        this bank raid, Jan-Carl Raspe bought travelers checks to the value of
        $2,350 at the Paris branch of the Amexco bank, and four days later re-
        ported them all lost at the Beirut branch of the same bank. Some four
        weeks later someone who could identify himself as Raspe, perhaps Raspe
        himself, cashed them all in London.

Chapter 14: Killing

232   "The language throughout is immoderate, emotional, at times inco-
        herent": In the publications of the RAF there is a sustained vehemence
        increased by a prodigal use of italics and exclamation marks (no fewer than
        twenty-one following one all-capital slogan) and semantically weak words
        like "shit" to express emotion only. It seems that the authors did not trust
        words to carry their own meaning, yet at the same time were afraid that
        they inevitably do.
        ". . . they maintain that most people do not know what they really want
        or what is really good for them": Adolf Hitler in *Mein Kampf* also asserted

that most people do not know what they really want or what is really good for them. And he too rejected parliamentarianism and announced his willingness to use illegal means to achieve his aims, which were, like those of the RAF, to foist his will on others against their own will and to create a totalitarian state.

240 "Ingeborg Barz . . . and her boyfriend Wolfgang Grundmann": Grundmann was one of several "urban guerrillas" who had been associated in the student protest days with the underground paper *Agit 883.*

246 "The police and the public expected more bombs and more killings, especially on June 2": Public fears of a violent attack on June 2 were not entirely disappointed. There was a bomb scare in Stuttgart. The alarm turned out to be false, but it was thorough while it lasted.

252 "Then they were sure, they said, that they had got Ulrike Meinhof": Klaus Rainer Röhl had tried to help Ulrike. He used a contact to get her asylum in East Germany, but the application was turned down. He then tried to see Willy Brandt, who did not see him but referred him to the head of the Chancellor's office, Horst Ehmke, who was the son of the Röhl family's Danzig doctor. Ehmke refused a safe-conduct for Ulrike. He advised that she should simply give herself up. Röhl pointed out to him that Ulrike might be afraid to walk into a police station in case she was shot on sight, so he asked if she could surrender to Josef Augstein in Hanover, as Homann had done. Ehmke did not positively agree to this but also did not discourage the plan. When Ulrike was eventually arrested in Hanover, Röhl wondered whether she was on her way to Augstein. In the light of her subsequent actions and reactions after her arrest, this does not seem likely.

Chapter 15: The Game Is Up, the Games Go On

257 ". . . some Arab gunmen of 'Black September' . . . killed eleven of the Israeli athletes": Five terrorists were also killed. Three were taken prisoner (and were rescued seven weeks later by blackmail when two Black September members hijacked a Lufthansa Boeing 727 between Damascus and Frankfurt and took it to Libya, where Qadhafi did not refuse it permission to land). A list of the Arab gunmen's demands which reached the Public Prosecutor of Karlsruhe included the release of some German terrorist prisoners, among them Ulrike Meinhof.

258 "They gave him the means . . . so that he could find a guru": Michael Baumann later wrote a book about his life as a political gangster called *How It All Started (Wie alles anfing).* It was banned a few days after its publication, although terrorist sympathizers despise it and even rumor that it was "ghosted by the Political Police."

260 "But on the night of June 4-5 somebody else 'got on with it' ": Schmücker's body was found in the Grünewald by American soldiers on June 5, 1974. Six people were brought to trial in Berlin for this crime. One made a confession. For two others the defense lawyer made the plea that they "had not understood the seriousness and possible consequence"

of the mock trial of the victim. An investigation into the Schmücker affair was conducted by Stefan Aust, the rescuer of the Röhl twins, for the North German Television program *Panorama*. His conclusion was that it started as a "stupid, cruel, childish game" and got drastically out of hand—an assessment that might be regarded as fitting for the whole "anti-authoritarian" protest movement from the mid-sixties to the mid-seventies and possibly beyond. Aust has also pointed out that though the judges and condemners of Schmücker called themselves Movement Second June, they were not necessarily the same people who committed any of the other acts claimed by a movement of that name, and that there were several separate groups as well as a shifting membership.

261 ". . . the other five were flown . . . to Aden with DM 20,000 each": One of them was Gabriele Kröcher-Tiedemann, who was later to join the terrorist party which raided the offices of OPEC in Vienna in 1976.

262 " 'In order to get rid of this thing about Jews that we've all had to have since the Nazi time' ": Extreme political action as a means to the satisfaction of personal feelings is specifically prescribed by Marcuse: "One of the tasks is to lay bare and liberate the type of man who wants revolution, who must have revolution because otherwise he would fall apart" (*Five Lectures*, p. 74).

Chapter 16: Crocodile Tears

263 "During the initial period of imprisonment . . . and representatives of Amnesty International": Paul Oestreicher, a vicar of Blackheath, near London, and chairman of Amnesty International in Britain, visited the terrorist prisoners in the Stammheim jail to try to persuade them to call off their hunger strike in the winter of 1974–75. He maintained that to him the life of a terrorist was no more expendable than the life of a politician such as Peter Lorenz. But so also, in his view "as a Christian pacifist," the terrorists' proposition that some people must be killed for humanity's sake was unacceptable. He told me that he found all the prisoners to be "supremely self-righteous, convinced of their own moral and intellectual superiority."

266 "If the hunger strikers would not take it . . . be compelled by thirst to take the milk": Dr. Gustav Heinemann, soon after his retirement as President of the Federal Republic, wrote to Ulrike Meinhof during one of the hunger strikes, reminding her that she had used him as a lawyer in a defamation suit, and imploring her and her "friends" to stop putting their lives at risk with this form of protest. "The complaints against the conditions of your imprisonment which you have associated with your hunger strike are—at least now—largely illusory," he wrote. She replied that the hunger strike would be called off if all "political" prisoners were "concentrated in one institution" and no longer isolated from each other.

269 "The state prosecution did not appeal, so Bäcker's acquittal stood": A bill for a new law making it worthwhile for certain types of offenders to cooperate with the police in securing the conviction of more serious offenders

was introduced several times but rejected. Nevertheless, it plainly did not harm a prisoner if he did cooperate.

270   ". . . and one, Holger Meins, eventually died, his death thereafter being consistently blamed on the judiciary and the state authorities": In a farewell letter shortly before his death, Holger Meins wrote, "Struggling against the pigs as a human being for the liberation of man, as a revolutionary, fighting to the last, loving life, disdaining death. That's my idea of serving the people." At his funeral Rudi Dutschke proclaimed, "The struggle goes on, Holger!"

274   "Then on Thursday, April 24, 1975, at 11:30 A.M. . . . .": About this time Baader got into such a state of excitement that he had to be given a sedative.

278   ". . . in which he proved himself an anticapitalist of sorts": Wessel had his suits and shoes handmade in London.

"The four members of the 'Holger Meins Commando' left to stand trial": They were brought to trial at Düsseldorf on May 6, 1976.

Chapter 17: Judgments

280f   "If the RAF had had any effect at all . . . it was only perhaps to have swung the electorate a little to the right": Some say that the most serious effect was the passing of certain new laws specifically to meet unusual situations which arose during the prosecution of terrorists and the searching out of their helpers; and that these laws endangered the democratic rights of all prisoners. The official government reply to this criticism was that these laws, defining, for instance, what is and is not permissible in the relationship between a lawyer and his imprisoned client, were not new but only clarifications of points of law already existing to the same effect in the Constitution. Another effect has been the building up of an information bank, computerized and up to date, by the security forces in Wiesbaden, which must prove a powerful instrument in the fight against not only terrorism but all crime inside Germany and beyond it in the wider sphere that Interpol has to deal with.

281   "Gudrun Ensslin . . . was told about fifteen minutes later that she could not see Ulrike Meinhof, as she was dead": Ulrike Meinhof and Gudrun Ensslin were used to spending several hours together every day. Neither would mix with the ordinary women prisoners, though freely permitted to do so. At the time of her death there were 150 books in Ulrike Meinhof's cell. She subscribed to seven newspapers and periodicals. She also had a radio, television set, and record player, although these were not normally permitted to prisoners, and since January 1976 she had been serving her sentence as a committed prisoner for her part in the freeing of Baader.

282   "In some English newspapers the suggestion that Meinhof was murdered by the State . . . was aired as perfectly plausible": A few weeks after the death of Ulrike Meinhof, certain lawyers began to publicize their belief that she had been raped and strangled. They offered "evidence" which was in part untrue, and for the rest provided better proof that she had not been

murdered than that she had. They maintained, for instance, that semen was found in her underclothes. This was not true. Because albumen was found, a test for detecting the presence of sperm was specifically asked for and carried out. The result was negative. No trace of sperm was discovered. Furthermore, there were none of the signs of violence in the region of the genitalia such as can be expected in cases of rape. There were bruises lower down the legs; but these, far from proving the likelihood of attack, were of the sort that can be looked for as part of the expected picture in a case of suicide by this method of hanging. The body is likely to jerk as it hangs, and the legs to knock against the chair or whatever it is that the suicide jumps from or kicks aside. In this case it was a chair. The lawyers and other complaining parties objected that the authorities had at first said there was no chair in the cell. This again was untrue. The authorities never said anything of the sort, and there certainly was a chair in the cell. Then the objectors maintained that there was a thread of saliva found on the chest of the corpse, which proved, they said, that Meinhof must have been naked at the time she died. But in fact she was wearing a shirt open on the chest, and the saliva fell on the skin only where the skin was exposed.

Two autopsies were performed. The first was the official one, carried out on the day the body was found. The two state-appointed specialists who made the investigation found that Meinhof had committed suicide. Under the fingernails they found fragments of material that matched the stuff the towel was made of which Meinhof had torn up to make her rope. Under this material no traces of someone else's skin were found, such as might have lodged there if she had struggled with an assailant before her death. Because the nails had been cut short in the first autopsy, this was one finding which the second investigation, carried out by an expert chosen by Meinhof's friends, could not confirm. But the objection raised by the lawyers that parts of the body had been removed in such a manner that the second autopsy could not be complete, was without foundation. Parts of the lung, liver, etc., had been cut away as they always are for postmortem examination, but not so largely that the second investigation could not be as accurate as the first. Indeed, though this privately chosen expert was not discouraged by the friends of Meinhof from finding evidence of murder, he was only able to confirm a classic case of suicide. Nevertheless, the rape and murder theory was adhered to by those who had thought it up. They said that if she had died by hanging there would have been bleeding in the eyes, and the fact that there was none suggested rather that she had died by strangulation, and that the fracture of the hyoid bone at the base of the tongue was also more typical of a throttling than a hanging. But again, both these facts—no eye bleeding and the broken hyoid bone—proved suicide rather than murder, for very few who hang without benefit of state executioner achieve a quick end; suicides by hanging almost always die of strangulation.

But those who desired to make a martyr of Meinhof would not be deterred by evidence anyway. And if those who started these rumors of violent assault and murder were themselves sympathetic to the urban guerrilla movement, they could be expected to deny that Meinhof committed suicide or was a suicidal type. The RAF and its sympathizers pretended that the members of the group acted for political motives only, never out ot private emotion. A suicide was a denial of that lie; it challenged the pretense that they were sterilized of all feelings except the fervor for revolution.

A Selected List of Members and Associates of German Terrorist Groups (July 1976)

ALLNACH, Kay-Werner: Born 1950. Student-teacher friend of Margrit Schiller. Arrested February 2, 1974. Deserted by defense lawyer Groenewold on refusal to continue hunger strike.

ASDONK, Brigitte: Born October 1947. Student. Participant Berlin bank raids. Arrested October 8, 1970, with Horst Mahler.

BAADER, Andreas Bernd: Born May 1943. Leader of RAF. Convicted 1968 of arson, partly served sentence, released while appeal pending, fled country when appeal failed, returned and rearrested Berlin, freed with guns by Ulrike Meinhof and others, May 1970. Again arrested June 1, 1972. Tried in special courthouse with Meinhof, Ensslin, and Raspe at Stammheim for murder, bank robberies, forming criminal association, etc.

BÄCKER, Hans-Jürgen: Born April 1939. Electrician. Tried 1974 for participation in May 1970 freeing of Baader, found not guilty.

BARZ, Ingeborg: Born July 1948. Secretary. Girl friend of Wolfgang Grundmann. Missing since February 1972, believed murdered.

BAUMANN, Michael: Born August 1947. Early member Movement Second June. Left Germany.

BECKER, Eberhard: Born March 1943. Lawyer, member of Heidelberg partnership involved with SPK. Husband of Marieluise Becker (Ensslin's lawyer at Stammheim). Arrested June 4, 1974.

BECKER, Verena: Born July 1952. Student. Sentenced December 1974 to 6 years' jail as member of Movement Second June. Freed in exchange for kidnapped politician Peter Lorenz, flown to Aden.

BERBERICH, Monika Klara: Born October 1942. Junior lawyer in Horst Mahler's "Socialist Lawyers' Collective." Arrested October 8, 1970.

Sentenced 1974 to 12 years' jail for bank robbery and membership in criminal association. Escaped from Lehrter Strasse prison, Berlin, July 7, 1976, with Plambeck, Rollnick, and Viett. Rearrested July 21, 1976, in Berlin.

BÖSE, Wilfried: Born February 1949. "The little fat one" to other members of RAF. Arrested by French police 1975, handed over to German authorities, released. Killed at Entebbe July 4, 1976, by Israeli rescuers of hijack victims.

BRAUN, Bernhard: Born February 1946. Involved with SPK and Movement Second June. Arrested June 9, 1972.

DELLWO, Karl-Heinz: Born April 1952. School failure. Involved with SPK. Participant raid on German embassy, Stockholm, April 24, 1975.

ECKES, Christa: Born February 1950. Junior lawyer in Groenewold's Hamburg office. Suspected participant Hamburg bank raid August 1973. Also arms offenses. Arrested February 4, 1974.

ENSSLIN, Gudrun: Born August 1940. Leader of RAF. Convicted 1968 of arson with Baader and two others, partly served sentence, released while appeal pending, fled country when appeal failed, returned to Germany early 1970. Rearrested June 7, 1972. Tried with Baader, Meinhof, Raspe at Stammheim for murder, bank robberies, forming criminal association, etc.

GOERGENS, Irene: Born April 1951. Illegitimate daughter of American soldier. State home inmate. Meinhof protégée. Arrested October 8, 1970, with Mahler.

GRASHOF, Manfred: Born October 1946. Army deserter. Member Berlin Kommune I. Involved in shootout with police in Hamburg apartment when chief of Hamburg Special Baader-Meinhof Commission was killed, March 2, 1972.

GRUNDMANN, Wolfgang: Born June 1948. Associated with Berlin underground paper *Agit 883*. Arrested with Manfred Grashof. Released October 1976.

GRUSDAT, Eric: Born April 1936. Motor mechanic. Doctored stolen cars for Mahler, Baader, etc. Participant Berlin bank raids. Arrested December 4, 1970.

HAAG, Siegfried: Born March 1945. Heidelberg lawyer, gone underground. Wanted for arms smuggling. Arrested November 27, 1976.

HAMMERSCHMIDT, Katharina: Born February 1943. Student. Early

Baader-Meinhof associate in Berlin. Fled abroad late 1971. Returned and surrendered to police mid-1972. Released on remand six months later. Died of tumor 1975.

HAUSNER, Siegfried: Born January 1952. Member SPK "Working Circle Explosives." Helped Meinhof lay bombs in Hamburg Springer offices May 1972. Participant in raid on German embassy, Stockholm, April 24, 1975, where he wounded himself with own bomb and died soon afterward.

HERZOG, Marianne: Born October 1939. Journalist. Early associate of Baader-Meinhof in Berlin and Frankfurt. Said to have attempted to free Astrid Proll from prison.

HOMANN, Peter: Born 1936. Artist and journalist. Lived with Meinhof in Berlin before freeing of Baader May 1970. Then went with her and others to Jordan, where he soon broke with Meinhof and her fellow factioneers and left the group.

HOPPE, Werner: Born February 1949. Dock worker, television trainee, self-cured drug addict. Arrested after shootout with police in which Petra Schelm was killed, July 15, 1971.

HUBER, Ursula: Born July 1935. Wife of Dr. Wolfgang H., née Schäfer. Leader of SPK. Made explosives in her Heidelberg laboratory. Arrested July 7, 1971.

HUBER, Wolfgang: Born January 1935. Psychiatrist founder of SPK. Arrested July 7, 1971.

JANSEN, Heinrich: Born February 1948. Participant in Berlin bank raids with RAF in September 1970. Remained with RAF in West Germany until arrest on December 23, 1970.

JÜNSCHKE, Klaus: Born September 1947. Student member SPK. Arrested March 2, 1971. Tried at Kaiserslautern with Grashof and Grundmann.

KLEIN, Hans-Joachim: Born December 1947. Associate of Stuttgart lawyer Croissant. Participant in raid on OPEC offices, Vienna, January 1976, where he was wounded but flew with other raiders and hostages to Algeria.

KRABBE, Hanna-Elise: Born October 1945. Member SPK's successor organization, IZRU. Arrested Stockholm April 24, 1975, as one of German embassy raiders.

KRÖCHER-TIEDEMANN, Gabriele: Born May 1951. Member Movement Second June. Arrested after shootout with police in Bochum.

Exchanged for kidnapped Peter Lorenz. Reemerged from South Yemen to participate in OPEC raid, Vienna, January 1976, with "Carlos" (known as "The Jackal"), Hans-Joachim Klein, and others.

LANG, Jörg: Born March 1940. Formerly in Socialist Lawyers' Collective with Croissant in Stuttgart. From early 1976 said to be new leader of RAF, replacing Baader.

LUTHER, Angela: Born April 1940. Member Movement Second June and RAF. Helped lay bombs Augsburg and Heidelberg with Möller, Baader, Meins.

MAHLER, Horst: Born January 1936. Founder of Berlin Socialist Lawyers' Collective and of RAF. Went with Meinhof and others to Jordan after Baader freeing, 1970. Participant in bank raids. Arrested October 8, 1970. Sentenced 1972 to 14 years' jail.

MAHRLÄNDER, Alfred: Born August 1942. Student member of SPK. Arrested July 1971.

MEINHOF, Ulrike Marie: Born October 1934. Journalist. Helped free Baader, May 1970. Went underground. After stay in Jordan with Baader, Ensslin, Mahler, and others, returned to Germany and participated in bank robberies, bomb laying, etc. Leader of RAF. Arrested June 15, 1972. Sentenced November 1974 to 8 years' jail for participation in Baader freeing. Tried in special court at Stammheim with Baader, Ensslin, Raspe. Committed suicide May 9, 1976.

MEINS, Holger Klaus: Born August 1941. Student of cinematography. Leading member of RAF. Arrested with Baader and Raspe June 1, 1972. Died in prison as result of hunger strike, November 11, 1974.

MÖLLER, Irmgard: Born May 1947. Suspected of being involved in shootout in Hamburg when a policeman was killed October 22, 1971. Has accused Gerhard Müller of being the killer. Arrested July 9, 1972.

MÜLLER, Gerhard: Born June 1948. Arrested with Ulrike Meinhof June 15, 1972. Has dissociated himself from RAF since coming to trial in Hamburg, 1975. Key witness for the state at Stammheim.

OTTO, Roland: Born 1951. Participant in bank raid. Arrested May 10, 1975, after shootout with police in which Werner Sauber was killed and Karl Heinz Roth wounded.

PLAMBECK, Juliane: Born 1953. Member Movement Second June. Arrested with Fritz Teufel September 13, 1975. Charged with Lorenz kidnapping and murder of Judge von Drenkmann. Escaped from Lehrter Strasse prison, Berlin, July 7, 1976.

POHLE, Rolf: Born January 1942. Specialized in buying arms for terrorist organizations, including RAF, using false papers. Caught and imprisoned, but exchanged for Peter Lorenz and flown to Aden. Rearrested in Greece and returned to Germany, October 1976.

PROLL, Astrid: Born May 1947. Younger sister of Thorwald P., who was convicted of arson with Baader, Ensslin, and another. Arrested May 1971. Released from prison to sanatorium, fled, and disappeared.

RASPE, Jan-Carl: Born July 1944 in Austria. Member Berlin's Kommune II. Sociologist. Leading member of RAF. Tried at Stammheim with Baader, Ensslin, Meinhof.

REINDERS, Ralf: Born August 1948. Early associate of violent Berlin political underground, later of SPK. Leader of Movement Second June, suspected of Lorenz kidnapping and murder of Judge von Drenkmann. Arrested September 9, 1975.

ROLL, Carmen: Born September 1947. Member SPK "Working Circle Explosives." Arrested March 2, 1972, after shootout with police in which Thomas Weissbecker was killed.

ROLLNICK, Gabriele: Born 1953. Sociology student. Charged with Lorenz kidnapping. Escaped from Lehrter Strasse prison, Berlin, July 7, 1976.

RÖSSNER, Bernd Maria: Born October 1946. School failure. Traveled in Far East. Returned to Germany and met Karl-Heinz Dellwo. Arrested when participating on raid on German embassy, Stockholm, April 24, 1975.

ROTH, Karl Heinz: Born 1944. Student leader. Doctor. Associate of Baader and Mahler in early days of RAF but warned Stefan Aust against them. Wounded and arrested after shootout with police, May 10, 1975.

RUHLAND, Karl-Heinz: Born March 1938. Employee of Eric Grusdat. Participant in raids on banks and municipal offices. Arrested December 20, 1970, made detailed confession at his trial.

SAUBER, Werner: Born April 1947 in Switzerland. Son of Swiss millionaire. Berlin communard. Suspected of supplying arms to terrorists. During shootout with police on May 10, 1975, was shot dead and according to ballistic evidence wounded his companion Karl Heinz Roth in the shooting.

SCHELM, Petra: Born August 1950. Hairdresser girl friend of Grashof. Drove through roadblock with Werner Hoppe July 15, 1971, and was killed in subsequent shootout with police.

SCHILLER, Margrit: Born March 1948. Student member SPK. Arrested October 22, 1971, sentenced to 27 months' jail, released February 1973. Went underground again. Rearrested February 4, 1974. Accused Müller of murder of policeman.

SCHMÜCKER, Ulrich: Born August 1951. Member Movement Second June. Arrested sleeping in car with bombs May 7, 1972. After release accused by comrades of treachery. Shot, after mock trial, on June 4, 1974.

SCHOLTZE, Ulrich: Born December 1947. Student. Member of RAF for few months only in 1970.

SCHUBERT, Ingrid: Born November 1944. Doctor. Participant in Berlin bank raids. Arrested October 8, 1970, with Mahler. Sentenced to 13 years' jail. After Meinhof's suicide, taken to Stammheim to be calming company for Ensslin.

SIEPMANN, Ingrid: Born June 1944. Member Kommune I and Movement Second June. Worked for a time in Palestinian pharmaceutical center in Jordan.

STACHOWIAK, Ilse: Born May 1954. Joined RAF at 17. Arrested November 1971. After release went underground again. Rearrested February 1, 1974. Was living in Angela Luther's Berlin apartment when explosion wrecked it in June 1972.

STURM, Beate: Born 1951. A member of RAF for a few months only in 1970–71. Left of her own accord, having committed no crime. Gave vivid descriptions of the gang's underground life.

TAUFER, Lutz Manfred: Born March 1944. Member of SPK. Participant in raid on German embassy, Stockholm, April 24, 1975, when he was arrested.

TEUFEL, Fritz: Born June 1943. The "happenings" satirist and founder of Kommune I, Berlin. Arrested September 13, 1975. Charged with Lorenz kidnapping and bank robberies.

VIETT, Inge: Born January 1944. Kindergarten teacher, girl friend of Ralf Reinders, arrested with him September 9, 1975. Charged with bank robberies and Lorenz kidnapping. Escaped from Lehrter Strasse prison, Berlin, July 7, 1976.

WEISSBECKER, Thomas: Born February 1949. Early associate of Mahler's Berlin circle. No prominent part in RAF. Killed in shootout with police March 2, 1972.

WESSEL, Ulrich: Born 1946. Dandy son of deceased Hamburg businessman. Millionaire by inheritance. Member SPK. Participant in raid on German embassy, Stockholm, April 24, 1975, where blown up in bomb explosion.

A Note on Sources

Much of the material in this book is derived from the author's interviews with persons concerned in the events and contains information published here for the first time. Where the informant is not named, the author is respecting his or her wish to remain anonymous.

In addition to interviews, other sources are: unpublished documents; the published books and collections of documents listed in the Bibliography; underground publications listed in the Bibliography; and the following issues of newspapers and periodicals:

PART ONE
Der Spiegel, XXI: 16, 24, 48, 49, 50, 51; XXII: 13, 25; XXVI: 23, 24
Stern, April 19, 1968; June 18, 1975
Die Zeit, April 16, 1967; July 28, 1967; April 19, 1968

PART TWO
Frankfurter Rundschau, April 4, 6, 1968; October 13, 16, 22, 23, 29, 30, 1968; November 1, 1968; February 5, 1970; May 15, 19, 25, 1970
Der Spiegel, XXII: 25; XXVI: 24
Stern, June 11, 1972; June 5, 12, 1975

PART THREE
Frankfurter Rundschau, May 26, 27, 1970; October 26, 1975
Der Spiegel, XXIII: 23
Stern, June 18, 1975

PART FOUR
Frankfurter Allgemeine Zeitung, August 29, 1975
Frankfurter Rundschau, June 11, 1970; April 20, 1971; May 6, 1971; July 5, 17, 23, 1971; October 23, 1971; November 2, 10, 11, 12, 1971; May 16, 1972; June 1, 2, 8, 19, 1972; August 9, 1972
The Observer (London), July 2, 1972
Der Spiegel, XXV: 48; XXVI: 3, 5, 7, 8, 23, 24, 25, 26; XXIX: 32; XXX: 5, 6
Stern, June 11, 1972; April 30, 1975
Stuttgarter Nachrichten, June 26, 1972

Süddeutsche Zeitung, January 30, 1976
The Times (London), June 30, 1972
Die Welt, all issues between and including May 20, 1975, and June 7, 1975;
January 28, 29, 30, 1976

PART FIVE
Das Da, April 4, 1975
Frankfurter Allgemeine Zeitung, April 30, 1975; July 4, 1975; February 6, 27,
1976
Frankfurter Rundschau, July 28, 1975
Neue Revue, May 12, 17, 26, 1975
The Observer (London), March 8, 18, 1975; May 18, 1975
Der Spiegel, XXVI: 26, 31; XXIX: 6, 18, 23, 32, 38, 39
Stern, April 30, 1975; February 5, 1976
Süddeutsche Zeitung, April 27, 28, 1975
The Times (London), March 5, 1975
Die Welt, February 28, 1976

Bibliography

1. *Publications by the RAF and its members, associates, and sympathizers*

Das Argument, Nos. 1–7. Peter Maier, Ulrike Meinhof, and Jürgen Seifert, eds. Münster: Studentischer Arbeitskreis für ein Kernwaffenfreies Deutschland, 1958. The student antibomb paper which Ulrike Meinhof helped to edit at Münster University.

Brückner, Peter, and Barbara Sichtermann. *Gewalt und Solidarität.* Berlin: Verlag Klaus Wagenbach, 1974. A collection of essays and documents presenting the arguments, pro and con, within the Left, over the murder of Ulrich Schmücker by his comrades of Movement Second June.

Die Entführung aus unserer Sicht. Berlin: Bewegung 2 Juni, 1975. Underground publication by the Movement Second June giving their views on their kidnapping of politician Peter Lorenz.

Der Kampf gegen die Vernichtungshaft. Komitees gegen Folter an politischen Gefangen in der BRD, 1974. A collection of articles and letters published by the "Committees Against the Torture of Political Prisoners in the Federal Republic of (West) Germany," sponsored and organized by some of the B-M terrorists' defense lawyers.

Kursbuch, various issues, in particular No. 32. Hans Magnus Enzensberger, ed. Berlin: Kursbuch Verlag. A leftist literary and political monthly. No. 32 contains detailed reports, essays, and analyses of the "isolation torture" of the arrested B-M gang members.

Mahler, Horst. *Horst Mahlers Erklärung zum Prozessbeginn am 9.10.72 vor dem 1. Strafsenat des westberliner Kammergerichts.* 1972. Underground publication reproducing terrorist Horst Mahler's lengthy declaration made before the West Berlin court at his trial in October 1972.

Marenssin, Emil, and Peter Paul Zahl. *Die "Baader Meinhof Bande" oder revolutionäre Gewalt.* Haarlem: Editora Queimada, 1974. Two long essays, the first about the B-M gang written in B-M argot, the second an echoing but more personal statement by a suspected terrorist.

Meinhof, Ulrike Marie. *Bambule.* Berlin: Verlag Klaus Wagenbach, 1971. Ulrike Meinhof's television play.

RAF (Rote Armee Fraktion). *Die Aktion des schwarzen September in München.* 1973. Underground publication praising the massacre of Israeli athletes by the Black September at the Olympic Games in Munich, 1972.

————. *Über den bewaffneten Kampf in Westeuropa* ("Concerning the Armed Struggle in Western Europe"), published as *Rotbuch 29;* also known as "Strassenverkehrsordnung." Berlin: Verlag Klaus Wagenbach, 1971. One of the few books ever banned in West Germany (on the ground that it incited armed insurrection). Also known by its underground cover name, *Road Traffic Ordinances.* Ascribed to Horst Mahler. Declamatory, emotional, and overemphatic in the B-M style.

————. *Dem Volk dienen* ("Serve the People"). 1972. Underground publication by the B-M gang, complaining against social ills on behalf of "the people."

Schubert, Alex. *Stadtguerilla.* Berlin: Verlag Klaus Wagenbach, 1971. Contains a reprint of the RAF publication *The Concept Urban Guerrilla.*

Vaneigem, Raoul. *The Revolution of Everyday Life* (a translation from the French, by John Fullerton and Paul Sieveking, of *Traité de Savoir-vivre a l'usage des jeunes générations*). London: Practical Paradise Publications, 1972. An outpouring of philosophical antiphilosophy: declamatory, emotional, sometimes witty. Advocates such youth-popular ideas as violent revolt against the consumer society and intense living in the moment. Its tone and mood provide an immediate insight into the atmosphere of student protest in the sixties.

Vesper, Bernward, ed. *Voltaire Flugschriften.* Frankfurt: Edition Voltaire, 1967–68. An irregular series of paperback booklets, edited by the sometime fiancé of Gudrun Ensslin, on a variety of subjects, all from a leftist viewpoint, including (No. 12, *Bedingungen und Organisation des Widerstandes: Der Kongres in Hannover*, 1967) the congress at Hanover held after the June 2, 1967, shooting of student Benno Ohnesorg by a policeman in Berlin during the riots sparked off by the visit of the Shah of Iran; also (No. 21, *Der israelische-arabische Konflikt*, 1967) the Israeli-Arab conflict as assessed by Ulrike Meinhof and Isaac Deutscher; also (No. 27, *Vor einer solchen Justiz verteidigen wir uns nicht*, 1968) the statement made by Frankfurt arsonists Baader, Ensslin, Proll, and Söhnlein at their trial on the reasons why they would not defend themselves.

2. Published collections of documents

Betrifft: Verfassungsschutz '74. Bonn: Federal Ministry of the Interior, 1974. An issue of an annual publication of the Ministry of the Interior on the work of the West German police special branch for political crimes, counterintelligence, antiterrorism, etc.

Buchholtz, Hans-Christoph, and Thomas von Zabern, eds. *Dokumentation über die Art der Fahnungs Massnahmen im Zusammenhang mit der Lorenz-Entführung*. Berlin: Liga für Menschenrechte, 1975. A collection of documents on police actions in West Berlin after the Lorenz kidnapping.

Dokumentation über Aktivitäten anarchistischer Gewalttäter in der Bundesrepublik Deutschland. Bonn: Federal Ministry of the Interior, 1975. A collection of circulars and letters written by arrested members of the B-M gang and their lawyers Groenewold and Ströbele, found in the cells of the prisoners or in RAF hideouts in various cities.

Grützbach, Frank, ed. *Heinrich Böll: Freies Geleit für Ulrike Meinhof, ein Artikel un seine Folgen*. Cologne: Verlag Kiepenheuer & Witsch, 1972. Böll's article "Free Conduct for Ulrike Meinhof" written for *Der Spiegel*, along with a collection of newpaper articles and open letters in answer to it.

Jacobsen, H. A., and H. Dollinger. *Die deutschen Studenten*. Munich: Deutscher Taschenbuch Verlag, 1969. Gives a detailed chronology, lists various proposals for university reform, reports speeches and discussions.

Lönnendonker, Siegward, and Tilman Fichter, eds. *Dokumentation FU Berlin*, vols. ii–iv. Berlin: Press Office of the Free University of

Berlin, 1975. A chronological record and collection of documents, with a slight left-wing bias in the selections and presentation.

Meinhof, Ulrike. *Dokumente einer Rebellion; 10 Jahre "Konkret" Kolumnen.* Hamburg: Konkret Buchverlag, 1971. A selection of Ulrike Meinhof's *Konkret* columns. Also contains the open letter to Ulrike Meinhof by her foster mother, Renate Riemeck, commenting on *The Concept Urban Guerrilla.*

Olzog, G., and A. Herzig. *Die politischen Parteien.* Munich: Günter Olzog Verlag, 1973. Gives short party histories, party manifestos, election results, and other facts.

Rauball, Reinhard, ed. *Die Baader-Meinhof-Gruppe: Aktuelle Dokumente de Gruyter.* Berlin: Walter de Gruyter, 1973. A collection of documents and other matter relating to the B-M group, including the judgment of the court on the Frankfurt arsonists.

Scheffer, Barbara. *Bericht über die Entwicklung und Perspektiven der frankfurter Wohngruppen.* Frankfurt: Verein Arbeits- und Erziehungshilfe E.V., 1970. Report by a social worker on the Frankfurt "apprentice" communes experiment with which Baader and Ensslin were briefly involved.

Sommersemester 1968—eine Dokumentation. Berlin: Rector's Office of the Free University, 1968. Short articles and documents on the eventful summer semester of 1968 at West Berlin's Free University.

3. *Selected Books*

Adorno, Theodor W., and others. *The Authoritarian Personality.* New York: Harper & Brothers, 1950. A massive work in which the authors try to prove that the authoritarian individual is likely to incline to the political right.

Alves, Marcio, Conrad Detrez, and Carlos Marighela. *Zerschlagt die wohlstands Inseln der III Welt: Mit dem Handbuch der Guerilleros von Sao Paulo.* Hamburg: Rowohlt Taschenbuch Verlag, 1971. Carlos Marighela's *Minihandbook of the Brazilian Urban Guerrilla* helped turn student rebels into terrorists in West Germany and elsewhere.

Der Baader Meinhof Report. Mainz: Hase & Köhler Verlag, 1972. Account of the B-M group. Contains police reports but is not otherwise reliable. No author named; right-wing bias.

Brosch, Peter. *Fürsorgeerziehung*. Frankfurt: Fischer Taschenbuch Verlag, 1971. The author was a childhood inmate of state homes, orphanages, and foster homes and was one of the "apprentices" who participated in the Frankfurt experiment of letting boys from state institutions live communally—which is the subject of his book.

Bunn, Ronald F. *German Politics and the Spiegel Affair: A Case Study of the Bonn System*. Baton Rouge: Louisiana State University Press, 1968. A clear account of this incident, showing its significance in German political history.

Carr, Gordon. *The Angry Brigade*. London: Victor Gollancz, 1975. The story of a terrorist group in England whose ideology was similar to that of the B-M gang.

Cockburn, A., and R. Blackburn, eds. *Student Power*. London: Penguin Books, 1969. A threatening book of emotional opinions.

Debray, Régis. *Che's Guerrilla War*. London: Penguin Books, 1975. How Guevara did what he did, by an admirer.

Dobson, Christopher. *Black September: Its Short, Violent History*. New York: Macmillan Company, 1974; London: Robert Hale & Company, 1975. The story of a terrorist arm of Al Fatah.

Fest, Joachim C. *The Face of the Third Reich*. New York: Ace Books, 1971; London: Pelican Books, 1972. An impressive study of Nazi Germany.

Friedeburg, Ludwig von, and others. *Freie Universität und politisches Potential der Studenten*. Berlin: Luchterhand Verlag, 1968. A history of West Berlin's Free University.

Fromm, Erich. *The Anatomy of Human Destructiveness*. New York: Holt, Rinehart and Winston, 1973. A Frankfurt School associate studies the destructive personality.

Goode, Stephen. *Affluent Revolutionaries: A Portrait of the New Left*. New York: New Viewpoints (a division of Franklin Watts), 1974. A lucid and objective account of the New Left, chiefly in the United States but also abroad.

Grosser, Alfred. *Germany in Our Time*. London: Pelican Books, 1974. Widely praised history by a much-acclaimed author.

Grunberger, Richard. *A Social History of the Third Reich*. London: Penguin Books, 1974. Full and highly readable description of life under a truly authoritarian government in the Germany of the parent generation of the terrorists.

Habermas, Jürgen. *Protestbewegung und Hochschulreform*. Frankfurt: Suhrkamp Verlag, 1969. A collection of essays and edited lectures and addresses on student protest and university reform by an erstwhile Frankfurt School associate.

———. *Toward a Rational Society: Student Protest, Science and Politics*. Boston: Beacon Press, 1971; London: Heinemann Educational Books, 1971. Contains important essays on the antiauthoritarian movement in West Germany.

Hitler, Adolf. *Mein Kampf*. Munich: Zentralverlag der NSDAP, 1938; Boston: Houghton Mifflin Company, 1940. "My Struggle," the teachings of Adolf Hitler. Resemblances to the views of contemporary terrorists, both of the Right and the Left, are striking and inescapable.

Horchem, Hans Josef. *Extremisten in einer selbsbewussten Demokratie*. Freiburg: Verlag Herder KG, 1975. An account of terrorist activities by a senior police officer.

Hunt, Sir David. *On the Spot*. London: Peter Davies, 1975. In which an erstwhile British ambassador to Brazil reveals that the terrorist groups which kidnapped ambassadors in South America were motivated only by nihilistic emotion and love of violence for its own sake.

Jacka, Keith, Caroline Cox, and John Marks. *Rape of Reason*. London: Churchill Press, 1975. Three teachers at a London Polytechnic describe an attempt by leftist students to take control of the college by disruptive practices which clearly exemplify the "fascism of the Left."

Jay, Martin. *The Dialectical Imagination*. Boston: Little, Brown and Company, 1973; London: Heinemann Educational Books, 1973. A history of the Institute for Social Research known as the Frankfurt School, 1923–1950.

Korsch, Karl. *Marxism and Philosophy*. London: NLB, 1970; New York: Monthly Review Press, 1971. One of the gospels of the student movement in West Germany. (The list of the prophets of the New Left in Europe whom the students esteemed and quoted but did not much read would include Frantz Fanon and George Lukaçz. Many did read Albert Camus.)

Marcuse, Herbert. *Eros and Civilization*. Boston: Beacon Press, 1955; London: Sphere Books, 1969. One of the books by this prophet of the New Left most esteemed by the student rebels of the sixties.

———. *Five Lectures*. Boston: Beacon Press, 1970; London: Penguin Books (Allen Lane), 1970. Includes the two lectures given by Marcuse at the Free University, Berlin, in 1967.

———. *One Dimensional Man*. London: Sphere Books (Abacus edition), 1972. Perhaps the chief gospel of the student movement, the New Left, and the terrorist theoreticians of Germany.

Röhl, Klaus Rainer. *Fünf Finger sind keine Faust*. Cologne: Verlag Kiepenheuer & Witsch, 1974. "Five Fingers Are Not a Fist": a history of *Konkret* by its publisher, Ulrike Meinhof's divorced husband.

———. *Die Genossin*. Munich: Verlag Fritz Molden, 1975. "The (female) Comrade": a novel, but plainly a partly fictionalized biography of Ulrike Meinhof by her divorced husband.

Rühmkorf, Peter. *Die Jahre die Ihr kennt*. Hamburg: Rowohlt Taschenbuch Verlag, 1972. "The Years That You Knew": a poet's autobiography, made up of a collection of diary entries.

Shirer, William L. *The Rise and Fall of the Third Reich*. New York: Simon & Schuster, 1960; London: Pan Books, 1964. A standard work on the history of Nazi Germany and the Second World War.

Spender, Stephen. *The Year of the Young Rebels*. London: Weidenfeld & Nicolson, 1969. A poet who was a leftist student in the thirties writes about the leftist student rebels of the sixties.

Stern, J. P. *Hitler: The Führer and the People*. Berkeley: University of California Press, 1975; London: Fontana Books (Collins), 1975. A fascinating study of the language of Nazism. Provokes interesting comparison with the language of other forms of political extremism.

Trotsky, Leon. *The Defence of Terrorism*. London: George Allen and Unwin, 1921. An aggressive classic. The author asserts that violent means of effecting political change are only permissible when used by the Left.

Index

318

INDEX

Jordan (cont.)
   guerrilla training, 179-80; Meinhof tries to
   send her daughters to, 221, 223, 226
Jubilation Persians, 38, 285
Jünger, Ernst, 121, 122
Jünschke, Klaus, 230, 231, 238, 245, 299

Kafka, Franz, 123
Kaiserslautern, bank robbery, 236-38
Kampen, 145, 148, 151, 263
Kapluk, Manfred, 132
Karlsruhe, 267; bombing, 245
Kassel, bank robberies, 203
Kennedy, John F., 143-44, 147
Kennedy, Robert, 11
Keser, Rosemary, 236
Khartoum, Black September raid, 11, 16
Khrushchev, Nikita, 135-36
Kiesinger, Kurt Georg, 71, 161, 287
King, Martin Luther, 48, 161
Klein, Hans-Joachim, 16, 17, 299
Kochel, 21
Kommune I, 22, 27, 29-32, 37, 44, 47, 53,
   61, 88, 89; pamphlets, 54-56
Kommune II, 22, 28, 173
Konkret, 47, 48, 71, 91, 129, 131, 133-34,
   140-41, 151-53, 161, 233; fifteenth an-
   niversary, 175-76; financial crisis, 144;
   Meinhof leads opposition to Röhl's editor-
   ship, 165-71; Meinhof leaves, 167-71;
   Meinhof with, 135-36, 138-41, 145, 158-
   59, 162; Meinhof's writings in, 33-34,
   36-37, 136, 141-44, 147, 151, 153, 157,
   165-66; sex in, 144, 145; tenth anniver-
   sary, 146-47
Konkret Berlin, authors' collective, 161,
   162, 165, 167, 168
KPD (Kommunistische Partei Deutschlands, Communist Party of Germany,
   banned 1956), 130, 132, 133
Krabbe, Hanna-Elise, 277, 278, 299
Kreisky, Austrian Chancellor, 17
Kröcher-Tiedemann, Gabriele, 16, 17, 293,
   299-300
Kropotkin, Peter, 288-89
Kuby, Erich, 24-25, 135, 288
Kunzelmann, Dieter, 32, 34-35, 47, 61, 99,
   262; in Jordan, 180; witness at trial, 268
Kurras, Karl-Heinz, 39, 43, 62; not guilty in
   Ohnesorg killing, 44-45

Lang, Jörg, 266-68, 300
Lang-Göns, 193

Langhans, Rainer, 44, 53, 262; in Kommune
   I, 21-22, 30; trial, 45, 62
Lawyers for Baader-Meinhof gang, 263-70,
   272, 273
Lemke, policeman, 234
Lenk, Thomas, 116
Leonhardt, Rudolf Walter, 290
Liebknecht, Karl, 88
Link, Werner, 123-26
Linke, Georg, 103-4, 232-33
Lorenz, Gertrud, 102-4
Lorenz, Peter, 16; kidnapped, 260-62
LSD (Liberaler Studentenbund Deutsch-
   lands, Student Liberal Party of Germany),
   50
Lübke, Frau, 38, 44
Lübke, Heinrich, 38, 44, 45
Ludwigshafen, 240
Luther, Angela, 244, 246, 258, 300
Luxemburg, Rosa, 88, 267, 283, 288

MacLeod, Iain, 252-53
Mahler, Horst, 14, 52, 105, 172, 174, 175,
   204, 225, 266, 286, 300; arrested, 186; in
   Baader-Meinhof gang, 180-86; and
   Baader's arrest in Berlin, 101; Baader's
   lawyer in Frankfurt trial, 84, 85, 87;
   Concerning the Armed Struggle in Western
   Europe attributed to, 233; demands action
   against Berlin police, 30-32; expelled by
   Baader's group, 268-69; in Jordan for guer-
   rilla training, 179; release attempted, 198,
   260, 261; search for guns, 99-102; in
   Socialist Lawyers' Collective, 99; trial for
   1968 demonstration, 51; trial in Berlin,
   and sentence, 268, 269
Mahrländer, Alfred, 231, 236-37, 300
Malle, Louis, 21
Mann, Thomas, 123
Mao Tse-Tung, 28, 151, 200
Marburg, 131; University of, 125-26, 128
Marcuse, Herbert, 43, 56-61, 75, 81, 84, 92,
   151, 286-87, 293
Marighela, Carlos, "Minihandbook of the
   Brazilian Urban Guerrilla," 175, 181,
   185, 199
Meier, Peter, 129, 135
Meinhof, Ingeborg, mother of Ulrike,
   110-15
Meinhof, Johannes, grandfather of Ulrike,
   109
Meinhof, Ulrike, 18, 71, 97, 99, 258, 267,
   273, 276, 289, 300; Das Argument,
   129-30; arrested, 12, 251-52, 257, 292; in